Novels by Stephen Coonts

Flight of the Intruder*
Final Flight
The Minotaur
Under Siege*
The Red Horseman*
The Intruders*

Nonfiction Books by Stephen Coonts

The Cannibal Queen: An Aerial Odyssey Across America*

*Published by POCKET BOOKS

Stephen
Coonts

War in the Air:

*True Accounts of the 20th Century's
Most Dramatic Air Battles—
by the Men Who Fought Them*

POCKET BOOKS
New York   London   Toronto   Sydney   Tokyo   Singapore

POCKET BOOKS, a division of Simon & Schuster Inc.
1230 Avenue of the Americas, New York, NY 10020

Copyright © 1996 by Stephen P. Coonts and Martin Greenberg

War in the air : true accounts of the 20th century's most
    dramatic air battles—by the men who fought them /
    [collected and edited by Stephen Coonts].
        p.   cm.
    ISBN 0-671-88191-4 (pb)
    1. Air warfare—History—20th century.   2. Fighter pilots—
United States—20th century. I. Coonts, Stephen, 1946–
D437.W37 1996
358.4'3'0922—dc20
[B]   96-33736
                                                  CIP

First Pocket Books trade paperback printing December 1997

10 9 8 7 6 5 4 3 2

POCKET and colophon are registered trademarks of
Simon & Schuster Inc.

Cover design by Steven Ferlauto
Cover photo courtesy of Jeffrey L. Ethell

Printed in the U.S.A.

Contents

CONTENTS

x

Foreword

The other day someone asked me about this book. "It's about airplanes, right?"

Wrong. This volume is a collection of true stories about men flying airplanes in battle. This book is no more about airplanes than Tennyson's "The Charge of the Light Brigade" is about horses.

Since the airplane is a creation of twentieth-century man, the stories compiled in this anthology are of necessity about this century's wars, thus the fliers are men. As this foreword is written, women are gaining access to the cockpits of combat aircraft in the United States. Presumably other nations will also open the trade of combat aviator to those women who volunteer and prove they have what it takes. For better or worse, women will be in the thick of the next war when it comes.

So what does it take? What qualities must a man or woman possess to succeed in aerial combat? First one must define success. Success to me means the ability to conquer your enemy, to shoot him down or bomb him, and survive the encounter. Said another way, to succeed one must be able to fly the aircraft, employ it as a weapon, hit what one aims at, and then fly home to fight again. As the stories in this book will make graphically clear, success is a lot easier to define than to achieve.

Yet even after the most careful reading of these excerpts from larger works, it will still be unclear precisely what qualities of physical ability, character, intelligence, and aptitude make up an aerial warrior. Excellent health and perfect vision would seem to be required, until one reads of Mick Mannock, who was essentially blind in one eye and still shot down seventy-three German airplanes, or the Luftwaffe's Hans Rudel, who flew for several months before World War II ended with just one leg, or of Douglas Bader, who lost both legs in a prewar crash and still became one of the leading aces during the Battle of Britain.

Courage? Ah, but what is that? If you will define it as the ability to keep climbing into a cockpit day after day knowing that the enemy will be trying his best to kill you, and you still go and do your best regardless, then I will grant you courage.

Still, courage alone is not enough. Flying is a craft, and war flying is a dangerous trade, but success in aerial combat comes only to those who have ripped aside the complacent veneers of civilization and are willing to fight, willing to kill. This drive to fight is not intellectual, a learned response, nor is it some bully's love for the sucker punch. This willingness to take the offensive and kill for what you believe to be right must be ingrained deep within your psyche. Nintendo did not invent this. To succeed as a fighter or attack pilot you must have this streak of the savage or you will be the one who falls.

Technological progress in aviation will not change this. Perhaps we have paid too much attention lately to grizzled veterans who scoff, "Oh, you young fellows have it easy with all this push-button stuff. Not like it was in the old days when it was just stick and rudder and a gunsight."

No, it's not like the old days. Aerial combat today demands more skills, a higher level of training, the ability to master extremely complex equipment, the ability to think very, very quickly because modern war aloft is fought at dazzling speeds, occasionally at multiples of the speed of sound. The speeds are such that a ham-handed or panicky pilot can literally pull his $40 million airplane apart in midair. The aircraft grow ever more complex and difficult to fly—years must be devoted to mastering the trade. Yet the fundamental truth, that merciless imperative, remains: you must aggressively seek the enemy, engage him, kill him, and get home before your fuel is exhausted.

Amazingly, fighter tactics haven't changed much between

World War I and the 1991 Gulf War—as this is written, our latest. Oh, the tactics have been altered to accommodate improved aircraft performance and weaponry, but the basics are still the same. A World War I ace listening and watching a jet fighter pilot talk with his hands would understand intuitively. This truth escapes many desk-flying military bureaucrats, who should know better. After every war in this century, including World War I, World War II, Korea, Vietnam, and the Gulf War, some general has declared that dogfighting is obsolete. The U.S. Navy swallowed this imbecility so completely in the 1950s that the F-4 Phantom was designed without *guns*. Everything changes, everything remains the same.

Since they were first used in combat, airplanes and the men who fight in them have attracted the public's eye. It is difficult to hide in an airplane. The craft is up there on center stage in front of God and everybody. Like his landings, a pilot's successes and failures are public events. His skill, his courage, his willingness to fight, are always on display to his fellow aviators, and to the enemy.

European propagandists realized during World War I that the exploits of successful fighter pilots would buck up the morale of the folks at home. Indeed, the aces of the day seemed the very embodiment of the military ideal: they were victory incarnate and, by happy accident, like the goddess wore wings. So in Europe and later in America they were lionized in the popular press and converted into something larger than life. (Today the celebrity press performs this metamorphosis for rock-music and film stars.) In a way it was a shame because the truth was quite large enough.

Some of these men accepted heroic fame as their due and reveled in the role. Perhaps for some the adulation and hero worship supplied part of what it took to keep climbing into that airplane when flesh and nerve kept screaming "enough."

For others the publicity and praise were grotesque embarrassments. They saw themselves as tradesmen, professional soldiers, and they were doing the usual bloody job that good professional soldiers do. Some of them had deep reservations about the killing. Some accepted the slaughter of fellow human beings as a patriotic duty necessary to win the war for their country. Some just refused to think about it. Whichever, the killing affected them all. And all suffered from the stress of combat, the necessity to risk one's life day after weary day. To single one man out as a hero worthy of a nation's hosannas while ignoring others with equal courage, some of whom died damn hard for their country, seemed somehow obscene.

Regardless of puffery, flying in combat was more than the blood, more than killing and dying. The risks imparted a richness to life that made everything that had gone before mere prologue and everything that might come after boring anticlimax. To fly, to kill, and to still be alive that evening was life on the edge, life at full throttle, life pungent and powerful and mysterious and infinitely valuable. American ace Raoul Lufbery was tugging at the corner of something profound when he said, "There won't be any 'after the war' for a fighter pilot."

Indeed, which of life's joys or triumphs could compare to returning from aerial combat with the flush of victory on your face and the narrowness of your escape on your lips, once again to feel the earth under your feet, the caress of the summer breeze, to smell the new-mown grass, to be welcomed by good friends and brave men, and that night drink the wine and eat the bread of the living? What more could life offer? Fame? Political success? Money? The love of a woman? Bah! *Nothing* could possibly compare to the intoxicating joy of taking great risks and surviving on the strength of your own skill and courage.

Nothing!

Until the next morning when you vomit your breakfast because you are going to have to go do it all over again. Until your nerves burn out on 200-proof life and your hands shake so badly, you can't hold a cigarette or remember simple things or concentrate on any task for more than a few seconds. Until the nightmares begin every time you close your eyes. Until your luck just flat runs clean out. Still, until then . . .

After World War I, pulp publishers found that tales of aerial combat sold well. Writers who had never been closer to the Western Front than the Lower East Side scribbled tales of aerial adventure that were read and reread by every boy who could lay hands on them. The pilots and aircrewmen of World War II grew up with the aces of the first war and their fictitious brethren, men with eyes like eagles and ice water in their veins, men who could fly through a thunderstorm blindfolded or bomb a railway station in stygian darkness and hit the darned thing, men who could dance the night away with a count's daughter and shoot down every Hun with a plane the following dawn, men who were—well, by God, they were *men*.

World War II was rougher on its airmen. The planes were faster, more complex, death came more quickly, randomly, and now civilians were targets. London, Dresden, Berlin, Tokyo, Hiroshima . . . the litany of great cities mercilessly bombed by merciless men took the luster off the flying tales.

Still they survived. For in fact, truth was better than fiction. Glory was a fabrication of propagandists and pulp writers, but the manner in which life is distilled inside a cockpit to its true essence was not made up. Life is meant to be *lived*, not hoarded. In the 1950s and even into the 1960s another generation of youngsters grew up on stories of fighter pilots. These boys became the pilots of the Vietnam War, the final obscenity where valor and honor and courage were given their true weight by the public these men sought to serve—almost nothing.

It was always so. War was never something glorious, something grand—war is and always was a filthy, bloody business begun by swine politicians for political objectives rooted in hypocrisy, hubris, and greed. And yet, embedded in the worst that men could do to other men were occasional moments where the best in man could shine. In the crucible virtues were refined, purified, the lesser stuff fluxed off. In the depths of the inferno most men were somehow induced to give the very best that was in them even to their last breath.

Nowhere is this curious fact more apparent than in the stories of the World War II bomber crews who day after day and night after night attacked the German war machine. The ten or so men who made up a bomber crew flew together, and all too often bled and died together. Theirs was a bond more sacred than any marriage vow. Their war was fought inside a freezing, heaving, slow, thin-skinned airplane. Their war was against flak, cannon shells, machine-gun bullets, fire, weather, mechanical failures, fate itself. Their war was against the demon fear and the horrible things it could do to good, brave men who had seen its terrible face once too often. Like their fighter-pilot brethren, to a man they were all volunteers. You will read about them in this volume in a selection from Philip Ardrey's *Bomber Pilot*.

At the heart of this volume are the stories of the men who flew alone, the fighter pilots, and of their triumphs and disasters aloft. It is axiomatic that a fighter pilot must shoot down the enemy and avoid being shot down himself. Amazingly, the ability to do this with any consistency is a rare quality. Studies of victory statistics among air forces have repeatedly shown that as many as 40 percent of the kills are made by as few as 5 percent of the pilots. Experience and excellent situational awareness are major factors, yet an intangible that is extremely difficult to spot or measure in the peacetime training environment is also involved. Does the pilot fly to find and kill the enemy, or does he fly to avoid being killed? Said another way, is this pilot the hunter or the hunted?

One unknown U.S. jet-fighter pilot labeled himself a hunter with this comment: "A MiG at your six is better than no MiG at all."

To categorize this quality as aggressiveness is to oversimplify. The intangible essential to success is a mixture of self-confidence, bloodlust, thirst for battle, all coming together as a willingness— indeed, a burning desire—to fight. Of course this fighting spirit must be tempered with an acute, prudent awareness of the tactical situation, yet too much caution makes the pilot ineffective as an aerial warrior. The fighting spirit must be innate. The other necessary flying skills can be acquired through thorough, proper training.

The fighter pilots you will meet in this book indubitably have this fighting spirit shaped, tempered, and finely honed to an edge that will allow them to win, again and again and again. Successful attack pilots also have it—they would never press through to their targets time after time without it.

From World War I to Vietnam, from England to the South Pacific, the fighter pilots are here. Also salted in are some exquisite nonfighter gems: the naval war in the Pacific, Gordon W. Prange's *Miracle at Midway;* the Vietnam era, Jack Broughton's *Thud Ridge* and John Nichols' *On Yankee Station.* Two selections I would classify as fighter stories involve helicopter pilots, Hugh L. Mills, Jr., and Robert Anderson's *Low Level Hell* and Robert Mason's *Chickenhawk.* The most honest piece of writing you have read in years, and perhaps the best thing in this book, is the selection from *The Heart of a Man,* which was merely a private diary that U.S. Navy A-4 pilot Frank Elkins kept during the Vietnam War.

The final selection in the book, "The Last Ace," is an original piece, never before published, based on my interview with Steve Ritchie. The opinions expressed in the introduction to that piece (and all the others) are mine, not Steve's.

With the exception of the last piece, each selection included in this anthology is but a short excerpt from a damn fine book. Each selection was chosen because I thought the writing good and because it seemed to illuminate, for me anyway, some facet of the air-combat experience. I have made no attempt to include stories representative of every major branch of combat aviation in this century—an impossibility, due to the necessity to cram it all into one book. For the same reason whole wars have been skipped, such as the 1991 Persian Gulf War and the Spanish Civil War.

These are not delicate little love stories with a world of meaning in a gesture or a glance, nor are they abstruse essays on good and evil layered like an onion. Nor are they about airplanes.

These stories are raw life, the straight stuff, the good stuff, true stories of brave men in desperate combat, naked in the sky. Some are written by the men who lived the adventure. All are written in the style of the era from which they came. They embody the very core of human values—faith, courage, perseverance, loyalty, trust . . . I hope after you read them that you look up each time you hear an airplane in the sky.

Stephen Coonts

The First Air Hero

from *The Zeppelin Fighters*

BY ARCH WHITEHOUSE

The first genuine, certified air hero was a young Royal Navy pilot named Reggie Warneford. In 1915 Warneford received the Victoria Cross and the joyous adulation of the British for his magnificent feat of destroying a Zeppelin.

Bombing at night from a height that the aircraft of the time could not reach, the huge Zeppelins terrorized people who had read far too much of H. G. Wells and other futurists who predicted hell raining from on high. It would, but in a future war. Fortunately the hydrogen-filled Zeppelins carried small bombloads and were wildly inaccurate. To escape British artillery the Germans usually bombed England from above a cloud layer. On several occasions luckless Zeppelin skippers missed the entire island with their weapons. Still, the specter of Teuton leviathans cruising the night sky miles above the earth and scattering death willy-nilly shook the British public badly.

While the orchestra plays Wagner, enter Reggie from stage left.

SURPRISINGLY ENOUGH, THE FIRST BRITISH AIRMAN TO DOWN A Zeppelin is seldom mentioned in general histories of this all-important segment of military aviation. Even today, if you ask any elderly Englishman the name of the airman who brought down the first Zeppelin, he will with no hesitation of any sort reply, "Oh, that was that chap Leefe Robinson. He brought it down one night, and it fell all ablaze at Cuffley. Got the VC for it, he did. We'll never forget that night."

How easily they forgot a young Royal Naval Air Service pilot, Reggie Warneford, who on June 7, 1915, destroyed the Army dirigible L.37 over Ghent, whereas Leefe Robinson's victory was

1

not scored until September 3, 1916. But Warneford made his "kill" over Belgium, and Leefe Robinson's was staged high above the outskirts of London where millions looked up and beheld the first of a series of defeats that eventually drove the military dirigible out of the skies.

Reginald Alexander John Warneford was a gay composite of the British Empire of those days. His parents were jovial Yorkshire folk who had shuttled about the world on engineering missions, and young Warneford, born in India, was schooled at the English College in Simla, but later went to England where he attended the Stratford-on-Avon Grammar School. The family next moved to Canada, and Reggie, who had developed a mechanical skill, particularly with engines, joined the Merchant Marine and was serving with the India Steam Navigation Company when World War I broke out. He resigned immediately and made his way to England where he joined the Second Battalion of the much-publicized Sportsman's Regiment, an infantry unit consisting chiefly of well-known sporting and athletic figures.

There was considerable prestige in this regiment, but in England, as in several countries, it was found that most headlined athletes were psychologically attuned for sport only, not for war. Fearing the conflict would end before the athletes could be whipped into combat condition, Warneford applied for a transfer to the Royal Naval Air Service. Whether he was an ideal candidate has been widely discussed. His best friends have generally agreed that Reggie was too cocksure, inclined to be boastful and frankly, no great shakes as a pilot. His first commanding officer, a Commander Groves, soon decided that this lad would break his neck long before he got into action. However, one or two intuitive instructors managed to curb his impetuosity, and by the time he had advanced to the Central Flying School at Upavon he had proved to be a daring young airman.

By May 1915 Warneford had won his RNAS wings and was shipped to Number 2 Naval Squadron, then located at Eastchurch (Thames Estuary). There his superior officers decided that he would be much better off where there would be some action to absorb his animal activity. He was sent across the Channel to Number 1 Naval Squadron, then under the command of Wing Comdr. Arthur Longmore, who became an air chief marshal in World War II. At Dunkirk Reggie continued his wild ways, resisting all discipline, and becoming the squadron nuisance. Longmore soon decided to turn him loose and let the Huns discipline him.

On his first flight out of Dunkirk he was given an ancient Voisin biplane, and an observer who, if he still lives, must remember that hair-raising experience. Shortly after taking off Warneford spotted a German observation plane circling over Zeebrugge. He went into immediate pursuit and ordered the observer to use the light machine gun with which he had been provided. They followed the enemy aircraft all the way back to its field, but by that time the British gun had jammed, and ignoring the flight controls, Warneford tried to get into his observer's cockpit to remedy the stoppage. The antics of the plane under such conditions can be imagined, and it is related that Warneford had to help his observer climb down out of the plane when they returned to Dunkirk.

Wing Commander Longmore then provided Warneford with a Morane Parasol, a high-wing monoplane, originally designed as a two-seater, but which, in a few instances, had been modified as a single-seater and flown as a fighter-scout. Young Reggie was sent off in one of these machines to do his worst, and from all accounts rolled up a remarkable record, chasing enemy planes, bombing gun emplacements, and attacking troop movements. So wild were these forays, Warneford soon wore out his mount, and Commander Longmore had to find another. In this it can be seen that Warneford was forming a service pattern that was to be followed by Capt. Albert Ball and Lt. Frank Luke, a young Arizonian.

At 12:20 A.M. of June 7 Wing Commander Longmore was warned by the Admiralty that three Zeppelins that had been over Britain were on their way back. Here was a chance of a lifetime.

3

Wilson's flight was warned and a broad plan, previously agreed on, was put into action. Warneford and another sublieutenant, Rose, were sent off in single-seater Moranes. Wilson and Mills took big bomb-carrying Henri Farmans to attack the Zeppelin sheds at Evere, near Brussels.

Warneford, who had never been off the ground at night, was flagged off first about 1 A.M. The Morane flew beautifully and Reggie was at 2,000 feet before he realized what he had volunteered for. He stared wide-eyed all around and tried to find his small grouping of instruments. A length of scarlet worsted that was knotted to a center-section strut flicked insistently, and he knew from this primitive instrument that he was in a dangerous slide-slip. Then, gradually, as his eyes grew accustomed to the yellow-gray nothingness beyond his Triplex windscreen, he could read all his instruments. Already he was at 3,000 feet!

Rose was not so lucky. He became lost in the low mist, the light on the instrument panel went out, and he had to make a forced landing in an open field near Cassel where he turned over but was not seriously hurt.

Warneford searched for the rest of the group from Dunkirk, but no other aircraft appeared to be in the sky. He listened to the even *chug-chug-chug* of his rotary engine and felt his face being wasp-stung by condensation drips coming off the center section. He was fascinated by the poisonous-looking blue-yellow flame of his exhaust, a feature he had not seen before. He checked with his compass, made sure he was on the proper bearing, and began another search.

Content, if somewhat bored with the comparative inaction, Warneford kept a close watch, hoping to find two more sets of exhaust flame that would guide him to where Wilson and Mills were heading for their rendezvous. He wondered what an airship shed looked like from the air at night. Then, he suddenly saw a strange glow a few miles to the north. He squinted and looked again. Although he was attracted by another blue-yellow exhaust, he wondered what Wilson and Mills were doing up there near Ostend . . . and whatever was that long black mass floating above them?

Wilson and Mills had made immediate contact after taking off and, after clearing the low fog around Furnes, had headed for Brussels nearly seventy-five miles away. The skies were clear in that direction, and Wilson decided to fly straight for Evere which lay on the north side of the old Flemish city. Both Henri Farman pilots found their target with no difficulty. Wilson was soon caught in the blazing bar of a searchlight and some antiaircraft fire, but he used a flashlight to give the impression he was a friendly airman coming in for a landing. Uncertain what to do, the Germans did nothing, and Wilson made a clean run-in, released his rack of 20-pound bombs, making a beautiful path-finder job for Mills who followed Wilson in. Between them they torched a great shed and an almost new dirigible, one marked L.38.

On this eventful night L.37, commanded by an Oberleutnant Von der Haegen, had been sent on a routine patrol with L.38 and L.39. L.38 returned early because of engine trouble, only to be burned in her shed by the RNAS airmen. There was nothing particularly important or offensive about L.37's mission. It had been arranged mainly to give a number of airship designers, specialists, and technicians from the Zeppelin factory some firsthand knowledge of the various problems experienced by the crews on active service.

L.37 was 521 feet long, and her eighteen main gas ballonets carried 953,000 cubic feet of hydrogen. She was powered by four 210–horsepower Maybach engines, and manned by a select crew of twenty-eight skilled airshipmen. For defense, her designers had provided four machine-gun posts that were built into the outboard engine gondolas. These positions gave good visibility, a fairly wide arc of fire, and efficient defense along both sides of the airship, but there was no gun position anywhere along the upper side of the dirigible.

After flying north for a few minutes, Warneford stared in amazement as he realized he had encountered a Zeppelin, but it seemed half a mile long. He had to twist his head from side to side to take in the leviathan proportions. Several glistening cars hung from its underside, and the gleam of the fantail exhausts indicated that the rubberized covering was daubed a yellow ocher. Warneford wondered what kept anything as large as that in the air.

But this was no time for cogitation. The Zeppelin's machine guns suddenly opened up and slugs clattered through the frail wing of Morane Parasol Number 3253. Somewhat puzzled, Reggie wisely heeled over and cleared out of range. It should be explained that this model of the Morane Parasol carried no machine gun of any kind.

The fog was clearing and the Ostend-Bruges Canal was sharply defined below, and with that position clear in his mind Warneford decided that the dirigible was heading for Ghent, but suddenly the big snub-nosed airship shifted course and came straight for him. Two more streams of tracer-flecked machine-gun fire were threatening. Two more bursts came from the forward gondolas and converged only a few yards from the Parasol. The RNAS pilot gave the Le Rhone all she could gulp, and tried to climb, but the crisscrossing tracers penciled in a definite warning, so Reggie had to peel off and dive.

As he studied the situation he may have turned to a light Belgian carbine, carried in a leather boot beside his wicker seat. He may have steered the Morane back into a position below and behind the mighty elevator-and-rudder framework. He may have gripped the control stick between his knees and triggered a few .303 shells at the massive target. He may have, but this is strictly conjecture. We do know he had six 20-pound bombs in a simple rack that could be released one by one by a toggle-and-wire device.

Warneford stalked L.37 for several minutes, but whenever he came within range or view the German gunners sprayed the sky with long bursts of Parabellum fire, and he was driven off time after time.

L.37 began to rise fast, for Von der Haegen had apparently

dumped some water ballast over Assebrouck, leaving Warneford still scrambling to get above his present 7,000 feet. Von der Haegen then increased his speed and nosed around for Ghent. Although he knew he was outclassed, Reggie refused to give up the chase, and he settled down, determined to keep the dirigible in view, and hoped to gain some much-needed altitude.

Von der Haegen was obviously racing for safety, and while he maintained his height, Warneford was helpless, but the German airship commander realized this was no ordinary patrol and he fretted about his passengers, the technicians, when he should have concentrated on maintaining a safe tactical procedure.

At 2:25 A.M. the Morane pilot, still stalking and trying to get above the Zeppelin, was cheered to see the big airship nose down and apparently head for a break in the 7,000-foot cloud layer that spread toward Ghent. By now Reggie had browbeaten his Morane up to a position where he could use his 20-pound incendiary bombs. In a few minutes L.37 was actually below him and for the first time he saw that its upper cover was painted what seemed to be a dark green, and he was thankful no gun turrets were showing along this upper panel.

Again, he was astonished by the size of this monster as he moved in for an attack glide. She was so big he felt he would have no trouble in making a landing on her topside. Below, Ghent lay a dull smudge, and when the gnatlike Morane nosed down for that 500-foot-long upper panel he must have felt slight and puny against the aerial leviathan.

He set a straight course along the top of the airship and began pulling the bomb toggle.

"One . . . two . . . three!" he counted, and felt the Morane jerk with the release of each bomb. He fully expected the Zeppelin to explode immediately, but nothing happened!

"Four . . . five . . . ," he continued to count, and then a blinding explosion ripped through the upper cover, baring the blackened tracery of the framework.

Whongff!

Spellbound, Reggie continued his run-in until the little Morane was swept up on a savage belch of flame and concussion. She whipped over with a violence that would have hurled Warneford out of his cockpit had it not been for his safety belt. He gasped in astonishment, rammed the stick forward and tried to force the aeroplane into a dive. Chunks of burning framework hurtled by as he floundered out of that aerial convulsion and streaked down through a curling pall of choking smoke. Over the next few minutes he was absorbed in skimming clear of the debris, getting back on an even keel, and frantically adjusting his air and gas mixture to dampen out a series of warning pops from the Le Rhone engine.

A few minutes afterward the doomed airship fell on the Convent of St. Elizabeth in the Mont-Saint-Armand suburb of Ghent. One man on the ground was killed and several badly burned, but the helmsman of the Zeppelin had a miraculous escape. According to some eyewitnesses he jumped clear of the tumbling wreckage at about two hundred feet, landed on a roof of the convent, crashed on through as though it had been made of matchwood, and landed in an unoccupied bed, suffering only minor injuries. He was the only man aboard the ill-fated airship to survive. However, survive he did, and is said later to have opened a beer hall where for years he related his adventure and confirmed Warneford's official account.

But what about the young British pilot who was now tossed across the flame- and smoke-streaked sky with a recalcitrant engine? He gingerly tested his plane controls and gradually brought the Morane back on an even keel. He fully expected his monoplane wing to part company from the fuselage, so violent had been the concussion. Then when the Le Rhone began to behave and respond, she snorted her wrath and quit cold. Warneford watched the gleaming wooden prop wigwag to a halt, and he had to ram his nose down to prevent a stall.

He did not have to look about, he *knew* he was at least thirty-five miles inside the German lines. There wasn't an earthly chance of stretching a glide, and it was obvious that the best he could hope for was a safe landing, and a long spell in a German prison camp.

Despite the darkness, the unfamiliar topography, and the lack of any ground lighting, Reggie landed his beat-up Morane safely in an open field—a turfed stretch shielded along one side by a long strip of woods. There was an old farmhouse nearby, but no one emerged to question his arrival, and no German troops appeared to take him prisoner. His initial impulse was to destroy the Morane, but he first tried to find out what had caused the Le Rhone to stop.

What now occurred may be a legend, but it was often told in those days. Warneford was a better than average mechanic and certainly knew the rotary engine, and it took him but a short time to discover that a length of fuel line running from the tank to the fuel pump had broken. There was still enough fuel to get him back across the line, either to Dunkirk or Furnes. A quick search through his pockets produced a cigarette holder. The wide outer end was perfect for making a temporary repair, and the two ends were bound secure with strips of his handkerchief.

In his official report, hurriedly scribbled after his arrival back at Furnes, there is no mention of this, just, "I was forced to land and repair my pump." Obviously, there was more to it than that for it must have taken some substitution and improvisation. In fact, Reggie spent about twenty minutes remedying the break and starting the engine again. An experimental tug on the prop assured him that fuel was being drawn from the tank to the carburetor device used on rotary engines. Fortunately, the engine was still warm, and after running through the starting sequence twice to draw vapor into the cylinders, Reggie cut in the switch and snapped her over. The Le Rhone caught immediately, and he had to scramble to duck under the wing and climb into the cockpit, but all went well. He taxied around for a good takeoff and in minutes was roaring away.

As he approached the coast again he flew into more fog, so he cruised up and down until he found a hole and glided through. He had little idea where he was, and on landing was told he was at Cape Gris-Nez, ten miles below Calais. He was welcomed warmly, given more gasoline, and permitted to call his squadron headquarters at Dunkirk. He told his story briefly, and was advised to sit out the bad weather and return when it cleared.

By the time Warneford returned to his squadron the news that a German Zeppelin had been sent down in flames had seeped out of Ghent, and within hours his name was ringing from one end of the Empire to the other. His photograph was flashed on hundreds of theater screens to the delight of cheering audiences.

Within thirty-six hours King George V awarded the Victoria Cross to Warneford, and the French government added their Cross of the Legion of Honor, but Flight Sublieutenant Warneford lived only ten more days to enjoy the laurels of victory. He was sent to Paris on June 17 to be decorated, and after the ceremony was ordered to Buc to pick up a new Farman biplane. The machine had been assembled hurriedly, and most of its standard equipment had not been fitted.

An American newspaperman, named Henry Needham, had asked to go along to Furnes where he planned to write a special story about Warneford and his Zeppelin victory. Reggie cheerfully agreed, and they climbed into the biplane and took off. Almost immediately, the Farman started to pitch and behave strangely, finally rolling over completely out of control. When it was on its back Warneford and Needham were thrown out and killed. Some reports have it that Reggie made a wild takeoff that was too much for the Farman; the tail was wrenched off and the rest of the machine fluttered over on its back. It was also said that neither man had bothered to fasten his safety belt.

Following Warneford's victory, the war news and rumors were well garnished with reports of other Zeppelin conquests. One of the most fantastic, that persisted for weeks, was that of a Frenchman who had tried to down a dirigible over Paris by using a machine gun. When that method of attack failed, he boldly rammed the raider in midair by flying his Morane Bullet straight through the aluminum framework, crashing out the other side. After that, so the story went, the Zeppelin folded in the middle and dropped in a French cornfield. There was no truth in the report, but faked photographs of this astounding adventure were on sale for weeks throughout France.

An Overrated Pastime

from *Flying Fury*

BY JAMES MCCUDDEN

James Byford McCudden enlisted in the Royal Engineers at the age of fifteen. Three years later, in 1913, he transferred to the new Royal Flying Corps to be near his brother, a sergeant-pilot, and became an aircraft mechanic. Accepted for flight training in 1916, he survived the primitive course of instruction and returned to France. In the first excerpt that follows, circa November 1916, he is learning his trade in BE-2s, a pusher-fighter with a top speed of about one hundred miles per hour. In the second excerpt from January and February 1918, he is an accomplished ace flying SE-5s, the best single-seat aircraft the British had.

After he had shot down fifty-seven German aircraft and been decorated with the Victoria Cross by the king, James McCudden wrote his memoirs. First published in 1918, this long-out-of-print masterpiece reveals an extraordinary young man.

We find a self-confident, happy young man as at home among the enlisted fitters who worked on his aircraft as he was among the class-conscious officers, a perfectionist who tuned his own guns and engine, a well-adjusted extrovert who loved the camaraderie of the mess yet didn't brood excessively on the many friends he lost along the way or his own probable end, a dry wit whose idea of a great leave was to see every show in London. And Jim McCudden was a hunter who could lead a scheduled patrol in the morning then go out at noon alone to stalk German observation planes "just for fun." For you see, McCudden loved aerial combat. He found the kill-or-be-killed game in the sky the ultimate sport.

Perhaps if Jim McCudden had not spent so much of his youth in the barracks and mess halls of professional soldiers, perhaps if he had been older when he went into the crucible,

*we jaded survivors of this modern, violent age could under-
stand him better. Alas, we have only his joyful recounting of
battles aloft, of close calls, of evenings spent in the company
of fellow warriors whom he loved. He comes to us as a knight
from the age of chivalry mounted on a winged charger, vi-
brantly alive and athirst for battle.*

*Three days after completing his memoirs, McCudden, now
a major, was given command of a fighter squadron in France.
He left for the front in an SE-5 he had tweaked himself. On
taking off from a French airfield his engine stopped and he
tried to turn to glide back to the field. The plane stalled,
flipped, and crashed; McCudden was killed. He was just
twenty-three years old.*

WE CONTINUED DOING OUR DAILY PATROLS AND SOON GOT TO
know our new patrol area. Nothing happened of interest until
the morning of 9 November 1916.

The morning dawned bright, with good visibility, and as I
dressed I remarked to Noakes that the Hun pilots were just
about dressing too, saying among themselves how they were that
morning going to strafe the *verfluchter Englander*.

Six of us left the ground about 7:30 A.M. and got our height
going towards Albert, intending to go round to Bapaume and
then fly north to Arras with the intention of cutting off a good
slice of Hunland and strafing any Hun that we found west of us.

By the time we got to Bapaume, our patrol had dwindled
down to three machines—Lt. Albert Ball, Noakes, and myself.
So from Bapaume we flew bravely north, for up to the present
we had not encountered any of the numerous Hun scouts that
were reported to be always obnoxious in that sector.

We had just flown over Achiet-le-Grand at about 11,000 feet
when I saw six specks east of us. I drew Noakes' attention, and
so we made off west a little as we were a long way east of the
lines. Long before we got to Adinfer Wood the Hun machines
overtook us, and directly they got within range we turned to
fight.

One Hun came down at me nose on but then turned away,

13

and in doing so I got a good view of the Hun, which I had never seen before. It had a fuselage like the belly of a fish. Its wings were cut fairly square at the tips, and had no dihedral angle. The tail plane was of the shape of a spade. We learned later that these machines were the new German Albatros D.1 chasers.

By now we were fairly in the middle of six of them and were getting a rather bad time of it, for we were a long way east of the line, so we all knew that we had to fight hard or go down. At one time I saw a fat Hun about ten yards behind Ball absolutely filling him with lead, as Ball was flying straight, apparently changing a drum of ammunition, and had not seen the Hun.

I could not at the time go to Ball's assistance as I had two Huns after me fairly screaming for my blood. However, Ball did not go down. Noakes was having a good time too, and was putting up a wonderful show.

The Huns were cooperating very well. Their main tactic seemed to be for one of them to dive at one of us from the front and then turn away, inviting us to follow. I followed three times, but the third time I heard a terrific clack, bang, crash, rip behind me, and found a Hun was firing from about ten yards in the rear, and his guns seemed to be firing in my very ears. I at once did a half-roll, and as the Hun passed over me I saw the black and white streams on his interplane struts. This fellow was the Hun leader, and I had previously noticed that he had manœuvred very well.

By now, however, we had fought our way back to our lines, and all three of us had kept together, which was undoubtedly our salvation, but I had used all my ammunition and had to chase round after Huns without firing at them. However, the Huns had apparently had enough too, and as soon as we got back to our lines they withdrew east.

I now had time to look over my machine on my way back to the aerodrome and saw that it was in a bad way. My tail plane was a mass of torn fabric, and various wires were hanging, having been cut by bullets. We all landed, and on getting out of our machines were congratulated by our OC, who had been informed of the progress of the fight by telephone from our Archy section, who had seen the latter part of the fight and had said that it was the best they had seen for a long time.

I really think that fight was one of the best I have ever had, although we were outnumbered and the Huns had better machines than we had.

I had a good look round my machine and found that the Huns had scored twenty-four hits. This was the greatest number I have ever had. I do not believe in being shot about. It is bad or careless flying to allow one's self to be shot about when one ought usually to be able to prevent it by properly timed manœuvres.

The same afternoon I went out on another machine to do an offensive patrol and, having encountered a two-seater over Gommécourt, fired all my ammunition at him to no avail, so I landed at the nearest aerodrome for some more, after which I left the ground again to look for the beastly Hun.

Whilst getting my height at about 4,000 feet, and feeling rather bucked with life, I thought I would try a loop; so I pushed the machine down till the speed got up to 90 mph, took a deep breath and pulled the stick back.

Halfway up the loop I changed my mind and pushed the stick forward, with the result that I transferred my load from my flying to my landing wires. The resultant upward pressure was so great that all my ammunition drums shot out of my machine over my top plane and into the revolving propeller which, being a "pusher," of course was behind me.

There was a mighty scrunch and terrific vibration as three out of my four propeller blades disappeared in a cloud of splinters. I at once switched off and removed my gun from my knees, where it had fallen after having been wrenched from its mountings and thrown into the air owing to the terrific vibration caused by my engine doing 1,600 revolutions per minute with only one propeller blade.

I now found that I wanted full right rudder to keep the machine straight, and discovered, on looking round, that the lower right-hand tail boom had been cut clean in two by one of the flying propeller blades, and all that was holding my tail on was a diagonal 10-cwt tail-boom bracing wire.

The machine was wobbling badly as the engine was still turning round slowly, and I had just about wits enough left to pick out a field and make a landing successfully.

As soon as I stopped running along the ground the machine tilted over on one wing, as the centre section bracing wires were broken, and there was nothing, now that the machine was at rest, to keep the wings in their correct position. I got out of the machine and thanked God for my salvation.

A few minutes later an officer from Number 3 Squadron, on horseback, rode up to pick up my pieces, for as he had seen various portions of an aeroplane flying about the locality, he had come to inspect the biggest piece. I remained by the machine until the tender from Number 3 Squadron arrived with a guard for the machine, and I then went to Number 3 Squadron and telephoned to my squadron what had happened, so they promised to send a car for me at once, and a breakdown party in the morning.

My old comrades in Number 3 Squadron were very pleased to see me, and happily that evening they were giving a farewell dinner to one of the sergeants who had just won a commission. His name was Leech, and he was afterwards killed in France after having gained a DSO. We made a very cheery evening of it I can assure you and had some real fun.

About midnight my tender from the squadron arrived, so off I went on a thirty-mile journey back to La Hameau, where we arrived at 3 A.M. The next morning I saw our CO, who was pleased to have me back, as a rumour went round that I had been seen going down in flames near Gommécourt. How these ridiculous rumours do go round!

On 28 January 1918 my machine was ready, having been fitted with my special high-compression pistons, and as the engine gave many more revolutions on the test bench than did the standard 200 hp Hispano, my hopes of surpassing the Maybach-Rumpler looked like materializing.

The morning was pleasant and I left the ground at 9:30 A.M. As soon as I opened the throttle I could feel the increase in power as the fuselage at my back pressed me forward hard in its endeavour to go ahead quickly. After I had left the ground, the increase of my machine's climb was very apparent, and although I will not mention exact figures, I was up to 10,000 feet in a little more in minutes than there are days in the week. After that morning's patrol, during which I had several indecisive fights, I knew that my machine was now a good deal superior to anything the enemy had in the air, and I was very pleased that my experiment, of which I had entirely taken the responsibility, had proved an absolute success.

On the last day of January I was alone at 19,000 feet over Cambrai when I saw below and west of me a patrol of five Hun scouts at about 14,000 feet over Bourlon Wood. I thought if I leapt on them quickly and then got away that I should at least get one of them before I had to run to the lines, for whilst on my flights I had to be very diplomatic as to whom, how, and where I attacked, for I had to live up to my doctrine, which is to down as many as possible of the enemy at the least risk and casualties to one's own side.

Down I went, and quickly got behind the leader, into whom I fired a burst at very close range. He at once went down vertically with pieces of three-ply wood falling off his fuselage, and he was seen to strike the ground by our Archie gunners. I hadn't time to watch him as I was fighting four more scouts now, and had my attention very fully occupied. However, I got into position behind a Pfalz, and after a short burst from the good old Vickers he went down in a spiral dive and crashed also.

The remainder now evinced signs of alarm, and as my motto was to hit hard and hit quickly, I fired at another Albatros who spun away. Then I found an Albatros behind me firing for all he knew. But soon I reversed the position, and was getting a lovely burst into him when both guns stopped. On looking round I saw that the Lewis had finished its ammunition and the Vickers' belt had broken, and so now I had no guns working, but I felt awfully brave, and as the remaining Pfalz and Albatros were very dud, I started chasing them about with no gun, and once very nearly ran into the tail of the Pfalz at whose pilot I could have thrown a bad egg if I could possibly have got one at that moment. However, I chased these two artists as far as south of Cambrai, and then my caution once more making itself felt, I turned west and soon landed at my aerodrome.

I at once rang up Archie to confirm if possible the destruction of these two scouts, which they did, and Captain Dixon, who had witnessed the fight, said that it was the queerest thing that he had seen since I shot that LVG down from a height of ten feet near Havrincourt, on the morning of December 29, on which occasion I was told afterwards the Hun's undercarriage nearly got mixed up with an Archie gun that was well elevated.

At times, fighting the Hun seems rather an overrated pastime, but still there are occasions when fellows sit in the mess and absolutely roar with laughter when something occurs to them that happened in the air. For instance, on one occasion I saw a Rumpler approaching our lines, and as he saw us he turned away and dived a little, but not at all steeply, and then suddenly all his four wings fell clean off, and—reader!—can you not imagine the feelings of the Hun crew when their photographic Rumpler shed all its wings. They *must* have felt let down, poor devils, and probably it did not seem a bit funny to them.

The cold and frosty weather that we had been having was now breaking up, and the air was assuming that delicious warmth of the French February. I have myself spent four winters in France and, having to be very observant, I have studied the weather a great deal, and in my experience I think that the weather as a rule is milder in France in February than in April.

Early in February I went up to test the weather to see if it was good enough for our offensive patrols to leave the ground, and I was only up ten minutes, going towards Havrincourt Wood at about 11,000 feet, when I saw a Hun two-seater running away to the east. He had apparently seen me before I had seen him, for I was not expecting Huns over, as the visibility was not too good, but I suppose he was out for some urgent information.

Opening the throttle of my specially tuned engine, I overtook the LVG just as though he were going backward, for I should judge my speed to be twenty miles faster on the level than his. Although the LVG tried hard, I presented him with a very excellent burst from both guns, and he went down in a vertical nose-dive, then past the vertical onto his back, when the enemy gunner shot out of the machine for all the world like a stone out of a catapult. The unfortunate fellow seemed all arms and legs.

The LVG went down on his back for a long time and finally crashed to matchwood in our lines at Velu Wood. So now, having ascertained that the weather was good enough for patrol, I flew home to my aerodrome, where I landed just twenty minutes after starting out, having destroyed an enemy machine from a height of 11,000 feet, twenty miles away from my aerodrome. Gee! What a world!

The same afternoon I was out again alone, and although I chased a Rumpler, who was very high, doing a reconnaissance, he had too long a start in height for me to overtake him in time before he was miles over the safety of his own lines.

On the 3rd February I was again up alone, and soon met one of the Hannovers, which have the biplane tail. I engaged this machine for a while, and at last drove him down east of Marquion with steam pouring from his damaged radiator, but he was under control.

During the last two months I had done a great deal of fighting in the air, and, although I had done a lot at the head of my patrol, I had done still more by myself while carrying out my own system of fighting the German reconnaissance aeroplanes that come over our lines for specially valuable information. During the winter months I had been fighting very high, always in fact above 16,000 feet, and I ask you to try to realise what it is like flying 20,000 feet at one hundred miles an hour for two hours at a stretch in the very midst of winter.

Nothing happened of much interest until the 16th of February, when I led my patrol towards the lines at 10 A.M. We were going to do an offensive patrol, in conjunction with some Bristol Fighters who were going to Le Câteau on reconnaissance. My patrol were to fly in the vicinity west of Le Câteau in order to clear the air for the Bristol Fighters on their homeward journey.

We allowed the Bristols a certain time to get their height and cross the lines, and then we went over a few miles south half an hour later. We crossed the lines at 16,000 feet over Bantouzelle, and then flew due east.

I have never seen so many Huns over the lines as that morning, for the visibility was good, and the old Hun always pushes up all his available machines on a day of good atmospheric clearness at a certain time in order to gain temporary command of the air over a certain sector, for just half an hour or so.

However, the Huns this morning were not offensive, as I expected them to be, and as we got behind the lines the Huns flew north, south and east. Soon after crossing we saw the "green-tailed" Hun marked "K" flying alone, no doubt cooperating with some of his patrol, who were most probably somewhere near in readiness for his call.

We flew east, and very soon arrived beyond Caudry, and here I turned to wait for the Bristols. We were then east of all the Hun scout patrols. I was now anxiously looking east for little specks and black Archie bursts, denoting that the Bristols were over their objective doing their work, but there was no sign at all of them.

I now perceived a Rumpler a little east of my formation, and above, just hoarding up plenty of height to go over our lines on long reconnaissance. The Rumpler came towards us, no doubt thinking we were German scouts, for we were over fifteen miles east of the trenches, and then perceiving his mistake, he turned off east, nose down, and I went off in pursuit. Slowly I caught up with him, for the Maybach Rumplers were undoubtedly very fast, and having got into position, fired a good long burst from both guns, after which the two-seater's nose dropped vertically.

Then all his four wings fell off and scattered to a thousand pieces and the fuselage went down with the speed of a meteor, its engine emitting volumes of blue smoke. The fuselage hit the ground east of Caudry, and the wing wreckage went floating down slowly, and, no doubt with the aid of the easterly wind, scattered itself on the country surrounding the Hun aerodrome west of Caudry, where it seemed the Rumplers' home was.

After this I zoomed up and saw all my patrol a little west of me, for I had outdistanced them while chasing the Hun, my engine being more powerful than theirs.

It now seemed that the Bristols had not come across the lines yet, so we flew west, and then saw a DFW just east of Vaucelles Wood, a little higher than we were. We flew towards him, and I very soon got a good position and fired a splendid burst from both guns, the DFW at once bursting into flames and whirling down to earth, 15,000 feet below, like a blazing comet. A few thousand feet above the earth the two-seater fell to pieces and the wreckage fell just south of Vaucelles Wood, where it burnt for a long while on the ground.

We now turned away and saw a little LVG slightly north of us. We soon did an enveloping move and surrounded him. I secured my firing position, and was just about to open when I glanced up and saw Junor diving steeply on the LVG, his guns going *Ra-ta-ta-ta*, *Br-br-br-br*, *a-Ra-ta-ta-ta-ta-Rat*, and I was then obliged to turn away, for he would have dived into me had I not cleared out.

One has to be very careful when fighting in formation, for most young pilots in their few first fights see nothing but the Hun, and don't trouble about avoiding their comrades.

Soon between the whole patrol we pushed the LVG down, emitting clouds of steam, but he was under control. While I was looking at him, I suddenly realized that there was a war on, for *cack*, *cack-cack-cack*, *zip*, *zip*, *bang crash*, and I felt the bullets hitting my dear old SE. On looking up I saw the "green-tailed" Albatros high above me. He had come down from a good height and tried a long-range snipe, but beyond hitting my machine did no other damage.

We had one or two indecisive skirmishes, and the time being short, we went towards our lines. While on our way I looked over my machine, and found that one of my elevators was out of action, the control wire having been cut. However, I still had another elevator which worked, so I had no cause to worry. On crossing our line I saw just in front of me a Rumpler flying west. He saw us and turned SE, but I soon caught him, and, getting into position, fired a long burst at him, after which he went down in a right-hand spiral, out of control, and when about 5,000 feet above the ground he burst into flames and hit the ground near Gouy and lay blazing furiously, a charred monument of my fiftieth aerial victory.

We flew back to the aerodrome, for we had had a morning's fine fun, and as soon as I had reported to the squadron office, I went out again on Galley's machine, for the morning was still young and the visibility good. As I left the ground and climbed up east I experienced all these joys only known to the pilot who has done a lot of Hun stalking, though perhaps that same thrill is not unknown to big-game hunters.

Having gone as far as St.-Quentin, I turned north, and after ten minutes or so saw a hostile two-seater west of me and well above. I was now at 15,000 feet, so I remained between him and his line, so that I could climb up to his height without his seeing me, otherwise had I gone at him as soon as I had seen him I should only have alarmed him, and he would have scampered off east over his lines like a rabbit.

Very slowly I approached his height, but Galley's machine, which I was flying, was not anything like as good as my own, which at that moment was having a new elevator fitted at the aerodrome. The Hun was now just east of Bapaume, at 16,000 feet, and was heading northeast towards Douai, in an endeavour to outdistance me, but soon I caught him, and, after a very short burst from both my guns, the Rumpler dived and, after going down five hundred feet, every one of his four wings fell off and went fluttering down like a lot of wastepaper, while the fuselage went down with that wobbling motion which a stick has when one sees it fall.

I thought how ghastly it must be to have to fly over enemy lines on a machine which one knew would fall to pieces as soon as one did a small dive. I now flew back to the aerodrome, having again in the space of one day destroyed four enemy two-seaters. After lunch I again flew to the lines on my own machine, which had now been repaired, and although I saw several Huns I did not find a good chance of attacking them with any hope of a decision.

The next morning, February 17th, I left the ground about nine-thirty and got my height going towards Arras, and soon saw that enemy aerial activity was pronounced. I climbed to 15,000 feet east of Arras, and then saw two enemy two-seaters south of me, so I flew to the attack and found that the machines were an LVG escorted by a Hannover, the latter of which at once ran away. I secured a firing position behind the LVG, and after a good burst from both guns he went down out of control in a long diving side-slip, but he went too far east to watch him crash, so I could only claim him "out of control."

On turning away I found that a portion of my Vickers gun had broken, so I was now obliged to sacrifice 15,000 feet of valuable height in order that I might have the broken portion renewed at my aerodrome. Of course I could have stayed up and used my Lewis gun alone, but still when one has two guns going it gives one a great deal more confidence.

After my guns were going well again, I left the ground in search of prey. I had been up for about forty minutes when I saw a Rumpler cross our lines at 17,500 feet. He was above me, for I was at 17,000 feet. I followed him all the way to Arras and then back to Bourlon Wood, where we arrived at about 18,000 and 18,300 feet, respectively, the Rumpler still being above, for by now I had found that this Rumpler had about the best performance of any that I had seen up to that time.

At Bourlon Wood the Hun turned west again, and I followed

him as far as Bapaume, and again back to Bourlon Wood, over which we now arrived at 20,000 feet, with the Rumpler still a little above, for up at 20,000 feet it is impossible to zoom up to an opponent who is 200 feet above. By now the old Hun, realizing that he was still safe, turned once more west and flew to Péronne and again back to Bourlon, where we now arrived at 21,000 feet, with the Hun still a little higher. Then he started to fly, nose down, east, as apparently he had completed his task.

At last I was able to get a good position, after chasing him for fifty minutes, but on opening fire at close range, both my guns stopped at once, the Vickers owing to a broken belt, and the Lewis because of the intense cold. I could not rectify the Vickers, but after reloading the Lewis it fired fairly well. By now the Hun was diving fairly steeply and presented a very easy target, so I fired another burst from the Lewis, but apart from seeing my tracer bullets enter his fuselage it had no apparent effect.

We were now down to 10,000 feet, west of Cambrai, in a very short time, and seeing many other enemy machines about, I turned away.

I felt very ill indeed. This was not because of the height or the rapidity of my descent, but simply because of the intense cold which I experienced up high. The result was that when I got down to a lower altitude, and could breathe more oxygen, my heart beat more strongly and tried to force my sluggish and cold blood around my veins too quickly. The effect of this was to give me a feeling of faintness and exhaustion that can only be appreciated by those who have experienced it. My word, I did feel ill, and when I got on the ground and the blood returned to my veins, I can only describe the feeling as agony.

There are times while flying when one experiences such hardship and suffering that one is inclined to say, "No more flying for me," but after passing that state one becomes keen again and the fascination of the whole thing begins afresh.

I was very disappointed about the last Rumpler getting away, for I did try so hard to get him, and on that flight alone I spent over an hour between 17,000 and 22,000 feet.

One day about this time much amusement was caused by one of our pilots, now a prisoner, who had been fighting a Hun. When he came down he rushed into the mess, shouting, "Come and see my machine, you chaps! I've got some Hun blood on it!"

We all went out expecting to see his machine covered in Teuton gore, and found some sticky red substance on the undersurfaces of his wings. We had a look at this and found that it was some rust preventative which had run off the cross-bracing wires inside the wings. Poor old Mac—he was so disappointed, too!

The Hero's Life

from *Fighting the Flying Circus*

BY EDDIE V. RICKENBACKER

Eddie Rickenbacker was America's first air hero. He shot down twenty-six German planes in the final year of World War I, a score that only a handful of American pilots managed to surpass during World War II and none in the jet age since.

Rickenbacker was a recruiter's dream, a handsome, athletic young man with extraordinary reflexes and natural leadership ability who knew all there was to know about internal combustion engines. By the time America came into the war in 1917, Rickenbacker had won championships as a professional motorcycle racer and race-car driver. He enlisted in the U.S. Army and used his racing fame to wangle an assignment as General Pershing's personal chauffeur. Once in France he pulled more strings and got himself sent to a French flying school, where he took to flying as if he had been born with wings upon his back.

Rickenbacker flew the same way he raced—flat-out, right against the edge of the performance envelope. He enjoyed almost immediate success against the Germans. Like many fighter pilots since, Captain Eddie was not averse to acting as his own PR agent. In the excerpt that follows he stars in one of the very first movies about fighter pilots, filmed in 1918, appropriately enough, at the front. And they didn't use blanks in the guns. Then he does what he knew so well exactly how to do—shoot down German planes. But let's let Captain Eddie tell it.

THE NEW LIBERTY DULY ARRIVED, AND AFTER A BRIEF REHEARSAL of our parts in the coming show, we again had our machines run out on the field on the morning of October 21 and took our stations in the line. Captain Cooper was again placed in the

26

rear seat of the Liberty, with Jimmy Meissner in the front seat acting as his pilot. Jimmy was to keep his machine as near the actors as possible, always flying to the left side, so that the photographer might face the show and keep his handle turning with the least possible difficulty.

Reed Chambers sat in the front seat of the captured Hanover and piloted it. He carried two guns which would fire only tracer and flaming bullets, and with true movie instinct Reed was prepared to do his utmost to imitate with two guns the Roman-candle effect of the latest four-gun effort of the Huns whom he was supposed to represent.

In the rear seat of the Hun machine sat Thorn Taylor, the villain of the play. He was dressed in villainous-looking garments that would deceive even the most particular Hun. He too had a gun, one which swung on a tournelle and which would emit a stream of smoky and fiery projectiles when the climax of the action was reached. As a clever pièce de résistance Thorn carried with him, down out of sight of the camera, a dummy Boche pilot stuffed with straw. At the height of the tragedy Thorn was supposed to duck down out of sight behind his cockpit and heave overboard the stuffed figure, which would fall with outstretched arms and legs, head over heels to earth. This would portray the very acme of despair of the Boche aviators, who, it would be seen, preferred to hurl themselves out to certain death rather than longer face the furious assaults of the dashing young American air fighters.

As to the latter—I was supposed to be *it*. In my old Spad No. 1, with the Hat-in-the-Ring insignia plainly inscribed on the side of the fuselage and the red, white, and blue markings along wings and tail sufficiently glaring to prove to the most skeptical movie fan that this was indeed a genuine United States airplane—I was to be Jack the Giant Killer, with an abundance of smoky and fiery stuff pouring from all my guns every time the hostile machine hove in sight. A few films of a distant formation passing through the sky had been taken early in the game so as to delude the innocent public into the belief that I was going up to demolish the whole caravan with my lone machine. A series of falls and spins would put the one Hanover out of the fighting enough times to account for a whole formation of them. Then as the last desperate encounter took place, Thorn Taylor, after shooting all his spectacular ammunition well over my head, would force the dummy to commit suicide rather than longer endure the suspense of waiting.

It was a clever plot. The whole aerodrome was in raptures over the idea, and everybody quit work to gather on the field to witness the contest. I doubt if the later performances will ever have a more expectant, more interested, or so large an audience.

Jimmy and his camera operator got away safely this time, and right behind them the comedian and tragedians of the show winged their way. Arrived at 2,000 feet over the field we pulled up our belts and began the performance. It was necessary to keep an eye on the camera, so as not to get out of its beam while pulling off our most priceless stunts, and at the same time we had to be a little careful as to the direction in which our bullets were going. Captain Cooper was thrusting his head out into the slipstream manfully trying to keep my swifter-moving machine always within the range of his camera. As I came up under the Hanover airplane's tail I would let off a terrific stream of flaming projectiles which are perfectly visible to the naked eye and certainly ought to be caught by a camera even in the daytime. Thorn shot as lustily under me and over me as I approached and even Reed's front guns were spitting death in a continuous stream at the imaginary enemy planes ahead of him.

Over and over we repeated the performance, the Hanover dying a dozen deaths in as many minutes. At last, our movie ammunition beginning to near exhaustion, it became necessary to stage a big hit that denoted the climax of the play. Coming about above the Hanover, while Captain Cooper was grinding industriously away not over twenty feet from its side, I came down in a swift dive, made a zoom and a renversement on the opposite side of the Hanover, and kicking my rudder over, came back directly at the enemy, full into the gaping lens of the camera. Firing my last rounds of ammunition as I approached, I saw them go safely over the tops of both machines. As I drew into the closest possible distance that was safe for such a maneuver, I threw my Spad up into a zoom, passed over the vanquished Boche, and came back in a loop somewhere near my original position.

As I glanced at the Hanover I saw that she was doomed! A quantity of lampblack, released by the crafty Taylor, was drifting windward, indicating that something seriously wrong had occurred with the enemy machine. Such a dense cloud of smoke would satisfy the dullest intellect that he must soon begin to catch fire. Ah, ha! There she comes! I knew she was afire! Sure enough several bright landing flares suddenly ignited under the Hanover's wings throwing a bright gleam earthward, but were prevented from injuring the wings themselves by the tin surfaces above them. Finding existence on such a burning deck unendurable, the poor dummy gathered himself together in the arms of the stalwart Taylor, and with one tremendous leap he departed the blazing furnace forever!

While Taylor kept himself hidden below deck, Chambers, throwing out the last of his sack of lampblack, lifted over onto the side the doomed machine and gave a good exhibition of the falling leaf. Down—down it drifted, the daring photographer leaning far out of his cage to catch the last expiring gasps of the stricken Hanover—the last of the wicked formation of hostile machines that had dared to cross our frontiers early in the picture. And then—just as he was prepared to flash on the "good night" sign and entertain the departing audience with views of the best line of corsets to be had at reasonable prices at Moe Levy's emporium—just then the real climax of the play did appear.

We had wandered some little distance away from the vicinity of our aerodrome while firing genuine flaming bullets over each other, so that the falling missiles would not cause any injuries to property or persons below. Paying little attention as to just where we were flying, so long as open country was below us, we had not noticed that we were some miles south and west of our starting place and almost over the edge of a French aerodrome. Suddenly a puff of real Archie smoke in the vicinity of the Hanover told me that some enthusiastic outsider was volunteering his services in behalf of our little entertainment. Another and another shell burst before I could reverse my direction and get started to place my Spad close to the black machine wearing the Iron Cross of the kaiser.

Reed Chambers took in the situation at a glance. He pointed down the Hanover's nose and began to dive for a landing on the French aerodrome below us. At the same time several French Breguets left the field and began climbing up to assist me in my dangerous task of demolishing the Hanover.

Diving down to intervene before any more shooting was done, I succeeded in satisfying the Frenchmen that I had the affair well in hand and that the Hanover was coming down to surrender. Without further incident we all landed and got out of our machines. The French pilots, their mechanics, and poilus gathered about in a curious body while I laughingly hurried over to the side of Reed's machine and explained to the assembly the meaning of this strange performance. They all laughed heartily over their mistake—all except Reed and Thorn Taylor of the Hanover crew, who, from the expressions on their faces seemed to feel that the joke was on them.

Getting away again, the Hanover flew home under my protection. After it had landed I climbed up through the clouds where Jimmy and the movie man were still waiting for me. There I stunted for a while in front of the camera, giving some excellent views of an airplane bursting through the clouds and some close-up views of all the aerial tumbling that a Spad is capable of performing.

Next day Captain Cooper departed with his films for Paris, where he expected to turn them over to the American authorities and, if permitted, take a copy of them for public exhibition in Paris and the United States. A day or two after Christmas, on my way through Paris to New York, I learned that these pictures had turned out very well and would soon be shown in the movie palaces of the cities of America.

The following afternoon I escaped death by four red-nosed Fokkers by the narrowest margin ever vouchsafed to a pilot, and at the end of the combat flew safely home with my twenty-first and twenty-second victories to my credit. Curiously enough I had gone out over the lines alone that day with a craving desire to get a thrill. I had become "fed-up" with a continuation of eventless flights. Saying nothing to any of my fellows at the aerodrome, I went off alone with an idea of shooting down a balloon that I thought might be hanging just north of Montfaucon. While I did not get a shot at the balloon I got all the thrill I needed for several days to come.

It was about five-thirty in the afternoon when I ordered out my machine and set off for Montfaucon. As I neared the Meuse valley, I found the whole vicinity was covered with a thick haze—so thick in fact that the Germans had hauled down all their observation balloons. There was nothing a mile away that could be observed until another day dawned. Over to the south the sky was clearer. Our own balloons were still up. But no enemy airplanes would be likely to come over our front again so late in the evening.

While I was reflecting thus sadly, a bright blaze struck my eye from the direction of our nearest balloon. I headed around toward this spot in the shortest space of time. There could be but one explanation for such a blaze. A late-roving Hun must have just crossed the lines and had made a successful attack upon our balloon over Exermont!

He ought to be an easy victim, I told myself, as soon as he should start to cross back into Germany since I was on his direct line to the nearest point in his lines. He was now coming my way. Though I could not see him, I did see the bursting Archie shells following his course northward. He must pass well under me, and no doubt would be alone.

Just then a series of zipping streams of fire flashed by my face and through my fuselage and wings! I divined rather than saw what this was without looking around. Two, or perhaps more than two, enemy machines were diving on me from above. Utterly absorbed in planning what I should do to catch the other fellow I had been perfectly blind to my own surroundings. The Hun balloon strafer had a protective formation waiting for him. They had seen me come over and had doubtless been stalking me for many minutes without my knowing it.

These thoughts flashed through my mind as I almost automatically zoomed and did a climbing chandelle to escape the tracer bullets directed at me. I did not even stop to look at the position of my assailants. Knowing they were above, I concluded instantly that they had prepared for my diving away from them and that therefore that would be the best thing for me to avoid. I fortunately had reasoned correctly.

As I corkscrewed upward two red-nosed Fokkers, my old friends of the von Richthofen Circus sped down and passed me. But even before I had time enough to congratulate myself upon my luck, I discovered that only half of the formation had passed me. Two more Fokkers had remained above on the chance that I might refuse to adopt the plan they had determined for me.

One glimpse of the skillful maneuvers of these two upper Fokkers showed me that I was in for the fight of my life. I lost all interest in the progress of the balloon strafer that had destroyed one of our balloons under my very nose. My one desire was to get away off by myself, where thrills were never mentioned. The masterly way in which the Fokkers met and even anticipated every movement I made assured me that I had four very experienced pilots with whom to deal. Zigzagging and sideslipping helped me not one whit, and I felt that I was getting a wind up that would only sap my coolness and soon make me the easy prey of these four extremely confident Huns.

The two machines that had first attacked me remained below me in such a position that they invited my attack, while also preventing my escape in their direction. I made up my mind to start something before it was too late. Even though it meant getting into trouble, I decided that would be better than waiting around for them to operate upon me as they had no doubt been practicing in so many rehearsals. Noting a favorable opening for an attack on the nearest man below me I suddenly nosed over at him and went hurtling down, shooting from both guns.

I had aimed ahead of him, instead of directly at him, to compel him either to pass through the path of my bullets or else dip down his nose or fall over onto his wing—in either case providing me with a fair target before he could get far away. He either preferred the former course or else did not see my bullets until it was too late. He ran straight through my line of fire and he left it with a gush of flame issuing from his fuel tank. I believe that several bullets passed through the pilot's body as well.

Considerably bucked up with this success I did not seize this opportunity to escape, but executed a sudden loop and renversement, under the impression that my two enemies above would certainly be close onto my tail and preparing to shoot. Again I had guessed correctly, for not only were they in just the position I expected to find them and just where I myself would have been were I in their places, but they were also startled out of their senses over my sudden and unexpected assault upon their comrade. It is never an encouraging sight to see a comrade's machine falling in flames. It is enough to make the stoutest heart quail unless one is hemmed in and is fighting for his very life. But however that may be, my three foemen did not turn to continue the combat with me, nor did they even pause for an instant to threaten pursuit. All three continued their headlong dive for Germany with a faster and heavier Spad machine following them and gaining on them every second. My blood was up and I considered that I had been badly treated by the red-nosed Boches. I was three miles inside their lines, other enemy machines might easily be about—I had no time to look about to see—and I had just escaped from the worst trap into which I had ever fallen. Yet I could not resist the mad impulse of paying back the three Huns for the scare they had given me.

Though the Spad is faster than the Fokker, the fleeing Huns had a slight start over me and I did not immediately overtake them. One of the three gradually fell back behind the others. The ground was getting nearer and nearer and it was growing much darker as we approached the earth's surface. At about a thousand feet above ground I decided the nearest Fokker was within my range.

I opened fire, following his tactics as he maneuvered to avoid my stream of lead. After letting go at him some two hundred bullets, his machine dropped out of control and I ceased firing.

His two companions had never slackened their pace and were now well out of sight in the shadows. I watched my latest antagonist flutter down and finally crash and then awoke to the fact that I was being fired at by hundreds of guns from the ground. The gunners and riflemen were so near to me that I could distinctly see their guns pointed in my direction. I had dropped down to within a hundred yards of earth.

All the way back to the lines I was followed by machine-gun bullets and some Archie. Absolutely untouched I continued on to my field, where I put in my claim for two enemy Fokkers, and after seeing to the wounds of my faithful Spad walked over to the 94 mess for supper.

The Reprieve

from *Nine Lives*

BY ALAN C. DEERE

*During World War II New Zealander Alan C. Deere flew Spit-
fires for the RAF and was credited with destroying twenty-two
German aircraft. The excerpt that follows from his book,* Nine
Lives, *is one of the most harrowing aerial combat survival
stories in print. Deere had narrowly survived a midair collision
with another Spit several weeks earlier, but on July 11, 1940,
fate dealt him the card again. This time the other aircraft was
German. A nose-to-nose pass, both pilots pouring shells at
the other, neither willing to break off—this not-uncommon
scenario usually resulted in a spectacular collision that instantly
launched both men into eternity. Miraculously, the gods
granted Deere another reprieve. Here is the way he remembered it.*

JULY 11TH WAS PARTICULARLY HECTIC, AND BOTH FLIGHTS FLEW
continuous convoy patrols throughout the day. "B" Flight was
engaged on two occasions, with losses on both sides. On the
fourth trip of the day I ran into trouble while leading my flight
to investigate what was reported as unidentified activity five
miles east of Deal. We had just crossed the coast at a height of
1,500 feet when I spotted an aircraft flying at wave-top height.
It was a seaplane painted silver, and from a distance there appeared to be civilian registration letters painted on the upper
surface of the wing. I was wondering what to do about this
unexpected discovery when Johnny burst through on the R/T.

"Red Leader, there are about a dozen 109s flying in loose
formation, well behind and slightly above the seaplane."

"Thanks, Johnny," I replied, "that makes the seaplane enemy
so far as I am concerned."

The camouflaged 109s were difficult to pick up against the gray background of the sea and it was a moment or two before I could locate them.

"Okay, Yellow Leader, I see them. You take your section and go for the seaplane. We'll try and distract the escort; they don't appear to have seen us as yet."

I ordered Red section to follow me and, banking around to get behind the enemy fighters, dived into the attack. The Huns soon spotted us, or perhaps Johnny's section diving toward the seaplane, for as we leveled out behind them, the leader split his formation in two. One-half broke upward and to the right in a steep turn while the other half performed a similar manoeuvre, but to the left. "No fool this leader," I thought to myself. "That's a smart move." I remembered this manoeuvre later on when the RAF was on the offensive, and used it with telling effect against defending German fighters.

The Hun leader had timed his break perfectly and he had certainly put us at a disadvantage by splitting his force. There was only one thing to do: break formation and have a go, each pilot for himself. We were outnumbered by about six to one and were more likely to confuse the Hun in this way, thus diverting attention from Johnny, who had just given the order for his section to attack the seaplane.

Fastening on to the tail of a yellow-nosed Messerschmitt I fought to bring my guns to bear as the range rapidly decreased, and when the wingspan of the enemy aircraft fitted snugly into the range scale bars of my reflector sight, I pressed the firing button. There was an immediate response from my eight Brownings, which, to the accompaniment of a slight bucketing from my aircraft, spat a stream of lethal lead targetwards. "Got you," I muttered to myself as the small dancing yellow flames of exploding "De Wilde" bullets spattered along the Messerschmitt's fuselage. My exultation was short-lived. Before I could fire another burst two 109s wheeled in behind me. I broke hard into the attack pulling my Spitfire into a climbing, spiraling turn as I did so, a manoeuvre I had discovered in previous combats with

109s to be particularly effective. And it was no less effective now; the Messerschmitts literally "fell out of the sky" as they stalled in an attempt to follow me.

I soon found another target. About three thousand yards directly ahead of me, and at the same level, a Hun was just completing a turn preparatory to reentering the fray. He saw me almost immediately and rolled out of his turn towards me so that a head-on attack became inevitable. Using both hands on the control column to steady the aircraft and thus keep my aim steady, I peered through the reflector sight at the rapidly closing enemy aircraft. We opened fire together, and immediately a hail of lead thudded into my Spitfire. One moment the Messerschmitt was a clearly defined shape, its wingspan nicely enclosed within the circle of my reflector sight, and the next it was on top of me, a terrifying blur which blotted out the sky ahead. Then we hit.

The force of the impact pitched me violently forward onto my cockpit harness, the straps of which bit viciously into my shoulders. At the same moment, the control column was snatched abruptly from my gripping fingers by a momentary, but powerful, reversal of elevator load. In a flash it was over; there was clear sky ahead of me, and I was still alive. But smoke and flame were pouring from the engine, which began to vibrate, slowly at first but with increasing momentum, causing the now-regained control column to jump back and forwards in my hand. Hastily I closed the throttle and reached forward to flick off the ignition switches, but before I could do so the engine seized and the airscrew stopped abruptly. I saw with amazement that the blades had been bent almost double with the impact of the collision; the Messerschmitt must have been just that fraction above me as we hit.

With smoke now pouring into the cockpit I reached blindly forward for the hood-release toggle and tugged at it violently. There was no welcoming and expected rush of air to denote that the hood had been jettisoned. Again and again I pulled at the toggle but there was no response. In desperation I turned to the normal release catch and exerting my full strength endeavoured to slide back the hood. It refused to budge; I was trapped. There was only one thing to do: try to keep the aircraft under control and head for the nearby coast. The speed had by now dropped off considerably, and with full backward pressure on the stick I was just able to keep a reasonable gliding altitude. If only I could be lucky enough to hit in open country where there was a small chance that I might get away with it.

Frantically I peered through the smoke and flame enveloping the engine, seeking with streaming eyes for what lay ahead. There could be no question of turning; I had no idea what damage had been done to the fuselage and tail of my aircraft, although the mainplanes appeared to be undamaged, and I daren't risk even a small turn at low level, even if I could have seen to turn.

Through a miasmatic cloud of flame and smoke the ground suddenly appeared ahead of me. The next moment a post flashed by my wingtip, and then the aircraft struck the ground and ricocheted into the air, again finally returning to earth with a jarring impact, and once again I was jerked forward onto my harness. Fortunately the straps held fast and continued to do so as the aircraft ploughed its way through a succession of splintering posts before finally coming to a halt on the edge of a cornfield. Half-blinded by smoke and frantic with fear I tore at my harness release pin. And then with my bare hands wielding the strength of desperation, I battered at the Perspex hood which entombed me. With a splintering crash it finally cracked open, thus enabling me to scramble from the cockpit to the safety of the surrounding field.

At a safe distance from the aircraft I sat down to observe the damage to person and property. My hands were cut and bleeding; my eyebrows were singed; both knees were badly bruised; and blood trickled into my mouth from a slightly cut lip. But I was alive! I learned later from the technical officer who examined the wreckage after the fire had been put out that the seat had broken free from the lower retaining bar, thus pivoting upwards, and so throwing my knees against the lower part of the dashboard.

The aircraft had ploughed a passage through three fields, studded with anti-invasion posts erected to prevent enemy gliders from landing, and bits of aircraft and posts were strewn along the three hundred yards of its path. My Spitfire was now a blazing mass of metal from which a series of explosions denoted that the heat was igniting the unused ammunition, to the consternation of a knot of onlookers who had by now collected at the scene of the crash.

A woman, whom I had observed coming from a nearby farmhouse, approached me and said:

"I have telephoned Manston airfield and they say that an ambulance and fire engine are already on the way. Won't you come in and have a cup of tea?"

"Thank you, I will, but I would prefer something stronger if you've got it."

"Yes, I think there is some whisky in the house. Will that do?"

"Yes thanks, just what the doctor would order. I'm sorry about messing up your fields; let's hope the fire engine gets here before the fire spreads to that field of corn. Incidentally, how far are we from Manston?"

"Oh not far, about five miles by road. Your people should be here soon."

Turning to a small cluster of the more curious onlookers, who had crept closer to the wreckage, I said, "I advise you to stand well clear of the aircraft. There is plenty of high-octane fuel in the tanks and an explosion is a distinct possibility." This remark had an immediate effect and they hastily retreated to a safe distance.

Before long, an anxious MO arrived with the ambulance and examined me cursorily before conveying me back to Manston. The squadron had returned to Rochford by the time I arrived, so I was forced to spend the night there. If the doctor had had his way I would have been bedded down in the station sick quarters, but after a certain amount of persuasive talk on my part he released me to return to the mess. The following morning saw me airborne in a Tiger Moth trainer, accompanied by Flying Officer Ben Bowring, a prewar rugger compatriot, and headed for Rochford with thoughts of a couple of days off. There was to be no respite, however. "Prof's" first words on seeing me were:

"Thank heavens you're back, Al. Are you fit to fly?"

"Reluctantly, yes," I answered. "A bit shaken I must admit. Why the urgent note in your voice?"

"Well, we are damned short of pilots. Perhaps you haven't been told yet, but we lost two of your chaps in that show yesterday, both presumed killed."

Frankly, I had hoped for a day or two off the station, perhaps a quick sortie to London. I was pretty sore and a bit shaken, but quite obviously I couldn't be spared.

Down at dispersal Johnny greeted me with, "We are in quite a mess for aircraft. There are only four serviceable, so you needn't expect to fly this morning."

"I'm in no hurry," I answered.

Scramble

from *Ginger Lacey, Fighter Pilot*
by RICHARD TOWNSHEND BICKERS

James H. "Ginger" Lacey was a sergeant pilot during the Battle of Britain and one of the RAF's top scorers. He shot down a total of twenty-eight Axis aircraft and finished the war as a squadron leader in Burma, but in September 1940 he became famous as the man who shot down a Heinkel that had just bombed Buckingham Palace. Insult to the king and all that, don't you know. Here is how he did it.

FAMILIARITY WITH COMBAT, AND CONFIRMATION OF A MAN'S PROWESS in it, did not lessen the strain of aerial warfare. Indeed, for some, the longer they survived the greater seemed the probability that their turn to be killed could not possibly be much more deferred. Whatever the reason, there were many by now who reacted agonizingly to every announcement from the Tannoy, and Lacey was one of them. Every time the loudspeaker hummed its preliminary note on being switched on, he had to rush from his bed in the dispersal hut, or from the grass under his Hurricane's wing, where he was lying, and vomit. Whether the message turned out to be "AC Plonk to report to the orderly room immediately," "The film in the station cinema tonight is . . . ," or the anticipated "501 Squadron—scramble!" the effect was the same. His stomach muscles jerked convulsively, his fatigue-sodden body and mind could not control them, and he must be sick.

Flying six and eight times a day, never less than four times, week in and week out, had brought all the pilots to such a state of tiredness that they could not bother even to walk away from their aircraft on landing. In that blisteringly hot summer it was easiest just to lie on the grass in the shade of a Hurricane's or Spitfire's wing and fall instantly asleep. If the intelligence officer came to ask you for a combat report, you put one in, and with it your claims for aircraft destroyed or damaged. If nobody asked you, you did not trouble to volunteer the information; until, perhaps, the day was finished and memory dulled. In this way, many of the pilots were never credited with victories they had won. Time and again there was another scramble before an IO could make out combat reports on the mission just completed, and by the time the boys were back from that one, everyone had forgotten about the previous sortie . . . and so on, with scrambles piling up and each obliterating the details of its predecessor. Time after time, a pilot who had scored successes on an early sortie must have been killed on a later one before ever being able to make a report, which would, at least, have given him permanent credit for what he had done.

Not that the Battle of Britain pilots needed any sordid accretion of numbers after their names to proclaim their skill, bravery, and stamina. Just by being airborne, reacting to each German raid, they were saving the world: their presence was enough, on many occasions, to turn the enemy away before combat was joined. And the strain of operational flying was no less when no enemy was encountered, than when a vicious dogfight was being decided: for each time they flew they expected to see the German and attack him, and it was this as much as, perhaps more than, the moments of battle that frayed their nerves and robbed them of refreshing sleep and proper relaxation.

Some of them became so emotionally numb that they were like automata: morose, withdrawn, wanting neither food nor companionship, dragging themselves through each day in almost a stupor. Others, more highly strung, teetered constantly on the brink of frenzy: talking incessantly, smoking heavily, forcing themselves to loud laughter and feigned high spirits. But among the unfriendly silence on the one hand and the horseplay on the other were the majority: levelheaded, thoroughly professional, in control of themselves. Perhaps Lacey's laconic Yorkshire character was as much responsible for keeping him sane and alive through that period as his naturally brilliant eyesight and swift mental and physical reaction to quickly changing events. If it hadn't been for that damned, whining Tannoy, he would probably never have shown any outward signs of nervous wear. Each day made the situation more desperate, with an average loss of fifteen fighter aircraft and ten pilots, nearly all in 11 Group.

On the thirtieth of August, over the North Foreland, he fought an engagement with thirty or forty Me-110 Jaguars which did not stay to dispute the issue: he put two long bursts into one of them, saw it stagger into the low haze with smoke emerging from one engine, and reckoned that he had a "probable" at least. There was a twenty-minute break at base while the aircraft were refueled and rearmed; but the German Air Force was under orders to batter its way through the British defenses and prepare the ground for Hitler's final, devastating assault: 501 was soon in the air again, this time with the controller ordering, "Vector two seven zero. A hundred-plus bandits approaching Dungeness." And how right he was, for there were the He-111s and Me-110s in a countless swarm.

Lacey, Yellow Two, picked the 110 which was leading a big formation and attacked from ahead, opening fire at 400 yards and continuing until, as his combat report describes his actions, "collision was imminent. So I broke underneath, and when I pulled up, I saw that the Me-110 had left the formation and was going east with smoke coming from its port engine. Climbing, I found a He-111 just ahead, also going east, rather slowly, as though it had been damaged. I attacked, opened fire at 250 yards, and saw the undercarriage drop and the port engine catch fire. As I closed, long flames and thick black smoke made vision difficult. I had to break off, as I was attacked by several 110s. I continued fighting until I had no ammunition left."

But there was more in store before the thirtieth of August came to a close. Lacey recalls that "later on that day I had an interesting experience." It seems that a newsreel film unit was working on Gravesend aerodrome and wanted a picture of a squadron scramble. Agreeably, the CO allowed his pilots to get into their cockpits while the cameras whirred, preparatory to demonstrating a quick, dummy takeoff.

But even in those circumstances they had their R/T sets switched on, and with the cameras barely in position, the sector controller's voice dinned in the pilots' ears, "Scramble. Bandits in Thames estuary."

The delighted cameramen marveled at the cooperation they were receiving: the Hurricanes thundered across the airfield, climbed steeply, formed up, and headed eastward.

Over the estuary, 501 saw well over fifty He-111s, with several Do-17s and a big escort of Me-109s, flying due west. The CO led them into a head-on attack and they held their squadron formation, four vics of three, in the manner of head-ons of that day. "On the CO's word we all put our fingers on the trigger, not looking where we were shooting, but just keeping our formation and flying straight through the middle of the Germans. With ninety-six machine-guns blazing straight at them, it must have been pretty frightening. It had the desired effect and the Heinkels split all over the sky. We were then able to pick them out one at a time. This time, however, as we were going in, I started to be hit by very accurate fire. I could see bullets entering my wings, coming in from directly ahead, and also straight into the engine."

Oil sprayed all over the cockpit, from the punctured oil cooler at the bottom of the radiator. He pulled out to starboard, and as he banked, bullets were piercing his wings from beneath. He completed his turn and began gliding southward, away from the battle. Immediately, bullets hammered through his aircraft from the rear. "So whoever was doing the shooting was either very lucky or knew a lot about deflection, because it had been constantly changing."

He jettisoned his oil-smeared cockpit hood and "was about to bail out when I suddenly realized that I was going to fall in the Thames; and I wasn't particularly keen on that."

It was a heart-stopping moment. The air was full of hostile fighters and his speed was very slow now that he had no engine. If he did bail out, the odds were that some sporting Luftwaffe pilot would shoot at him as he hung beneath his parachute. Either way, he was a sitting duck. He could only hope that other Hurricanes and Spitfires were holding the attention of the enemy enough to divert them from pursuing aircraft which were already out of the fight.

The engine was showing no signs of catching fire, and the oil had run dry and was no longer spurting all over him, so he decided to stay in his machine, glide as far as the Isle of Sheppey, and bail out there. But when he arrived over this small piece of land he saw how unlikely it was that, without knowing the wind direction, he would succeed in landing on it. So he made for the mainland, aware by now that he had enough altitude to glide all the way back to Gravesend.

Pumping the undercarriage and flaps down by hand, he circled the aerodrome to lose height and made a perfectly judged landing. "And finished my run, with a dead engine, right smack beside the point from which I'd taken off. Much to the joy of the newsreel unit, who were busy taking pictures of my landing."

There were eighty-seven bullet entry holes on Lacey's Hurricane, and innumerable bigger gashes where lumps of metal, ripped internally from the aircraft, had been smashed right through it.

"I was awfully pleased with myself, having brought the aircraft back in that condition; until I eventually saw the engineer officer. His remark was, 'Why the hell didn't you bail out? If you'd bailed out of that thing, I'd have got a new aircraft tomorrow morning! Now, I've got to set to work and mend it.' "

Lacey's postscript is: "It certainly made me change my ideas about what was a good thing and what was a bad thing."

The pattern of the times is inexorable and appears to be never-ending. Rise at an early hour: 4 A.M., perhaps, certainly never later than six-thirty. Fly standing patrol somewhere around

"Hell's Corner," the southeast angle of England. Land· at Hawkinge. Scramble ... scramble ... and scramble again. One more standing patrol, waiting for an enemy who might or might not come. Back to Gravesend. Maybe, a night standby. If not, a hurried visit to someplace where there are ordinary people to mix with and take one's mind off revs and boost and deflection shots. Finally, a flop into bed and instant sleep, with always the semiconscious appreciation that tomorrow might be one's last day of life. Or the day after that. Sometime next week at the latest, surely, with the huge enemy formations coming and coming again, and the odds seldom better than five to one.

And still there is room for humor. The growing number of Poles, Czechs, Norwegians, Dutch, Belgians, and Frenchmen appearing on RAF stations gives rise to new problems and birth to new anecdotes. A favorite one is about the Polish airman who, on being told by a station commander that he is to be remanded for a court-martial, drops instantly in a dead faint. It is only when the interpreter explains that, at home, this usually means execution by a firing squad within four hours that the CO understands why it is that he cannot strike similar terror into the hearts of his British airmen. There is another, too, about the foreign nobleman, commanding a unit of his countrymen, who had to be dissuaded from his feudal method of dispensing justice: arguing against the necessity to hear evidence when a man is on a charge, he declares, "If *I* say he is guilty, he *is* guilty." The RAF likes those stories.

The fifth of September. "501 Squadron scramble!"

The familiar voice of the controller. "I've got some trade for you coming in from the south. Maintain vector one zero zero, making Angels twenty-five."

And the CO, matter-of-fact, sounding even indifferent: "Understood. Any idea how many Bandits?"

"Looks like sixty-plus."

"Good show."

A few seconds' pause, then some wit breaks R/T silence with

a terrifyingly realistic imitation of machine-gun fire, in the best music-hall style.

But you can't hide your identity from men with whom you share almost every waking second. The boss, sounding reluctantly amused, tells him to shut up.

The controller again. "What Angels now?"

"Just passing through Angels twenty-two."

"Okay. Level out. Trade approaching from south at Angels eighteen."

"Understood."

"I'm going to turn you, presently, and bring you in from up-sun."

"Thanks!" The irony in the leader's acknowledgment is not entirely accidental.

"Bandits three o'clock, range forty. Start turning now onto two seven zero."

The squadron wheel, turning to their right so that they will face the enemy, who is approaching from the south. They settle down to a due westerly heading, and the controller's voice gives them some more help. "Bandits now ten o'clock, range fifteen."

They begin to wriggle on their parachute packs, feeling the chafing of their harness straps as sweat starts involuntarily to run over their backs and chests. In their silk gloves, palms grow moist, while mouths feel dry and eyes burn with the concentration of staring, staring, always staring . . . at the man ahead and the man on your wing . . . at the burning, sunlit sky . . .

"Target should be eleven o'clock, range five—"

And instantly the leader's exultant "I've got 'em. . . . Tallyho! Tallyho!" And the tight wheel, with your heart pounding and your eyes smarting with the glare on those threatening cross-shapes, which are suddenly Messerschmitts and Dorniers and Heinkels in countless numbers. The air around you boils and seethes as you are tossed around and sucked down by slipstream and explosion. Here a bomber goes to smithereens in a mighty thunderclap that almost shatters your Perspex windscreen, as incendiary bullets hit its bomb bays. There a fighter in an inverted, flaming spin—God! You see it is a Hurricane and recognize the letters on its side . . . so much for your double date that evening to take those two girls to a dance . . . one of them would have to find another partner . . . and now there are three 109s on your tail and you are on the tail of one yourself. Who would get whom first?

Grip the stick, thumb poised over firing button. Ease the throttle back a shade . . . one . . . two . . . three . . . four seconds—would the brute never show signs of damage? Ah! That is better: a puff of smoke . . . another two seconds . . . a flicker of crimson along the edge of his cowling . . . then, suddenly, the 109 is on its back and a sprawling figure is dropping from its open cockpit.

Look in the mirror, throttle back, watch the three behind overshoot, open the taps again, get the rearmost in your sights . . . one, two, three seconds . . . a vomit of oil-streaked smoke, the Me staggers, a sliver of metal drums against your cowling . . . you see a wingtip sawn off as you give another burst . . . and the pilot doesn't get away from that one.

One hour and forty-five minutes later, you land back from the longest operational sortie you have flown to date, but with two more Me-109s confirmed to bring your score up to fifteen.

On the thirteenth of September, they were at Kenley, thirteen miles south of London and four from Croydon, where they had been posted on the tenth.

A fifty-minute patrol yielded nothing, and then the weather deteriorated.

But it wasn't long before Ops were on the telephone to the crew room to ask for a volunteer to take off and look for a Heinkel which was somewhere over London. "But," they warned, "owing to the unbroken cloud everywhere in the southeast, whoever goes will probably be unable to land: it will mean bailing out."

Lacey said he had always wondered what it was like to bail out, and off he went.

It was a long stalk, and he was airborne for two hours.

The controller guided him eastward, at 14,000 feet, above the solid layer of cloud that covered the whole of the southeast of England. A turn to the south, another to the east; a turn to the southeast, then east again. The controller's directions were concise and intelligent, but the Heinkel was elusive. Until . . .

"I saw it, slipping through the cloud tops, half in and half out of cloud, making for the coast. I didn't know where I was, because I hadn't seen the ground since taking off. I dived down on him and got in one quick burst, which killed his rear gunner. I knew he was dead because I could see him lying over the edge of the rear cockpit. Of course the Heinkel dived into cloud, and as I was coming up behind him, I throttled hard back and dropped into formation on him, in cloud. He turned, in cloud, two or three times, still making a generally southeasterly direction, and I'm quite certain he thought he had lost me or that I'd stayed above the cloud. Actually, I was slightly below and to one side. You couldn't see very well, in cloud, through the front windscreen of a Hurricane, but you could see through the side quarter-panel and I was staying just close enough to keep him in sight through this. I stayed with him in all his turns. He made one complete circle and then carried on southeasterly. Eventually he eased his way up to the top and broke cloud, presumably to see if the fighter was still hanging around. Just as he broke cloud and I was dropping back into a position where I could open fire, the dead gunner was pulled away from his guns and another member of the crew opened up on me, at a range of, literally, feet.

"I remember a gaping hole appearing in the bottom of the cockpit. The entire radiator had been shot away, and I knew it was just a matter of time before the engine would seize, so I put my finger on the trigger and kept it there until my guns stopped firing. By that time he had both his engines on fire and I was blazing quite merrily too. I think it was a glycol fire rather than an oil fire, but *what* was burning didn't particularly interest me: I knew that *I* was burning and I was going to have to get out.

"As soon as the guns ran out of ammunition, by which time

the He-111 was diving steeply through the cloud, I left the aircraft.

"I came out of cloud in time to see my aircraft dive into the ground and explode. While drifting down, I saw various people running across the fields to where it had crashed. There was one man passing almost underneath me, when I was about five hundred feet up, so I shouted. This chap stopped and looked in all directions, so I shouted again, 'Right above you.' He looked up, and I saw that he was a Home Guard.

"As he saw me, he raised a double-barreled shotgun to his shoulder and took aim. I knew it was a double-barreled shotgun because I was looking down the barrels; and they looked like twin railway tunnels!

"I shouted, 'For God's sake don't shoot,' and amplified it with a lot of Anglo-Saxon words that I happened to know and continued to exhort him not to shoot for the rest of my way down; and added a lot more Anglo-Saxon words.

"Eventually I fell in a field and just sat there, but he still kept me covered with his gun. I said, 'Hang on a minute while I get at my pocket and show you my identity card.' He put his gun down and said, 'I don't want to see your identity card: anyone who can swear like that couldn't possibly be German.'

"I was a little bit singed [his trousers were burned off to the knees] but had beaten out the fire on the way down, and my face was a bit burnt. Not very burnt, because I was always careful to pull my goggles down as soon as I saw an enemy aircraft. I'd seen too many of my friends in hospital who hadn't pulled their goggles down, and burnt eyes were a pilots' trademark that I was determined not to get."

He had come down near Leeds Castle, which was the officers' annexe of the Shorncliffe Military Hospital. Here he had an argument with a doctor who wanted to put him to bed; Lacey was determined that he would first telephone the airfield and inform the squadron that he was safe. But, owing to the bombing, there were so many telephone lines down that he had to abandon it after two hours of trying.

"So I told them that they must send me back, and I had to get back before the squadron packed up for the day, otherwise a 'Missing, believed killed' telegram would go off to my mother, and I didn't want her to have that kind of shock."

The doctor had told him to report sick on returning to camp, so he dismissed the ambulance at the guard room and walked to the officers' mess to report to his CO. By then, he had on a new pair of trousers which concealed the burns on his legs, "so I was able to go straight back on readiness."

It was only now that he learned that the Heinkel he had just shot down had bombed Buckingham Palace.

His log-book carries the entry, "Must remember to leave bombers alone in future. They are shooting me down much too often."

Spitfire Tales

from *Fly for Your Life*

BY LARRY FORRESTER

Fought in August and September of 1940, the Battle of Britain is probably the most famous aerial conflict of all time, and rightly so. The fate of a nation hinged on the outcome. In his biography of Robert Stanford Tuck, Larry Forrester caught very well the spirit of the British fighter pilots and the people they were trying to protect. The excerpt that follows details a few of Tuck's adventures in Spitfires.

"Bob" Tuck managed to shoot down twenty-nine German planes before he was himself shot down over occupied Europe. He spent the remainder of the war as a guest of the Germans.

THE VICKERS AIRCRAFT COMPANY HAD TAKEN OVER BROOKLANDS, the prewar motor-racing track, as a test field and experimental plant. Tuck was sent there one day to have a new camera-gun fixture installed in his aircraft. The job done, he hopped over to Northolt to have lunch with Group Capt. "Tiny" Vass, an officer he'd known since training days. In the middle of the meal the alarm went and the squadrons scrambled. Vass grabbed a phone and learned that a big battle was developing off Beachy Head, Sussex. At that moment the air-raid warning sounded. Station orders were that all nonflying personnel were to take shelter in slit trenches during raids.

Vass, a mountainous man with the strength of a farmhouse, grabbed Tuck's arm and propelled him out of the mess.

"Come along, Tommy. Down the bloody bunker!"

Protesting, Tuck was shoved into a damp hole where an NCO unceremoniously rammed a tin hat on his head. Looking out across the grass, he could see his aircraft—the only one left at dispersal. He started to clamber out but Vass grabbed his ankle and hauled him back. They argued for precious minutes before Vass finally shrugged and said, "Dammit, I can't give you permission to take off, not on your own. But . . . well, I can't be everywhere, I can't see everything that goes on, can I?" He turned his back and concentrated on surveying the sky to the east. Tuck went west—scrambling out of the trench and pelting across to his machine. He started it himself and was airborne within two minutes.

He picked up Hornchurch control and followed their directions. As he crossed the coast, far to the north and very high he could see a tremendous tangled mass of vapor trails, and tiny glints of metal . . . then the hurtling, weaving fighters, mere dots, flitting in and out of sight, like dust motes in the sun's rays. He advanced his throttle through the gate into emergency power and clambered up frantically to join in the fray. Soon he could distinguish 109s, Hurris, Spits, 110s, a few Ju-88s. . . . It was the biggest fight he'd yet seen, an awe-inspiring spectacle that made his throat tighten and produced an odd, damp feeling at the temples and wrists.

Then suddenly, far below him two 88s passed, very close together, striking out for home at sea level. He turned out from the land, away from the main scrap, and with a long, shallow dive got well ahead of them. Then he turned again, due west, dropped low over the water and made a head-on attack.

The port one reared up so violently as the Spitfire's bullets ripped into the cabin that its slender fuselage seemed to bend backwards, like the body of a leaping fish. Then one wing dipped. The plane cartwheeled and vanished in an explosion of white water. It was exactly as if a depth charge had gone off.

He pulled up sharply into a half loop, rolled off the top and dived hard after the second bomber. He passed above it, raced ahead, and came round again for another head-on attack.

Tracer came lobbing leisurely at him: from this angle it wasn't in streaks, but in separate, round blobs, like a long curving chain of electric lightbulbs. The stuff was strangely beautiful, the way it glowed even in the broad daylight. At first it was well out of range, but as the two aircraft raced towards each other, suddenly he was flying in the broad jet of the Junkers' forward guns, and the tracer seemed to come alive and spurt straight for his face at bewildering speed. He concentrated on his own shooting, and saw his stuff landing on the bomber's nose and canopy.

The enemy's silhouette, limned almost black against the sunlight, remained squarely in his sight, growing with incredible rapidity, and all the time those wicked blue flashes twinkled merrily on it. It came on and on like that, calm and beautiful and stately as a giant albatross, straight and unflinching as though it were some purely automatic missile, an unfeeling super arrow, scientifically, inexorably aimed so as to drive its point between his eyes.

He had the sudden unsettling conviction that this one was different from all the others. This one was more dangerous. It wasn't going to stop firing at him, it wasn't going to break off no matter how much lead he pumped into it.

This one could be death.

All this was happening, all these thoughts and feelings were crowding on him, in the space of a mere two or three seconds. But everything was so clear, so sharply focused. The moment seemed to stand still, in order to impress its every detail on his mind.

The silhouette grew and grew until it seemed to fill the world. He clenched his teeth and kept firing to the last instant—and to the instant beyond the last. To the instant when he knew they were going to crash, that each had called the other's bluff, that they could not avoid the final terrible union.

Then it was a purely animal reflex that took command, yanked the stick over, and lashed out at the rudder. Somehow the Spitfire turned away and scraped over the bomber's starboard wing. There could have been only a matter of inches to spare, a particle of time too tiny to measure. Yet in that fleeting trice, as he banked and climbed, showing his belly to his foe, several shells smashed into the throat of the cowling and stopped up the Spitfire's breath. The elaborate systems of pipes and pumps and valves and containers which held the coolant and the oil, and perhaps the oil sump, too, were bent and kneaded into a shapeless, clogging mass that sent almost every instrument on the panel spinning and made the Merlin scream in agony.

"With what speed I had left I managed to pull up to around fifteen hundred feet. I was only about sixteen miles out, but I felt sure I'd never get back to the coast.

"I can't understand why that engine didn't pack up completely, there and then. Somehow it kept grinding away. I was very surprised, and deeply grateful for every second it gave me.

"As I coddled her round towards home I glimpsed the 88 skimming the waves away to port, streaming a lot of muck. In fact, he was leaving an oily trail on the water behind him. I had the consolation of thinking the chances were that he wouldn't make it either."

At the time, Tuck was heartily glad to see the Junkers in as poor shape as himself, and he hoped fervently that the German would crash into the sea.

"I trimmed up and the controls seemed quite all right. The windscreen was black with oil. Temperatures were up round the clocks and pressures had dropped to practically zero. But she kept on flying after a fashion. Every turn of the prop was an unexpected windfall—that engine should have seized up, solid, long before this.

"I knew it couldn't last, of course, and I decided I'd have to bail out into the Channel. It wasn't a very pleasant prospect. Ever since my prewar air collision I'd had a definite prejudice against parachutes. But the only alternative was to try to ditch her, and a Spit was notoriously allergic to landing on water—the air scoop usually caught a wave and then she would plunge straight to the bottom, or else the tail would smack the water and bounce back up hard and send you over in a somersault. Bailing out seemed the lesser of two evils, so I opened my hood, undid my straps, and disconnected everything except my R/T lead.

"It got pretty hot about now. The cockpit was full of glycol fumes and the stink of burning rubber and white-hot metal, and

I vomited a lot. I began to worry about her blowing up. But there were no flames yet, and somehow she kept dragging herself on through the sky, so I stayed put and kept blessing the Rolls-Royce engineers who'd produced an engine with stamina like this. And in no time at all I was passing over Beachy Head.

"I began to think after all I might make one of the airfields. The very next moment, a deep, dull roar like a blowlamp started down under my feet and up she went in flame and smoke.

"As I snatched the R/T lead away and heaved myself up to go over the side, there was a bang and a hiss and a clump of hot, black oil hit me full in the face. Luckily I had my goggles down, but I got some in my mouth and nose and it knocked me right back into the seat, spluttering and gasping. It took me a little while to spit the stuff out and wipe the worst of it off my goggles, and by that time I was down to well under a thousand. If I didn't get out but quick, my chute wouldn't open in time.

"It wasn't the recommended method of abandoning aircraft—I just grabbed one side with both hands, hauled myself up and over, and pitched out, headfirst. As soon as I knew my feet were clear I pulled the ripcord. It seemed to open almost immediately. The oil had formed a film over my goggles again and I couldn't see a thing. I pushed the goggles up, then it got in my eyes. I was still rubbing them when I hit the ground."

It was an awkward fall and he wrenched a leg and was severely winded. He was in a field just outside the boundaries of Plovers, the lovely, old-world estate of Lord Cornwallis at Horsmonden, Kent, and several people had witnessed his spectacular arrival. The blazing Spitfire crashed a few hundred yards away in open country. An estate wagon took him to the house, where His Lordship had already prepared a bed and called his personal physician. But Tuck, once he'd stopped vomiting, insisted on getting up to telephone his base—and once on his feet, wouldn't lie down again. He had a bath, leaving a thick coat of oil on His Lordship's tub, then despite the doctor's protests, borrowed a stick and hobbled downstairs in time to join the family for tea.

But after that, very suddenly, exhaustion took him. They

helped him back upstairs and he slept deeply for three hours. When he awoke his leg felt better and his host's son, Fiennes Cornwallis, was waiting to drive him to Biggin Hill, where a spare Spitfire would be available.

"Drop in for a bath anytime, m'boy," said His Lordship.

Precisely one week after his parachute escape he was in trouble again. And lucky again.

He had with him Bobbie Holland and Roy Mottram. An unidentified aircraft had been reported off Swansea. A day or two earlier the big oil-storage vats at Pembroke Dock had been hit, and they were still burning fiercely. The great pall of smoke reminded him of that first day's fighting over Dunkirk. Between 3,000 and 4,000 feet there was a solid shelf of white cloud, and running through this was a distinct, oily black ribbon.

Control told them a small coaster coming up the Bristol Channel was being bombed by a Do-17 and gave them a course to steer. They dived below the cloud and found the ship, but couldn't see the raider. All at once a plume of spray sprouted just off the coaster's port bow. Still they couldn't spot the Dornier, but now at least they knew its approximate position and course. At full throttle they flashed over the ship and climbed through the cloud. The topside was smooth as a billiard table. Still nothing. Tuck called to the others to stay up top, on lookout, then nipped back underneath.

As he broke cloud and circled, he spotted the big, loggerheaded Dornier making another run on the coaster. Another white plume blossomed close by the little vessel. On the deck he could see a group of seamen fighting back gamely with a couple of ancient Lewis guns.

The Dornier saw the Spit curving in at him and quickly pulled up, into the cloud. Tuck followed him in, overtaking very fast. As the blinding whiteness struck the windscreen he throttled back hard—to stay behind him, with luck to catch the vaguest outline of his tail.

The best part of a minute passed. His straining eyes saw nothing. Then came a series of deafening thuds and the Spitfire kicked and leapt like a startled foal.

Christ, he was being clobbered . . . the Hun's rear gunner must have X-ray eyes! He kicked his rudder savagely, yawing about violently in an effort to get out of the fire, but couldn't. More thuds, more jolts and shuddering. He narrowed his eyes to slits and shoved his face forward, close to the windscreen. If it could see him, then he ought to see it! But—only the whiteness.

Then his port wing lifted joltingly, and glancing out, he noticed a couple of holes in it. He skidded to the right and at once saw, immediately below and very slightly ahead, the shadow outline of the bomber. He'd been sitting almost on top of it! He closed the throttle, dropped down and slid in directly behind it, ignoring the rear gunner's furious blasts. Then he opened up the engine and edged up on it. From what couldn't have been more than fifty yards he dealt it a long, steady burst. Then he rose a little to one side, and with his guns roaring again gently brought his nose down slantwise and literally sawed right across it, from starboard engine through the fuselage to port engine and out to the wingtip. The cloud thinned suddenly, and he could see holes as big as his fist appearing all over it. But at this low speed the recoil of the second burst threw him into a stall, and he went hurtling down into the clear air.

His engine was critically damaged, spluttering and rasping and leaking glycol. But as he regained control and brought the nose up he saw the Dornier plunge vertically into the water, less than half a mile from the little ship it had failed to hit.

He called up Bobbie and Roy and told them the score. Bobbie had gone steaming off somewhere after a shadow, but Roy came swooping down, slid in alongside, and took a good look.

"One *helluva* mess underneath," he reported—and he spoke with a chuckle in his voice, as if his leader were a schoolboy who'd just driven a cricket ball through the vicar's greenhouse. "I say, you're in *beastly* trouble and no mistake!"

The smashed engine was losing power fast. Tuck decided he was very unlikely to make the shore. It would have to be the chute again. Angrily he made ready to depart, sliding back the canopy, undoing harness and oxygen pipe.

"Going somewhere?" Mottram inquired.

Tuck reached out a hand to disconnect the R/T lead, but surprisingly, the engine began to provide spasmodic bursts of power. He hesitated. The shoreline drew closer. Then a last, gallant pop or two and the Merlin died. Dead ahead there were sheer cliffs with flat, browned grassland on top—St. Gowan's Head. He had about twelve hundred feet. Only seconds to make the decision, and his judgment had better be precise.

He decided he could just make it. He could stretch his glide and set her down on the clifftops. The ground looked rough: he'd have to make it a belly landing.

He held the speed at a hair's breadth above the stall mark and, forcing himself to relax, to be delicate and to "feel" every inclination of his aircraft, settled down once more to fly for his life.

"Ha! *Now* you've had it!" cried Mottram after they'd descended another two or three hundred feet. "Should've gone while you had the chance. You'll *never* get over these cliffs!"

Tuck shot him a hateful glance. Mottram, no respecter of rank, responded with a hoot of laughter and some rapid-fire V-signs. Predicting disaster was his way of giving comfort.

Right up to the last moment the issue was in gravest doubt. Mottram, irrepressibly pessimistic, stayed right on Tuck's wing-tip all the way, until the crippled Spitfire, fluttering in the first tremors of a stall, grazed the brink of the cliffs and bounced on its belly on sun-cracked, rutted ground. Then he yelled, "Jolly good!" and got out of the way.

Only as he wrestled to set her down again did Tuck remember, with sickening apprehension, that he'd undone his safety straps. No time to rectify that now—he could only hope he'd get away with black eyes and a broken nose, not crack his skull. . . .

Then the tail struck a bump and the Spitfire bounced up again, this time for all of a hundred feet. All hope drained away.

Now he would surely stall—a wing would drop, she'd plow in on her back. . . .

She seemed to stop in midair and drop vertically, like a lift, but shaking herself like a dog after a swim. He shoved the stick hard forward and worked the rudder feverishly to try to keep her straight.

Steel bands around his chest, thorax throbbing painfully, damp-faced and dry-mouthed. He was like a man lashed face upward on the guillotine—in another instant he would be watching death hurtling at him. But though the needle was for several seconds distinctly below stalling speed, the Spit didn't drop a wing. A creature of true breeding, she kept her poise—and suddenly she was responding, she was flying again, she was gliding down smoothly and steadily!

This time he was able to flatten out with a shade more speed, and consequently more control. Out of the corner of his eye he saw Mottram away to the left, very low, going round in a steep bank, watching him. Then he spotted a hedge across his path just ahead and thought, "That's handy, that'll break my fall a bit, I'll try to touch down right on it."

He judged it perfectly. But instead of passing through the leafy barrier, the Spitfire stopped dead, as if she had hit a wall.

She *had* hit a wall—a dry-stone dike hidden by the hawthorn. She came from eighty miles an hour to a standstill in about five feet, but Tuck went right on traveling, out of the seat—luckily not upward, not out of the cockpit, but horizontally, in the general direction of the instrument panel, on and on into an ocean of darkness.

When he awoke, he could remember nothing at first and couldn't think where he was. No pain, no sound at all. Something was pressing down on his head, though, and a strange piece of metal was wound around his leg. Odder still, he seemed to be all rolled up in a ball.

He stared at the twisted piece of metal and recognized it as the control column. He looked around some more and found he was sitting on the rudder pedals. Then he knew where he was: he was stuffed into the small space under the instrument panel.

There came to his ears, gradually, a faint hissing and dripping, and he caught a whiff of gas. That made him wriggle out very quickly. He walked about ten paces and sat down with a thump. It was a great effort to raise an arm and wave to Mottram's low-circling machine, but he managed it. Then he decided to have a nice, quiet snooze.

In hospital that night he persuaded a young nursing sister to let him go to the telephone in her office. He was talking to "Mac," the adjutant at Pembrey, when suddenly he was greatly surprised to find that he couldn't see anything, not even his hand holding the phone. He just managed to slur out, "Well, g'bye, ol' boy, g'bye," and fumble the receiver back on its hook. Then he did a forward somersault into oblivion.

Postaccident shock, they called it, and they kept him on sedatives for two days. When finally he was discharged, he suffered another shock: he had been posted from 92 to 257.

And 257 was a *Hurricane* squadron!

Spitfires Get the Kommodore

from *The Greatest Aces*
BY EDWARD H. SIMS

Most of the highly successful fighter pilots of World War II were shot down at least once, some many times. To tally an impressive record of aerial victories you had to be aggressive and fly hard, yet no matter how good you were, sooner or later it would be your turn to fall. Consequently it is not surprising that the highest-scoring aces of that war racked up most of their victories fighting on the defensive. If they were shot down over friendly territory, when their wounds healed they could fly and fight again. If they were bagged over enemy territory and survived, the odds were that they quickly wound up in a prisoner of war camp.

The Luftwaffe's Adolf Galland scored most of his 103 victories early in the war. He rose to command the entire fighter arm of the Luftwaffe, ultimately fell out with Goering over the proper use of that arm, and ended World War II in command of a jet fighter squadron. Even though he was good, superbly good, one June day in 1941 Spitfires shot him down twice.

IN 1941 ADOLF GALLAND WAS KOMMODORE OF ONE OF THE TWO German fighter *Geschwader* left in the West to oppose the RAF—most of the Luftwaffe having been transferred to the East for the offensive against Russia. His *Geschwader* was distributed over various fields in the Pas de Calais, and in those days he often led his fighters against the RAF. He came to know the names of some of the RAF aces, several of whom he met when they were shot down over France and accepted his invitation to dinner. German fighter pilots in 1941 were confident and capable, and their fighters were perhaps the best in the world. Morale was good and Galland led his squadrons whenever he could. And it is with this period, and a memorable day for Galland, that we are now concerned.

Saturday, 21 June 1941, was warm and sunny over the Straits of Dover. Close to the coast of Kent, and the French coast between Calais and Boulogne (the Pas de Calais), were the strategically located advanced fighter fields of the RAF and the Luftwaffe.

The two air forces, flying from the same bases, had met in all-out battle in the summer of the preceding year, when the German Air Force had failed to subdue the RAF and bomb England into submission. At the conclusion of that struggle, the Luftwaffe discontinued massed daylight bomber attacks and bombed England largely by night. In the summer of 1941 it was the RAF which had gone over to the offensive in an effort to relieve pressure on Russian armies in the East, and RAF fighters and bombers were carrying out daylight attacks on targets in France. Because the escorting fighters (Spitfires and Hurricanes) had limited range, targets bombed by the RAF were usually close to the coast. German fighters, which a year before had often flown as bomber escorts over England and London, were now playing an opposite role— attacking RAF bombers over France.

On the French side of the Straits, midway between Calais and Boulogne and a few miles east of Cap Gris-Nez, sprawled the Luftwaffe fighter station of Wissant, named after the French coastal village. On a clear day German pilots could see the chalk cliffs of Dover across the Straits, and, higher, the radar and radio towers which stood out clearly on the green Kentish shore. The distance was twenty-two miles.

At the beginning of this summer of 1941 only two Luftwaffe *Geschwader*, 2 and 26, defended France and Occupied Europe against the RAF assault, then being referred to in the Allied press as the "nonstop" offensive. *Kommodore* (commander) of Jagdgeschwader 26, which had its headquarters at nearby Audembert in a farmhouse, was Oberstleutnant Adolf Galland.

The morning of the twenty-first began without a hint of action. There were no reports of enemy activity. The breeze steadily increased from the Straits as the morning wore on and the rising sun warmed the green, rolling Calais hills. Galland was nervous. The weather was too good.

His *Geschwader* was composed of three *Gruppen*, each containing three *Staffeln*. The normal flying strength of squadrons was from eight to twelve fighters. Thus, using all nine squadrons, Galland could send up more than a hundred fighters. He also had a *Stabschwarm* (staff schwarm) of four, with which he normally flew as leader. (In general, a *Geschwader's* strength at this time could be estimated at 120 aircraft.) One squadron was based at Audembert with Galland; the other eight were stationed at three other nearby fields.

The double row of sheds housing the 109s at Audembert were effectively camouflaged to blend inconspicuously into the roll of surrounding farmland. Trees were painted on sides, netting was used extensively, and from only a moderate height installations became indiscernible. A few hundred feet west of the sheds, just south of the grass takeoff area, stood a white masonry chalet.

At seven-thirty that morning Galland was awakened in one of its five bedrooms. He washed and shaved and dressed in black, sheep's-wool flying boots and flying suit, and a brown RAF flying jacket. The first officer to report to him was the weather officer, who confirmed what he had already seen—flying conditions were excellent. He was also briefed on the latest information gleaned from intercepted radio traffic and prisoners of war. (The German Signals Corps supplied valuable information about RAF activities, down to details such as which squadron leaders had gone on leave.) For breakfast Galland drank a mixture of raw eggs and red wine. He could never eat much in the mornings. In spite of his nervousness, nothing was apparently happening on the other side of the Straits.

He resigned himself to paperwork relating to Friday's activities. The morning progressed and soon it was ten o'clock, then eleven. Outside, it grew warmer. Apart from an occasional roaring start-up, of one of the 109s by a crewman, the only sounds through the open farmhouse window this summer morning were those of breezes, birds, and insects. But Galland couldn't relax. It was a quarter past eleven.

The telephone rang. It was an officer in the plotting room, a wooden building a few hundred feet from the front door, left. *"Viele, über Kent,"* the voice said. Galland answered, *"Komme sofort."* In sixty seconds he was hurrying through the door of a ninety-by-ninety-foot plotting room. Inside the curved-roofed building, which was covered with green netting stretching away to each side, were a number of tables on which were charted plots from Freya radar stations on the coast. Galland went from one to another, scanned the situation map where all the data was combined into a single picture. The picture was clear enough; he immediately ordered an alert and a briefing and hastily departed, leaving instructions that he be informed of any change in the developing picture.

Time was very short, for the distance was not great. Crewmen hurriedly began checking the 109s to have engines warm and ready to go. The distant roar permeated the countryside, and frenzied activity on all sides betrayed the sudden change of pace of the fighter station; an atmosphere of imminent action had fastened its grip on the field. Galland meanwhile was explaining the prospect to hurriedly assembled pilots at the farmhouse. "We have detected three wings of bombers, probably with fighter protection, at three thousand meters. We expect them to penetrate the coast a few kilometers west of Dunkirk." Using a map, he continued, "We expect to intercept between here and here"—he indicated an area to the east, slightly inland. "All squadrons are assembling. If there's time, I will lead them all in a concentrated formation; if not, we'll attack in separate groups."

There were few questions, little time. Galland, wrapping a yellow scarf around his neck, and fifteen other pilots ran toward their 109s. Galland would lead the staff *Schwarm* of four, in addition to the *Staffel* of twelve. Since the *Gefechtsalarm* (battle alert) had sounded, all crewmen were present at their 109s. Galland greeted his crew chief, Unteroffizier Meyer, bounded into the cockpit of the ready 109 F.2, and after strapping himself in, started the engine by pulling the start button.

After quickly checking instruments and gauges, he signaled ready. A crewman standing nearby pointed a flare pistol into the air and fired. A small green ball of fire shot up a hundred feet. Galland closed his canopy, released the brakes, eased the yellow knob on the left of the cockpit wall forward with his left hand; the Daimler-Benz howled louder as the prop pulled the fighter forward. Other pilots—only a short distance back—taxied out behind. Galland taxied north to the southern edge of the field, turned right to reach the eastern edge, and halted. Close to him were three other fighters, the rest of the *Schwarm*. Behind the *Schwarm*, in twos and fours, came the *Staffel*, now all taxiing rapidly into position. It was 12:24 and Galland opened the throttle all the way. The 109 began to gather speed, leaping and lunging over the grass as all the power of the big engine thrust the light (5,500 pounds) aircraft faster and faster. Sleek, pointed-nosed, gray-green fighters, with three-foot black crosses behind the cockpits on the fuselages, followed the *Kommodore* lifting off the field into a blue western sky.

Galland pushes a button at the bottom of the instrument panel and the 109's wheels begin to fold. He eases back on the throttle, begins a slow turn still climbing, and checks in with operations. *"Die dicken Hunde,"* he hears, are continuing on course. (German controllers called a stream of bombers or bombers and fighters Fat Dogs, referred to fighters as Indians.) Galland closes the air scoop, adjusts the wheel on the left of the cockpit floor for proper climbing trim, and sets course at 110 degrees. His 109—with Mickey Mouse insignia on the side of its canopy—climbs initially at three thousand feet per minute. (As the air gets thinner, the rate slows.) Galland estimates it will take a little over five minutes to reach the desired height above the oncoming bombers—about 13,000 or 14,000 feet.

The airspeed needle at the bottom of the right side of the panel shows a climbing speed of close to 400 kph (top speed indicated on the dial is 750). Galland checks to be sure his engine and oil temperatures are within limits. The German system is easy. Water lines and gauges are painted in green, oil in brown, air in blue, fuel in yellow. The fire extinguisher is red. He flips the stick cover lid to ready his guns and cannon, and switches on the electrical gunsight button. Directly in front of his face, on a glass rectangle measuring four inches high and two wide, a yellow-white electric-light circle appears. At a hundred meters a Spitfire's wingspan (thirty-six feet) fills the circle. Galland can fire his two 20-millimeter wing cannon by depressing an uncovered button on top of the stick with his thumb and can fire two 7.8 machine guns by depressing the front of the black, hand-shaped stick handle. He is now ready for action; the yellow-nosed 109 *Schwarm* of four reaches higher and higher into the eastern sky, the *Staffel* in position behind . . . 6,000 feet, 7,000, 8,000.

The English bombers—twin-engined Blenheims—prepare to go into their bombing runs over an airfield. It is at Arques, near St.-Omer. The Blenheims, Galland is informed by radio, are already east (ahead) of Galland's climbing yellow-noses, so there will be no time for Galland to assemble the *Geschwader*. The controller at Wissant also reports large formations of RAF fighters located above the bombers. Galland acknowledges, continues his climb. Altitude 9,000, 10,000, 11,000 feet. He follows a course furnished by the plotters below, points slightly south of due east. He should be seeing the enemy formation and scans the sky ahead. Nothing is in sight. He checks the sky behind, continues on course. Up ahead . . . he can see St.-Omer. Then . . . just past St.-Omer on a road leading southwest he sees the airfield—and bombs bursting! It's under attack. The RAF bombers are over Arques at 11,000 feet. A pack of escorting Hurricanes and Spitfires are above. Galland and all the German pilots feel the tension of impending battle upon seeing the enemy; they move their throttles all the way forward and steepen their climb. Galland will get above the RAF fighters and into position to make a diving attack. The 109s roar upward higher and higher above the bombers, now off to the right. Galland leans into a wide right turn, keeps his stick back climbing, and pulls up above the escorting fighters and well above the enemy bombers, still below, right. The Blenheims appear to have finished their bombing and are turning homeward.

His *Staffel* is in position. But English fighters are between the 109s and the bombers. Can he get through the escort to get to the bombers? No other German fighters are yet attacking. He must dive through the escort, presses the mike button of his brown helmet: *"Angriff!"* Diving pass to the right. His port wing flips up, exposing a black-and-white cross, and the 109 accelerates downward and right as Galland pushes stick forward and applies right rudder. The 109s quickly stretch out in the dive. Airspeed rapidly increases. Galland keeps the nose well down and peers ahead and down through the gunsight glass. The Spits and Hurricanes, above the Blenheims, appear to be rushing up to meet him as they bank above their larger comrades but Galland pays them no attention. He is suddenly on them, flashes through the enemy fighter formation at 400 mph. Taken by surprise, the RAF fighters bank sharply to take on the 109s. But so fast are the German fighters diving that they are now down and far away from the enemy fighters and approaching the Fat Dogs.

Galland eases back on the stick, feels the drain of blood from his head, but keeps his eyes fixed on the Blenheim formation. One of the twin-engined bombers is off to the right, trailing behind the formation. Galland maneuvers feet and stick, leveling the 109, still hurtling forward at great speed, and rushes up from directly behind. The distance rapidly closes in a straight-from-behind approach. The dorsal turret gunner hasn't seen him. Galland keeps his eyes on the electric-light circle, his fingers on the trigger buttons . . . closer . . . closer. The wingspan of the Blenheim spreads wider and wider, now a line of diameter. Galland is on him.

Thumb and forefinger down! Cannon and machine guns roar amid vibration. Aim is dead on. Shells rake the bomber and the

Blenheim staggers under the sudden barrage. Pieces fly backward and there is a flash of flame—high octane!

Galland is so close he must bank away to avoid fiery death. He veers to the side and the Blenheim wings over and plunges . . . smoke pouring back behind streaks of flame. A parachute opens, then another. Two of the three-man crew are out. There is no return fire from victory number sixty-eight for Galland.

In the attack he has lost his comrades, who have selected targets of their own. Most of the *Staffel* seems occupied with enemy fighters, but Galland is alone, scans the sky, and climbs at full power back above the bombers. He will come down again in another diving attack if enemy fighters don't interfere. Gradually the lone 109 out to the side pulls above the boxes and milling fighters around them. Galland manages to stay out of the melee and now, back at 12,000 feet, is ready to make a second pass. He checks the rear . . . clear behind. A little higher . . . over 12,000 feet now, above the enemy fighters. Once more he dips stick and starts down in a diving pass. His speed quickly accelerates and down he flashes through the fighters again. But this time one of the RAF pilots spots the diving Messerschmitt, stands his Spitfire on a wing, opens the Rolls-Merlin engine wide, and starts down after him. Galland is diving faster, however, and pulls away, eyeing the bombers below through his sighting glass. Rapidly closing them as he levels out at great speed, he decides to attack the lead bomber, then make his way out and away in front of the formation. He has the necessary speed, maneuvers rudder pedals and stick to bring the 109 in dead astern of the leading Blenheim.

The bomber grows larger and larger in his sights as he comes on fast. The rear gunner hasn't time to take him under fire. The wingspan is stretching across the circle. Galland presses the buttons. Again cannon and gun shells streak straight into the victim, Galland so close behind he can't miss. His firing pattern concentrates in the starboard wing, and from the starboard engine dark smoke streams backward. Galland takes a second to watch as he pulls off to the side. The Blenheim begins to yaw

. . . it's falling out of formation to the right, leaving a dark trail of smoke. Once again the crew, or some of them, get out. Galland sees one chute, then a second. Victim number two. His sixty-ninth victim of the war.

Whump! Whump! Tracers, streaking by above, to the side. A second for the new situation to register. Smoke! He's hit. Fighter behind! Instantly he kicks rudder, dips stick, and does a diving turn down and away. The fuel injection of the Daimler-Benz again proves its worth. He dives into a patch of haze, and this and his quick change of direction save him. (The Me-109s enjoy a tactical advantage over Spits and Hurricanes in a sudden dive, when centrifugal force momentarily interrupts the flow of fuel to the engine; the Daimler-Benz is equipped with fuel injection and in such dives continues to perform normally. That brief moment, the distance gained, is enough to enable Galland to get away. British pilots often attempted to nullify the German advantage by rolling or half-rolling as they dived in pursuit.)

Galland checks behind. He has evaded the Spit but has lost much altitude. And smoke leaves a long, white, funnel-like trail behind his F.2. He can see his right radiator is shot up and coolant is pouring out. The engine is certain to overheat. He pushes his stick down, looks behind again, and begins to search the landscape below for a place to get down. The engine begins to run roughly. Engine temperature steadily rises. No more coolant. The liquid-cooled engine will soon be finished. Directly below, he sees an open place in the landscape, two miles east of Calais. He looks carefully . . . airfield. Calais-Marck! He was so busy fighting he hadn't known his position. The engine is now throbbing and clanking, louder and louder. Galland eases back on the yellow throttle knob, but at the very moment the Daimler-Benz stops completely. The whirling three-blade prop out front turns slower and slower and then freezes. No power!

The airfield is just below, fortunately. Checking behind, thankful no enemy fighter has spotted his crippled 109, Galland circles to stay directly over the field. He will circle until very low and then bank in a last turn which will take him out and around to its edge where he is down to a few hundred feet. Silently the Messerschmitt circles downward. The whistling of the wind and the billow of white smoke accompany him as he calls on his training as a glider pilot. No wheels. He will belly in canopy open. He prepares to jump out as soon as the 109 stops sliding. Fast descending, he glides out to the field's edge and makes the last turn, levels the wings, dips the stick, and noses her down over the grass. Stick back, slower and slower, seventy-five feet, fifty, twenty-five . . . solid bumping, sliding, crunching. The 109 rushes over the ground, sliding straight, slows and comes to a halt. Galland is up and out of the cockpit as soon as the fighter stops. Men are rushing out from all directions. He is down safely on a German field.

His first request to onrushing field personnel is that they radio Audembert for a light plane to come and pick him up, which is done immediately. (Audembert is only ten miles down the coast to the southwest.) He walks around the battered 109. The prop is bent under, belly thoroughly skinned, and the right radiator, about two feet back from the propeller under the nose, is badly shot up. The Spit must have come up from behind and low!

Galland answers questions about the action and tells of his two victories. Field personnel prepare to move his damaged 109, and an Me-108 looms into sight in the western sky. It is from Audembert and Galland is soon on his way back to the base—in time for a late lunch. There he learns his wingman, Hegenauer, has been shot down, too. It has been a hard day . . . two victories in a few minutes but both he and his wingman shot down. The action is thoroughly discussed by excited German pilots.

After lunch, Galland—with no injuries—returns to his desk and paperwork and red tape. The weather is still perfect . . . but surely the RAF has had enough for one day. He works on until three o'clock. Half past the hour, and then four. And then . . .

The telephone. Plotting house. Large formations once again assembling across the Straits. Galland hurries over and soon is among the tables looking at radar plots . . . enemy formations, several heading toward France. From the plots it appears they'll cross in fifteen to twenty miles south. For the second time that day Galland sounds the *Gefechtsalarm* and pilots hurry into action. With whom shall he fly? His wingman is missing. He hasn't had time to arrange things. For one of the few times in his career Galland decides to take off alone. It's against the rules of fighter combat. Perhaps he can join one of his *Gruppen* when airborne. And so, without waiting to find a wingman, Galland races out to his other Me-109, which has been made ready (two aircraft are always at his disposal) and is soon leaving a cloud of dust in his wake as he taxies out to take off.

The lone, roaring 109 soon lifts off the grass into the still-blue western sky. It is minutes after 4 P.M. Galland banks left into the south, toward the area where the enemy will cross in. Retracting landing gear, he makes a quick cockpit check, turns on his guns and sight—all in order—and continues a solitary climb into the south. He soon reaches 10,000 feet, then 11,000 and then 12,000. He checks with control . . . enemy formations should be a few miles ahead, a bit higher, and are thought to be fighters. He can't make them out, but below, forward, he sees Boulogne. The Daimler, at maximum climb, continues to pull the 109 upward into the south, and he reaches 15,000, 16,000, then 17,000 feet and is approaching Boulogne off to his right, still climbing. He searches the sky ahead . . . wants to find friends before the enemy. Southeast of Boulogne . . . dots . . . aircraft. His eyes remain fixed on the approaching specks . . . fighters. He can distinguish the silhouettes . . . Me-109s! It's Gruppe I of his *Geschwader!* He will join them. He's up to 20,000 feet, levels out, points the yellow nose of his fighter in the direction of his comrades. Then off to the left of the 109s he sees another formation of fighters . . . Spitfires! He sees only six and they're at lower altitude. He has the altitude advantage and, quickly changing his mind, stands the 109 on its left wing to curve in above them. Perhaps he can dive down at speed, utilizing the element of surprise, and bring down the last in the formation, get away before the others turn.

The Spits are now ahead and below and Galland noses down

into a dive which will bring him into position behind the sixth enemy fighter. He must get in and out quickly. Airspeed increases as he holds the nose down, carefully sighting through the glass. The trailing Spit is in view . . . still small in the pale yellow light circle. He eases slightly back on the stick as the 109 approaches 700 kph, levels out, and comes in behind the enemy. Blood drains from his head, he is pressed down hard in his seat as he pulls stick back further, fast coming in from behind on the Spit, now growing bigger and bigger in the sighting circle.

The RAF fighter stays in the same flying altitude just long enough. The thirty-six-foot wingspan widens, now fills the circle. A hundred meters. Galland presses both buttons. The cannon and 7.8 shells smash into the larger Spitfire. Debris flies backward. Smoke streaks from the engine. Almost at once Galland knows his foe is finished. The enemy pilot probably didn't know what hit him. The Spit's wing goes up and over he flips, the roaring Merlin engine points earthward, and down plunges Galland's seventieth victim—his third of the day. Galland dives away to avoid the flight path of other Spits. He checks behind, sees nothing, and watches the falling Spitfire plunge to the ground a few miles southeast of Boulogne. Unlike his regular 109, which he flew in the morning, this one has no camera and he wants to see where the Spitfire crashes.

But he pays the price for a lone-wolf attack. For the second time in the day he is startled by ominous sounds. *Whumph! Whumph! Whumph! Whumph!* He can hear, feel the 109 taking hits . . . many hits. A sudden pain in his head, his right arm! Desperate, trapped, Galland rams the stick forward, dives straight down, down—and pulls out, banking. At last he's out of the line of fire, but too late. The 109 is mortally crippled and Galland is bleeding profusely. His frantic evasive action has shaken off the pursuing fighter, but the engine is banging loudly and vibrating heavily. Soon it will be finished. Galland switches it off to lessen chances of fire, which all pilots dread, especially 109 pilots, who sit in front of the fuel tank. The 109 begins its glide downward silently, just as another did earlier that morning.

On the right side of the cockpit and fuselage is a large gaping hole, through which the wind rushes in; there are holes in the wings. The enemy fighter's aim was deadly accurate. But the 109 responds to the controls and Galland feels he can make another belly landing. He is still high, over 17,000 feet, and points the nose northward. Ominously, fuel and coolant begin leaking onto the cockpit floor. Galland, head and arm bleeding, notices the liquid on the floor and realizes his danger. Then, *whump!* The enemy again? He looks back. Flames stretch out behind. The tank, behind, is afire! His breath almost stops as he notices small streams of liquid fire running between his legs from behind the seat into the cockpit. He must get out!

Galland jerks off his seat straps, reaches up with his left hand to release the top of the canopy. The *Kabinennotabwurf* doesn't work! The top won't fly off, is jammed! He pushes up hard with both hands. No movement. The fire is hotter. He must get out or burn to death. He pushes with all his strength, straight up. Flames now reach up from the bottom of the cockpit. He has seconds. Still he can't open the canopy. With all his strength in a desperate leap he throws his whole body against the roof. The front section of the top finally lifts, is caught by the wind, and hurtles back and away in the slipstream. Galland at the same time pulls back on the stick, stands in his seat, and tries to spring out of the cockpit as the 109 stands on its nose. He gets part of the way out, but his parachute, on which he sits, catches on the back part of the canopy, which hasn't dropped away as it should have. And as he stands struggling, half in and half out in the biting wind, the 109 stalls, falls down and away on a wing, and goes into a spin. Galland, still caught, falls with the burning plane. The force of the wind pushes his body backward against the very part of the cockpit from which he needs to free himself. His parachute is stuck into it. Desperately, he tries with hands and feet as he turns and falls to pull free, but he's stuck fast. The fighter falls on downward, his feet burning, his body violently buffeted as the 109 spins. For some strange, unexplainable reason Galland's mind turns to his electric train set—he has an elaborate installation at Audembert and he received two new engines that morning. Through his mind at this critical second flashes the thought he won't be able to try them out. Strange how the mind works!

With hand reaching out and gripping the aerial mast and feet kicking, Galland makes a final desperate effort to free himself. And then, without knowing how it happens, he is falling free. He's alone, hurtling downward, turning over and over as he falls. With relief, but suffering shock, Galland grips the release handle of his chute! With a start, he realizes what he's doing just in time. He's about to get out of his parachute harness, in midair! If he had pulled the *Schnelltrennschloss*, he would have fallen free without his chute. Shaken, he carefully grips the rip-cord handle *(Aufreissgriff)*, pulls. For a moment he fears his chute is not working. Then, with a jolt that straightens him up, feet downward, the chute opens and he is oscillating back and forth, softly and noiselessly floating down.

It's quite a contrast to the desperation and terror of only seconds ago. He is still high. Below a green summer landscape stretches in all directions. He notices his burning Me-109 smash into the ground about a mile away, thinks how close he came to going in with it. Then a Spitfire looms in view, flashing through the sky ahead, and apparently takes some pictures of him descending. Others are farther away and he hears them firing. Boulogne is easily visible to the west. He is coming down on top of a big forest . . . the wind is taking him toward the edge. He mustn't land in the trees . . . down, down; the wind carries him toward the edge; it will be close. He's over the forest, drifts toward a hedgerow. A large poplar tree is directly in his path. He passes below but the canopy of his chute strikes the limbs and collapses. As the air spills out, his descent quickens and he strikes the ground falling too fast. A sharp pain stabs him in the left ankle. Luckily the ground is wet and soft—a meadow—or he would certainly have been hurt badly. Even as it is, he's not in good condition.

Until now he hasn't realized he is badly burned, but lying on the ground, bleeding from the head and right arm, his ankle dislocated, burned over the bottom part of his body, he begins to realize his condition. He makes an effort but can't stand up. His ankle is swelling rapidly, energy draining away. He can hardly move. He can feel pieces of metal in his head. He just lies there, glances around half-dazed. At some distance he notices a French farmer, and then another, and slowly they approach. Galland is helpless and at their mercy. Soon there are several others with them, but they are extremely cautious and approach slowly. Galland speaks: "I'm German and I'm wounded. Please help me." One of the French onlookers is a woman; all are elderly. Another man speaks: "He will die very soon. We must call the Germans. If he dies before the Germans come, they will say we killed him."

Galland, understanding the conversation, replies, *"Ich werde nicht sterben. Ich bin sehr kräftig."* (I will not die. I am very strong.) The Frenchmen look at him in surprise. Several reach down and begin to drag him to a nearby farmhouse. When they finally arrive at the house, Galland asks, *"Haben Sie etwas cognac?"* They have none but they have some eau-de-vie. It's in a dirty bottle but Galland takes a long drink. One of the old men starts down the road to inform a group of German Todt Organization workers, the nearest Germans.

In a few minutes a car approaches. Galland can see they're Germans and is relieved. Quickly they ask, *"Wohin sollen wir Sie bringen?"* Galland tells them to take him to his fighter station. They tell him he should go to the hospital. Galland insists and they help him into their car and drive him to Audembert, 26 Geschwader headquarters. At his arrival there is excitement and relief. Galland even has a cognac and a cigar and feels somewhat better. But they soon pack him off to the nearby naval hospital at Hardingham, where his good friend Dr. Heim removes various pieces of metal from his head and patches him up. Heim suggests he stay a few days at the hospital. Galland, however, refuses to remain and is soon back at headquarters; he will remain in command, if necessary from the ground!

The Doolittle Raid

from *Thirty Seconds Over Tokyo*

BY TED W. LAWSON

First published in 1943, Thirty Seconds Over Tokyo *by Ted W. Lawson quickly became one of the most widely read aviation books of the century. It is the story of the Doolittle raid, sixteen B-25 Mitchell bombers launched from the deck of USS Hornet on April 18, 1942, for a strike on Tokyo, as told by one of the pilots. The raid was of no military significance—sixteen medium bombers each carrying one ton of ordnance could not conceivably do material damage to the Japanese Empire or the city of Tokyo, over a hundred square miles of densely packed humanity—yet it was launched anyway. A nation still stunned by Pearl Harbor needed a morale boost; this raid gave it to them in spades.*

Lawson's story is still a good one. In the pages presented here the inexperience of the fliers, their patriotic fervor, and the enormous respect they had for Japan's military capabilities leap at you. These attitudes mirrored the American public's at the time, which is one reason the book enjoyed such enormous success.

Doolittle hoped when planning the raid that the Hornet and her escorts could get to within four hundred miles of the Japanese coast before launching the B-25s to strike Tokyo and land at fields in China. Unfortunately a Japanese picketboat spotted the battle group when they were eight hundred miles out. An immediate launch followed, dooming the bombers to crash landings short of safety.

In Lawson's text, he states that the Japanese picketboat didn't report the sighting of enemy warships. U.S. authorities arrived at this conclusion due to the dearth of opposition to the raiders over Japan. Postwar investigation, however, revealed that a warning from the picketboat was received by

Japanese naval headquarters, which alerted Navy forces and launched an unsuccessful effort to find the Americans with land-based reconnaissance planes. The Navy also informed the Army of the sighting, reported as three carriers, because the Army was responsible for air defense of the home islands. In a fit of military hubris and overconfidence, the Japanese Army dismissed the warning, and did nothing.

FIRST THERE WAS A MUFFLED, VIBRATING ROAR, FOLLOWED IMMEDI-ately by the husky cry of battle stations. "Nig" jumped for the door and I went right after him. We were three decks down. Scrambling after Nig as fast as I could, I found other Army boys racing for the top. We flung questions at one another, but got no answers. And twice before I could get up on top, the *Hornet* vibrated and echoed with the sound of heavy gunfire nearby.

I got out on the flight deck and ran around a B-25 just in time to see the cruiser off to our left let go another broadside of flame in the direction away from us. And presently, down near the horizon, a low-slung ship began to give off an ugly plume of black smoke. Dive bombers were wheeling over it.

I must have asked two dozen questions in one minute. One of the Navy boys, hurrying past, said it was a Japanese patrol boat and that our gunnery had accounted for it within three minutes after engaging.

"Let's go!" somebody yelled at me above the bellow of the cruiser's guns, the crashing sea, the sound of the wind, and the cries of excited, jubilant men. I turned and saw it was Nig. He was racing back over the route we had covered just a few minutes before.

I was on his heels, saying nothing. This was it, and before we wanted it. We'd have to take off now. Not Sunday evening. Now, Saturday morning. We were forced to assume that the Japanese ship had had time to flash the warning about us. All hope of surprising the Japanese had now fled, I thought. Surprise was our main safety factor, Doolittle had often drummed into our heads. We had no way of knowing that no warning was sent. Apparently the ship either did not see the B-25s spread all over the deck of the *Hornet* or just couldn't believe that it was possible, or maybe the Navy sank it too soon.

The *Hornet* leaped forward, boring a hole in the head wind. I could feel its turbines take up a faster beat and felt that it was straining forward as fast as it could, to get us a minute closer— a gallon nearer.

I don't really remember what I stuffed in my bag. Whatever it was, it was handy to reach. Now I was thinking about our gas, and the junking of so many of our long-discussed plans. We had based so much of our hope of getting to China on the presumption that the Navy could run us up to within about four hundred miles of the Japanese coast. Even then it was going to be a tight fit.

Now we were going to take off about eight hundred miles off the coast. It took some figuring—quick figuring. And the sums I arrived at, in my buzzing head, gave me a sudden emptiness in the stomach. I thought of the preparations the Japanese must be making for us, and I thought of that turret that just wouldn't work. But most of all I thought of our gas.

"Army pilots, man your planes! Army pilots, man your planes!" the loudspeakers brayed. But I already knew the time had come.

I went right to my plane. The crew was there. I shoved some of the stuff in McClure's navigating compartment, just behind and a step lower than the pilot's compartment.

The flight deck of the *Hornet* was alive with activity, while the big voice of the looming island barked commands. The man I thought was responsible for our bad turret hurried by, and I stopped him long enough to tell him what I thought of him. And was sorry, as soon as I did. Nothing was important now except getting off that wet, rolling deck.

The Navy was now taking charge, and doing it with an efficiency which made our popped eyes pop some more. Blocks were whipped out from under wheels. The whirring little "donkey"—the same one that was supposed to have broken loose and smashed my plane—was pushing and pulling the B-25s into position.

In about half an hour the Navy had us crisscrossed along the back end of the flight deck, two abreast, the big double-rudder tail assemblies of the sixteen planes sticking out of the edges of the rear of the ship at an angle. From the air, the *Hornet*, with its slim, clean foredeck, and its neatly cluttered rear deck, must have looked like an arrow with pinfeathers bounding along the surface of the water.

It was good enough flying weather, but the sea was tremendous. The *Hornet* bit into the roughhouse waves, dipping and rising until the flat deck was a crazy seesaw. Some of the waves were actually breaking over the deck. The deck seemed to grow smaller by the minute, and I had a brief fear of being hit by a wave on the takeoff and of crashing at the end of the deck and falling off into the path of the careening carrier.

The *Hornet*'s speed rose until it was making its top speed, that hectic, hurried morning of April 18. The bombs now came up from below and rolled along the deck on their low-slung lorries to our planes. It was our first look at the 500-pound incendiary, but we didn't waste much time on it except to see that it was placed in the bomb bay so that it could be released fourth and last.

The Navy had fueled our planes previously, but now they topped the tanks. That was to take care of any evaporation that might have set in. When the gauges read full, groups of the Navy boys rocked our planes in the hope of breaking whatever bubbles had formed in the big wing tanks, for that might mean that we could take a few more quarts. The *Hornet*'s control tower was now beginning to display large square cards, giving us compass readings, and the wind, which was of gale proportions.

It was something of a relief when five additional five-gallon tins of gas were handed in to us. We lined them up in the fuselage beside the ten cans Doolittle had already allotted us. It was a sobering thought to realize that we were going to have to fly at least four hundred miles farther than we had planned. But my concern over that, as I sat there in the plane waiting to taxi and edge up to the starting line, was erased by a sudden relief that now we wouldn't have to worry about running into barrage balloons at night. This, of course, was going to be a daylight raid. It was only a few minutes after eight in the morning.

I suddenly remembered that none of my crew had had breakfast and that all of us had lost sight of the fact that we could have taken coffee and water and sandwiches along. I was tempted to send Clever below to get some food, but I was afraid that there would not be time. Besides, Doolittle's ship was being pulled up to the starting line, and his and other props were beginning to turn. The *Hornet*'s deck wasn't a safe place. I found out later that one of the Navy boys had an arm clipped off by a propeller blade that morning.

Doolittle warmed and idled his engines, and now we got a vivid demonstration of one of our classroom lectures on how to get a 25,000-pound bomber off half the deck of a carrier.

A Navy man stood at the bow of the ship and off to the left with a checkered flag in his hand. He gave Doolittle, who was at the controls, the signal to begin racing his engines again. He did it by swinging the flag in a circle and making it go faster and faster. Doolittle gave his engines more and more throttle until I was afraid that he'd burn them up. A wave crashed heavily at the bow and sprayed the deck.

Then I saw that the man with the flag was waiting, timing the dipping of the ship so that Doolittle's plane would get the benefit of a rising deck for its takeoff. Then the man gave a new signal. Navy boys pulled the blocks from under Doolittle's wheels. Another signal and Doolittle released his brakes and the bomber moved forward.

With full flaps, engines at full throttle, and his left wing far out over the port side of the *Hornet*, Doolittle's plane waddled and then lunged slowly into the teeth of the gale that swept down the deck. His left wheel stuck on the white line as if it were a track. His right wing, which had barely cleared the wall of the island as he taxied and was guided up to the starting line, extended nearly to the edge of the starboard side.

We watched him like hawks, wondering what the wind would do to him, and whether we could get off in that little run toward the bow. If he couldn't, we couldn't.

Doolittle picked up more speed and held to his line, and just as the *Hornet* lifted itself up on the top of a wave and cut through it at full speed, Doolittle's plane took off. He had yards to spare. He hung his ship almost straight up on its props, until we could see the whole top of his B-25. Then he leveled off and I watched him come around in a tight circle and shoot low over our heads—straight down the line painted on the deck.

The *Hornet* was giving him his bearings. Admiral Halsey had headed it for the heart of Tokyo.

The engines of three other ships were warming up, and the thump and hiss of the turbulent sea made additional noise. But loud and clear above those sounds I could hear the hoarse cheers of every Navy man on the ship. They made the *Hornet* fairly shudder with their yells—and I've never heard anything like it, before or since.

Travis Hoover went off second and nearly crashed. Brick Holstrom was third; Bob Gray, fourth; Davey Jones, fifth; Dean Hallmark, sixth; and I was seventh.

I was on the line now, my eyes glued on the man with the flag. He gave me the signal to put my flaps down. I reached down and drew the flap lever back and down. I checked the electrical instrument that indicates whether the flaps are working. They were. I could feel the plane quaking with the strain of having the flat surface of the flaps thrust against the gale and the blast from the props. I got a sudden fear that they might blow off and cripple us, so I pulled up the flaps again, and I guess the Navy man understood. He let it go and began giving me the signal to rev my engines.

I liked the way they sounded long before he did. Now, after fifteen seconds of watching the man with the flag spinning his arm faster and faster, I began to worry again. He must know his stuff, I tried to tell myself, but when, for God's sake, would he let me go?

I thought of all the things that could go wrong at this last minute. Our instructions along these lines were simple and to the point. If an engine quit or caught fire, if a tire went flat, if the right wing badly scraped the island, if the left wheel went over the edge, we were to get out as quickly as we could and help the Navy shove our $150,000 plane overboard. It must not, under any circumstances, be permitted to block traffic. There would be no other way to clear the forward deck for the other planes to take off.

After thirty blood-sweating seconds the Navy man was satisfied with the sound of my engines. Our wheel blocks were jerked out, and when I released the brakes, we quivered forward, the wind grabbing at the wings. We rambled dangerously close to the edge, but I braked in time, got the left wheel back on the white line, and picked up speed. The *Hornet*'s deck bucked wildly. A sheet of spray rushed back at us.

I never felt the takeoff. One moment the end of the *Hornet*'s flight deck was rushing at us alarmingly fast; the next split second I glanced down hurriedly at what had been a white line, and it was water. There was no drop nor any surge into the air. I just went off at deck level and pulled out in front of the great ship that had done its best to plant us in Japan's front yard.

I banked now, gaining a little altitude, and instinctively reached down to pull up the flaps. With a start I realized that they were not down. I had taken off without using them.

I swung around as Doolittle and the others before me had done, came over the nine remaining planes on the deck, got the bearing, and went on—hoping the others would get off and that the *Hornet*—God rest her—would get away in time.

There was no rendezvous planned, except at the end of the mission. Those who took off early could not hover over the ship until a formation was formed because that would have burned too much gas in the first planes. This was to be a single-file, hit-

and-run raid—each plane for itself. And at levels which still are hard to believe.

Once on our way, we immediately started topping the wing tanks with the auxiliary gas. We began with the big emergency tank. I knew all there was to know about the appetite of our Wrights, but it was still depressing to figure that they had burned the equivalent of eight of our five-gallon tins during the warming up and takeoff. Forty precious gallons gone before we were on our way!

About 2,200 miles of nonstop flying, I hoped, lay ahead of us. I tried now to visualize the end of the trip, the airport at Choo Chow Lishui. I thought again of the tremendous planning behind the whole raid when I recalled that I must not miss the signals at Choo Chow Lishui or the other Chinese fields I might be tempted to choose. All of them were close to Japanese-occupied territory. There was always the chance that even while we were en route the Japanese might seize these fields. If that happened, the Chinese were to signal "Don't land" by a simple but effective system.

But there were more pressing things to think about now as I kept the clean nose of the Ruptured Duck about twenty feet above the water and settled into the gas-saving groove. If all went well on the way in, I would hit Tokyo about a half hour after Doolittle. I figured that if by some improbable miracle the first few planes got in unmolested, every Japanese fighting plane and antiaircraft gun would be ready for me, and for the others behind me.

That made me think about the turret. I pushed the button on the interphone and told Thatcher to give it one more test. He did and said it was still on the blink. Then I switched on the emergency juice, but that wouldn't work either. I hadn't built up enough power as yet. Our two .50-caliber rear guns were pointing straight back between the twin rudders and would be unable to budge one way or the other in case of attack. I spoke to Thatcher again and said that, at least, we'd test the guns. So I raised the nose of the plane, and when the tail slanted down at the right angle, Thatcher fired a short burst into the water behind us.

"Say, boy, this is serious," Davenport, the copilot, said into the phone.

We plowed along at a piddling speed for a B-25. The controls were sloppy at that speed. Nobody wanted to say anything. We were busy, or thinking. The flying weather was good—alarmingly clear.

Suddenly a dazzling, twisting object rushed past our left wing. It was startling until I realized it was a five-gallon can discarded by one of the planes in front of me. I could see two planes, and Thatcher said he could see two behind us. The can would have downed us if it had hit a prop. What a climax that would have been!

An hour and a half after we took off, we came into view of a large Japanese merchantman. It was about three miles off to our left as we spun along just over the waves.

"Let's drop one on it," Davenport said into the phone.

"Let's do," somebody else said. I let them talk. I had better use for the bombs.

"Okay," McClure said, "but I bet that guy is radioing plenty to Tokyo about us." It was the only ship we saw on the way in, but no one doubted by now that the whole coast of Japan knew that we were en route.

Our emergency tank was used up by now and we were well into our other stores. We drummed along, expecting to see planes every minute, but saw none. I tried the turret again, and it worked. I had enough power. It had to be used clumsily in that the emergency power had to be turned on in the pilot's compartment. I couldn't see Thatcher in the back of the plane, so it had to be done over the phone. The emergency power would last such a short time that the turret would have to be used sparingly. Only during actual attack could I afford to turn it on.

We kept going in, and after two or three hours it got tiring. I was keyed up enough, but at our low level and sluggish speed it was a job to fly the ship. I called Clever on the phone, out in the snout of the bombardier's section, and asked him to turn on our automatic pilot. He did, but when I took my hands off the controls, the Ruptured Duck slipped off dangerously to the left. The automatic pilot wasn't working.

So Davenport and I took turns at the controls, and I happened to have them in my hands, at 2 P.M., our time, when we sighted the coast of Japan.

It lay low in the water in a slight haze that made it blend into the horizon. I had an ingrained, picture-postcard concept of Japan. I expected to spot some snow-topped mountain or volcano first. But here was land that barely rose above the surface of the water and, at our twenty feet of height, was hardly distinguishable. I headed straight for the beach.

Many small boats were anchored off the beach, and as we came in closer, I was surprised to see that they were motorboats and nice-looking fishing launches instead of the junks I expected. I had to keep low to avoid spotters as much as possible and to keep out of range of any detecting device which the Japanese might have. So I braced myself as we came close to the masts of the little boats offshore, waiting for a burst of machine-gun fire.

We thundered up to and just over them. Instead of bullets, I got a fleeting, frozen-action look at a dozen or so men and women on the little boats. They were waving at us. You see, the emblems on our plane were the old style: blue circle with white star and a red ball in the middle of the white star. Maybe that's what confused them. I'm sure we weren't being hailed as liberators.

White beaches blended quickly into soft, rolling green fields. It was the first land I had seen in nearly three weeks. It looked very pretty. Everything seemed as well kept as a big rock garden. The little farms were fitted in with almost mathematical precision. The fresh spring grass was brilliantly green. There were fruit trees in bloom, and farmers working in their fields waved to us as we pounded just over their heads. A red lacquered temple loomed before us, its coloring exceedingly sharp. I put the nose of the ship up a little, cleared the temple, and got down lower again.

It was all so interesting that I believe none of us thought much about our danger. What brought that to us, a few minutes after we came over the land, was the sudden sight and disappearance of a large flat building which literally erupted children as we came up to it. A lot of them waved to us. I caught a fleeting glimpse of a playground—and then a sharp, quick look at a tall flagpole from which fluttered the Japanese flag.

It was like getting hit in the chest very hard. This was for keeps. I listened with new interest to the voice of the engines. A lot of the unreal beauty left the land below us. We just could not have a forced landing now.

I clicked on the interphone and said, "Keep your eyes open, Thatcher."

"I'm looking," Thatcher said.

I found a valley leading more or less toward Tokyo and went down it lower than the hills on either side. But McClure checked our course and found that it was leading us off, so I lifted the nose over a hill and found another valley that compensated and straightened us out again. McClure held a stopwatch on the valleys that went off on tangents. He'd let me go fifteen seconds down one, then I'd hop the ridge and find one that brought us back on our imaginary beam. We kept very low.

Davenport, Clever, and I saw the Zeros simultaneously. There were six of them, flying in two tight V's. They were at about 1,500 feet, coming straight at us. Our eyes followed them as they came closer and closer. They looked like one of our American racing planes, with their big air-cooled engine and stubby wings. I kept just over the tops of a forest of evergreens.

The first echelon of Zeros swept up our transparent nose and disappeared in the metal top that shut off our view. The second V of Japanese planes was now doing likewise, but just before I lost sight of them overhead, the Zero on the left end peeled off and started to dive for us.

I clicked the interphone just as Thatcher did. "I saw him," he said.

I was relieved, until I thought again about the turret. I told Thatcher to tell me when he wanted the power on.

Five or six interminable seconds dragged by. Then I asked Thatcher if he wanted the turret on now.

"No, wait awhile," he said.

My mind was making pictures of that Zero diving on our tail with cannon and machine-gun fire. I called Thatcher again. There was no answer. I thought that something might have gone wrong with the interphone and that Thatcher even now might be yelling into a dead phone that he needed the turret. I was just about to take a chance and switch it on when Thatcher came back on the phone again.

"I don't know what the dickens happened to him," he said. "I can't see him now. I think he must have gone back in the formation."

We skimmed along. We went over the rooftops of a few small villages, and I began to worry. Twenty minutes was what it was supposed to take to reach Tokyo from the point where we came in. Now we had been over land for nearly thirty minutes, and no sign of the city. I saw one fairly large town off to the left, however, and I said to myself that if worst came to worst and we couldn't find Tokyo, I'd come back there and do at least some damage.

But just then we came up over a hill, dusting the top of another temple, and there before us, as smooth as glass, lay Tokyo Bay.

It was brilliant in the midday sun and looked as limitless as an ocean. I came down to within about fifteen feet, while McClure checked our course. I kept the same slow speed, gas-saving but nerve-racking when I thought occasionally of the 400-mph-plus diving speed of the Zeros.

We were about two minutes out over the bay when all of us seemed to look to the right at the same time, and there sat the biggest, fattest-looking aircraft carrier we had ever seen. It was a couple of miles away, anchored, and there did not seem to be a man in sight. It was an awful temptation not to change course and drop one on it. But we had been so drilled in what to do with our four bombs, and Tokyo was now so close, that I decided to go on.

There were no enemy planes in sight. Ahead, I could see what must have been Davey Jones climbing fast and hard and running into innocent-looking black clouds that appeared around his plane.

It took about five minutes to get across our arm of the bay, and while still over the water, I could see the barrage balloons strung between Tokyo and Yokohama, across the river from Tokyo.

There were no beaches where we came in. Every inch of shoreline was taken up with wharves. I could see some dredging operations filling in more shoreline, just as we were told we would see. We came in over some of the most beautiful yachts I've ever seen, then over the heavier ships at the wharves and low over the first of the rooftops. I gave the ship a little more throttle for we seemed to be creeping along.

In days and nights of dreaming about Tokyo and thinking of the 8 millions who live there, I got the impression that it would be crammed together, concentrated, like San Francisco. Instead it spreads all over creation, like Los Angeles. There is an aggressively modern sameness to much of it, and now, as we came in very low over it, I had a bad feeling that we wouldn't find our targets. I had to stay low and thus could see only a short distance ahead and to the sides. I couldn't go up to take a good look without drawing antiaircraft fire, which I figured would be very accurate by now because the planes that had come in ahead of me had all bombed from 1,500 feet. The buildings grew taller. I couldn't see people.

I was almost on the first of our objectives before I saw it. I gave the engines full throttle as Davenport adjusted the prop pitch to get a better grip on the air. We climbed as quickly as possible to 1,500 feet, in the manner which we had practiced for a month and had discussed for three additional weeks.

There was just time to get up there, level off, attend to the routine of opening the bomb bay, make a short run, and let fly with the first bomb. The red light blinked on my instrument board, and I knew the first 500-pounder had gone.

Our speed was picking up. The red light blinked again, and I knew Clever had let the second bomb go. Just as the light blinked, a black cloud appeared about one hundred yards or so in front of us and rushed past at great speed. Two more appeared ahead of us, on about the line of our wingtips, and they too swept past. They had our altitude perfectly, but they were leading us too much.

The third red light flickered, and since we were now over a flimsy area in the southern part of the city, the fourth light blinked. That was the incendiary, which I knew would separate as soon as it hit the wind and that dozens of small firebombs would molt from it.

The moment the fourth red light showed, I put the nose of the Ruptured Duck into a deep dive. I had changed the course somewhat for the short run leading up to the dropping of the incendiary. Now, as I dived, I looked back and got a quick, indelible vision of one of our 500-pounders as it hit our steel-smelter target. The plant seemed to puff out its walls and then subside and dissolve in a black-and-red cloud.

Our diving speed picked up to 350 miles an hour in less time than it takes to tell it, and up there in the front of the vibrating bomber I dimly wondered why the Japanese didn't throw up a wall of machine-gun fire. We would have had to fly right through it.

I flattened out over a long row of low buildings and homes and got out of there. I felt satisfied about the steel smelter and hoped the other bombs had done as well. There was no way of telling, but I was positive that Tokyo could have been damaged that day with a rock.

Our actual bombing operation, from the time the first one went until the dive, consumed not more than thirty seconds.

We were very low now, snaking back and forth, expecting a cloud of Zeros from moment to moment.

I pushed the interphone button and asked Clever if he was sure the bombs were all away.

"Sure," he said. McClure set our course due south. Thatcher, looking behind us, said that smoke was beginning to rise. I told him to watch out for planes and let me know when he wanted the turret.

I nosed down a railroad track on the outskirts of the city and passed a locomotive close enough to see the surprised face of the engineer. As I went by, I could have kicked myself for not giving the locomotive's boiler a burst of our forward .30-caliber guns, then I remembered that we might have better use for the ammunition. A string of telephone wires shone like silver strands in the sunlight. It wasn't difficult to imagine the excited voices coursing over them, giving our direction to those waiting for us ahead.

It was McClure who spotted the six Japanese biplane pursuits, ugly black crates that look as slow as observation planes. They were flying well above us in close formation. We watched them, waiting for them to dive, and hoped that if they did so our extremely low altitude would cause enough of them to crash before they could pull out.

But the planes stayed where they were, and we were in no mood to go up there and fight them.

There was the gas to consider. All our auxiliary gas was gone now. We were starting in on the wing tanks. With the city behind us, I dropped the speed.

Presently we were out over water again, for the coastline of Honshu, the main island on which Tokyo is located, slants to the southwest. We were going due south because it was part of the plan to confuse possible pursuers and to keep from tipping off our eventual intention of swinging westward to China.

Thatcher now got a chance to use his guns, but not on a

plane. A big yacht loomed up ahead of us, and figuring it must be armed, I told Thatcher to give it a burst. We went over it, lifted our nose to put the tail down, and Thatcher sprayed its decks with our .50-caliber stingers.

Not much later, as we edged along about twenty feet over the water, I looked ahead and four or five miles immediately in front of us three Japanese cruisers appeared. They were coming our way, fast. They spotted us about the exact instant we spotted them. I looked down at the water a moment, gauging my clearance, and when I looked up again, the three cruisers were turning with amazing precision, leaving big white wakes for tails, to face us broadside.

I wanted no part of them. I skirted deeply around them, and they didn't fire a shot.

McClure got us back on our course. Now, in line with the long-rehearsed plan, we altered our course to southwest. The island of Honshu has a lumpy, half-submerged tail of islands curling southwestwardly from it. Our marker was the volcanic mass named Yaku-Shima, which rises out of and forms a kind of eastern barrier of the China Sea.

We bored along our course through the long bright afternoon, all of us under considerable strain. Then, with a yell, we spotted what was unmistakably Yaku-Shima and the smaller nearby Sumi Gunto. I flew between their wide-set gorge, held the course a bit longer, and then turned due west. We were now on the twenty-ninth parallel and winging out over the China Sea for our still-distant Choo Chow Lishui.

That broke the ice.

"Wow! What a headache I've got," Davenport said into the interphone.

I guess everybody had one. I told Thatcher to keep his eye peeled on the rear. I said that this thing wasn't over by a long sight. He said he wasn't asleep.

We were flying so low and were so much on the lookout that once the plane edged toward the water when I looked up momentarily, and we came awful close to touching it. Our nerves twanged like guitar strings, so I told Davenport to do the looking around while I did the piloting, and after about ten or fifteen minutes, we reversed the jobs.

We could smoke now, and that helped a lot. The extra gas, of course, was all out of the ship, so there was no danger from the cigarettes. Thatcher passed up some of the chocolate bars from the rear, and we nibbled on them. But none of us had much of an appetite. Besides, they made us thirsty and we had no water. We had found one thermos bottle in the plane after the takeoff but had finished it before we got to Tokyo.

We saw an occasional fishing boat or yacht in the China Sea as the afternoon wore along and figured that they were probably radioing ahead to Japanese-held airdromes on the China mainland, giving them our direction.

About five o'clock in the afternoon, when we were halfway across the China Sea, we spotted two submarines being refueled. They were tied up to a tanker. I wished we had saved a bomb. There didn't seem to be much good using our machine-gun ammunition on them, either. There would be plenty of uses for it over Japanese-held China, I thought. It was just impossible for me to believe that we were going to get away from the raid as easily as this.

Clever crawled up from his bombardier's nose and climbed into our compartment.

"Were you scared?" he asked me.

I told him I sure was.

I guess we all wanted to be together, now. We smoked a cigarette and talked as best we could, and I tried not to notice that the weather was going bad. The engines were wonderful. I felt like getting out on the wing and kissing them.

Kimigayo

from *Miracle at Midway*

BY GORDON W. PRANGE WITH DONALD M. GOLDSTEIN
AND KATHERINE V. DILLON

June 4, 1942, marks the coming of age of U.S. naval aviation. On that day, amid the fog of misconceptions, uncertainties, and lost chances that define war, Dauntless dive bombers from USS Enterprise, Hornet, and Yorktown found the Japanese carrier battle group northwest of Midway Island in the Pacific and sank all of the Japanese flattops—Kaga, Akagi, Soryu, and Hiryu. The Japanese got in their licks before their last carrier went under, sinking Yorktown, but the battle was a lopsided win for the American Navy, one that turned the tide in the Pacific and marked the beginning of the end of the Japanese Empire.

The Americans had broken the Japanese naval codes and knew of the enemy's intent to attack, then invade, Midway Island. Admiral Chester Nimitz sent everything he had, three carriers and some escorts, to the northeast of Midway with instructions to attempt to surprise the Japanese fleet.

The battle opened with a strike by Japanese carrier planes on Midway Island on June 4. American planes soon located the Japanese fleet, and the three U.S. carriers launched strikes. After an ineffectual strike by Army Air Corps bombers flying from Midway, two squadrons of U.S. carrier–based torpedo planes, flown mostly by inexperienced pilots, found the Japanese carriers and immediately attacked. The obsolete TBD Devastators were slaughtered by Zeros and flak and didn't manage a single hit. All fifteen of Hornet's Torpedo Squadron 8's aircraft were shot down, and only one of the thirty crewmen survived, Ens. George Gay. Enterprise's Torpedo Squadron 6 lost ten of its fourteen aircraft, also to no avail. Then, in an extraordinary twist of fate, as Zero fighters circled at low altitude looking for more incoming torpedo planes while the Japa-

nese carriers refueled and rearmed their aircraft on deck for a strike at the American ships, three flights of Dauntless dive bombers from Yorktown and Enterprise arrived overhead, opened their dive brakes, and nosed over.

Here is that moment, as described by Gordon W. Prange and his associates in his magnificent history, Miracle at Midway.

FROM HIS HEIGHT OF 20,000 FEET, WADE MCCLUSKY HAD A CLEAR view from horizon to horizon, but however far he craned his neck, all he could see was the Pacific Ocean stretching for limitless miles. The time was 0920, and he had reached the anticipated point of interception, 142 miles from *Enterprise*. Far off to port, a subtle change in the texture of the sea hinted that Midway's shoals lay just over the horizon. Some of his pilots on the formation's far left could see smoke rolling up from the stricken base. But where was the Japanese Mobile Force?

Built rather like his own SBD Dauntless dive bomber—short and stocky—McClusky was almost a stranger to it, being a fighter pilot by training and experience. He had joined *Enterprise* in June 1940 as commander of VF-6 and became air group commander, in charge of all the carrier's airmen, on March 15, 1942. Since that date, he had familiarized himself with the Dauntless as best he could, snatching an hour here, a few minutes there, from his busy schedule. Now, leading thirty-two dive bombers into battle, he knew the plane fairly well, could take off from the carrier and land back on the flight deck, but he had never dropped a bomb from an SBD. So no one, McClusky least of all, would have termed him an experienced dive bomber pilot. What he brought to his job was a gift for command, composed in equal parts of personal fearlessness and the ability to feed unexpected data into his brain cells and click out a prompt, intelligent answer. Rear Adm. Raymond Spruance, who never tossed adjectives around recklessly, called McClusky "terrific."

Here was a situation which challenged him to the full. Should he assume that he had beaten the Japanese to the location and circle the area until Nagumo's fleet steamed into view? Conversely, should he continue toward Midway, in case he was behind the Japanese? His planes had eaten up too much fuel for him to send them winging out on an expanding square—the conventional air-search tactic—to seek out the missing enemy. Should he get his men home to *Enterprise* while the getting was good? Whatever he decided, he must do so in a hurry, for he could only spare fifteen minutes to search before fuel consumption would force him to take his flight back to the carrier.

After a quick consultation with his plotting board, McClusky decided to go on for an extra thirty-five miles on course 240°, then turn northwest parallel to the anticipated Japanese route. Captain Murray, skipper of *Enterprise*, termed this resolution "the most important decision of the entire action," and Nimitz agreed that it was "one of the most important decisions of the battle and one that had decisive results."

At 0955, about seven minutes after the SBDs swung northwest, McClusky spotted the long, white brushstroke of a ship's wake across the sparkling blue surface. Following the line through his binoculars, he saw what he took to be a cruiser speeding northward. McClusky rightly deduced that if the cruiser captain was in that big a hurry, he must be trying to catch up with the rest of the Japanese fleet. Therefore McClusky changed course from northwest to north and followed the speeding ship. His unwitting guide was the destroyer *Arashi*, which had become separated from the Mobile Force, being engaged in depth-charging *Nautilus* when Nagumo changed his course.

While trailing *Arashi*, McClusky lost one of his aircraft, that of Ens. Eugene A. Greene. The reason for this dropout remains a mystery. Greene and his gunner were reported to have climbed into their lifeboat about forty miles from the U.S. fleet, but after that all trace of them was lost.

The *Enterprise* dive bombers had been following McClusky about ten minutes in his stalking of the Japanese destroyer when the enemy fleet broke into view. But his troubles were by no means over. Just as Ens. Tony F. Schneider's group moved into the outer ring of Japanese screening vessels, his plane ran out of fuel, forcing him to turn south and land in the sea. He and his gunner spent three days in their life raft before a PBY fished them out and took them to Midway.

At almost the same moment that Schneider turned away, Lt. Richard H. Best, the blue-eyed, youthful-looking, and combat-seasoned commander of VB-6, caught a signal from Lt. (j.g.) Edwin J. Kroeger, one of his wingmen. Kroeger had run out of oxygen. Best could have instructed his wingman to break off and return to *Enterprise* at a lower altitude, but he had a good reason for reluctance to do so. Best knew that his fellow squadron commander, Lt. W. Earl Gallaher of VS-6, had to equip his unit with 500-pound bombs because, being the first dive bombers to take off, they did not have the deck space necessary for a run long enough to launch with 1,000-pound bombs. As a result, only Best's men packed the heavy wallop. Rather than lose the extra punch of Kroeger's 1,000-pounder, Best led his squadron down to 15,000 feet. There he removed his own face mask, indicating to his men that they could safely do the same. This movement brought Best below and ahead of McClusky, so that he could not observe any visual signal from his group commander.

McClusky broke radio silence to instruct Best to hit the carrier to port, and at the same moment he ordered Gallaher to attack the target to starboard. Deciding to head the starboard strike himself, McClusky added, "Earl, follow me."

Somehow, Best missed McClusky's radioed instructions and assumed his target to be the "left-hand" carrier. He so radioed McClusky.

At this time, Nagumo's carriers were lined up in no orderly formation. Two successive ship-by-ship turns to the northeast had left *Akagi* and *Kaga* to the southwest, *Kaga* "positioned in the direction of *Akagi*'s starboard bow," with *Soryu* somewhat to the northeast, and *Hiryu* in the same direction but far enough away that she escaped immediate attention. As VB-6 and VS-6 approached from the southwest, there seems little doubt that the carrier to starboard was *Kaga*, and to port *Akagi*.

As Best made for *Kaga*, he split his division in three parts, one to hit straight in, the second to port, and the third to starboard. This would catch the carrier in a squeeze and prevent concentration of her antiaircraft guns. Just as he began his run, McClusky plunged past him like a kingfisher. Best broke off his dive and took off toward *Akagi*, thus unavoidably delaying his strike by a few moments.

All during the torpedo bombing attacks, the Japanese had rushed preparations for their own strike on the enemy task force, prodded along by a message from *Akagi:* "Hurry up preparations for the second wave." Reports reached the flagship's bridge of more American planes coming in, but thus far the clouds concealed them. At 1020, lookouts spotted a dive bomber over *Kaga*, and *Akagi* went into a maximum turn.

At first Comdr. Minoru Genda, First Fleet Air Officer, was not too concerned, stating in retrospect:

> I thought dive bombers might be troublesome, but, from my own experience of seeing just a while ago that enemy skill was not so good, concluded that they, too, might not be so good. But, I had a concern in that our fighters were flying at low altitude following the previous engagement and they needed some time to climb up again to intercept enemy dive bombers.

Perhaps antiaircraft fire could drive them off, or the carriers maneuver out of their way.

But within the instant a *Kaga* lookout shouted, "Dive bombers!" Capt. Takahisa Amagai, *Kaga*'s air officer, felt a moment's professional admiration. "Splendid was their tactic," he observed, "of diving upon our force from the direction of the sun, taking advantage of intermittent clouds."

Communications Officer Lt. Comdr. Sesu Mitoya, standing on the flight deck near the tower, dove flat as the scream from the dive bombers rose to a bansheelike wail. The time was 1022. The first three bombs missed the target. Then Gallaher, roaring down to 2,500 feet to release, dropped his bomb starboard aft squarely amidst the planes massed for takeoff. Instantly the flight deck was a holocaust. As the aircraft tilted over on a wing or forward on the nose, the fuselage formed a chimney flue spouting flame and smoke.

The next two missiles failed to strike, and in this slight relief Lieutenant Fiyuma, the fire control officer, raced to the bridge, where Captain Okada stood staring into space as if he could not take in what was happening. Fiyuma reported all passages below were afire and most of the crew trapped. All power was cut off. Fiyuma urged Okada to leave the bridge and go with his staff to the anchor deck to escape, for the carrier was already starting to list. But Okada only shook his head dreamily. "I will remain with my ship," he said. Mitoya left the bridge to try to contact the engine-room crews through the ready room, and when he came back, there was no bridge, no Okada, no Fiyuma.

In his absence, the seventh and eighth bombs had struck near each other in the vicinity of the forward elevator. One of these crashed through the elevator and exploded among the planes on the hangar deck. These aircraft had been armed, fueled, and were ready to be lifted for the second wave, destined never to take off. Amagai saw the second hit explode directly over the head of the carrier's maintenance officer, and curiously enough the sight steadied his nerves and engendered a certain objectivity. All men must die, and this was the way he would like to go—in one instantaneous flash. *Let a bomb come upon my head, if it comes,* he thought.

What did fall on his head was command of *Kaga,* for the third direct hit struck a small gasoline truck near the island, and flaming debris killed everyone on the bridge. That left Amagai senior officer aboard, and he devoted all his energies to directing the fire fighting, in the hope that the ship might yet be saved. That hope was to prove vain. The ninth American bomb delivered the fourth and last hit, landing almost directly amidships far to port, and was almost redundant, for without light or power Amagai's efforts were doomed to failure.

Comdr. Mitsuo Fuchida was so intensely interested in the preparations to launch *Akagi*'s second wave that he did not consciously note the attack on *Kaga* immediately. At 1022, the bridge ordered the fighters to take off as soon as readied. The air officer, Comdr. Shogo Masuda, swung his white flag and the first Zero sped down the flight deck. Then a lookout screamed, "Hell divers!" Fuchida glanced up in time to see three planes plummeting down, seemingly aimed straight for the spot near the command post where he sat. He just had time to recognize the stubby silhouette of the Dauntless when three black dots dropped from the aircraft and seemed to float almost leisurely toward *Akagi*. Fuchida prudently crawled behind a mantelet.

According to American records, Best's unit of five dive bombers attacked *Akagi*. To the best of the authors' knowledge, Japanese eyewitness accounts and records were unanimous that only three were involved. Rushing down in a nearly vertical dive, Best saw a plane taking off as he peered through his gunsight. He released his missile at 2,500 feet, fused to ensure a four-foot penetration of a carrier flight deck. He was perfectly sure that he had secured a hit "just forward and on center line." In his book, Fuchida also stated that the first bomb struck. Yet in a personal interview he informed Prange that the first bomb missed. "It dropped on starboard side into sea, *brrrr*," he said in his flavorful English, "and in sea explode. Big water splash." *Akagi*'s damage chart shows that the first bomb was a near miss about ten meters off the port bow, and Genda remembered the waterspout which it sent over the bridge, drenching everyone and turning their faces black. According to Genda, Vice Admiral Nagumo and his staff "were surprised but not scared."

The second bomb struck near the amidship elevator, twisting it like a piece of futuristic sculpture and dropping into the hangar. Certain that the third bomb would be even more accurate and devastating, Fuchida rolled over on his stomach, pressed his face to the deck, and crossed his arms over his head for protection. The actual sound of impact was not quite as strong as the first hit, but it struck near the edge of the port flight deck, and *Akagi*'s damage chart notes, "Fatal hit. Several holes." Then followed a moment of uncanny silence.

Genda was surprised to feel so little shock from the two direct hits. This fact, plus his naturally forward-looking disposition, lulled him into a momentary calm. Akagi *has been hit, too*, he thought. *What a pity! We must not be downed*, he added to himself, *as we still have the Second Carrier Division*.

Genda's optimism was not entirely misplaced, for normally the two strikes would not have been fatal. But the dive bombers had caught the First Carrier Division with flight decks full of armed and fueled aircraft, with others in the same condition in the hangar decks waiting to be lifted. Moreover, there had been no time to return the 800-kilogram land bombs to the arsenal. It was induced explosions from this stacked-up destruction and a chain reaction of flaming planes which would shortly turn *Akagi* into what Kusaka called "a burning hell."

Even as Genda reminded himself of Yamaguchi's carriers, he looked toward *Soryu*. She, too, was sending up a billow of white smoke. Genda "was really shocked for the first time"; for once in his life both ideas and speech were knocked out of him.

If contemporary American reports of the battle of Midway could be accepted as gospel, nothing happened to *Soryu* at the hands of the dive bombers. Nobody sank her; nobody even tried to sink her. The problem seems to have been, as Walter Lord has observed, a misunderstanding of how big *Soryu* really was. Yet sink she did, so some group must have attacked her. And the preponderance of evidence points to *Yorktown*.

During the hour's delay between launch of Task Force Sixteen's dive bombers and *Yorktown*'s, Rear Adm. Frank Jack Fletcher received no amplifying reports. But Task Force Seventeen's staff put the time to good use, studying the initial Japanese plot, course, and speed. These calculations indicated that if Nagumo proceeded along these lines, he would be only ninety miles from Midway. This appeared a much closer approach than necessary, so squadron commanders were warned not to overfly the course line—to turn right, because the Japanese probably would reverse course.

Comdr. Murr E. Arnold, *Yorktown*'s air officer, planned that Massey's VT-3 and Lt. Comdr. Maxwell F. Leslie's seventeen SBDs of VB-3 should strike the enemy in unison. So he directed Leslie to orbit *Yorktown* to give the slower torpedo planes a fifteen-minute head start.

At a few minutes after 0900, Leslie lifted off and began his climb to 15,000 feet. Weather conditions could not have been more favorable: "The visibility was excellent, ceiling unlimited with scattered clouds at 3,000 ft. The sea was calm with little or no wind."

Lt. (j.g.) Paul A. "Lefty" Holmberg worried lest the battle be over before VB-3 could get into it. He himself almost missed the action. At takeoff, his aircraft, 3-B-2, was caught in Leslie's slipstream and his left wing brushed the gutter on the forward catwalk. Holmberg greatly feared that he would crash and fail to accomplish this, his first combat mission, for which he had trained so long. But he gained altitude and swung into position as Leslie's wingman.

Leslie was having his own troubles, thanks to a "bug" in the electrical bomb-arming mechanism. Shortly after reaching 20,000-foot cruising level, Leslie signaled his men to arm their bombs, pushing his own newly installed electric arm switch as he did so. Instead of activating the bomb, it dropped the missile into the sea. When the same thing happened to three other planes, Leslie had to break radio silence to warn the others to use the manual switch. Holmberg could see Leslie berating himself.

Although the accident was no fault of Leslie's, it would be difficult to imagine a more frustrating experience for an officer as conscientious as Leslie. Not only must he lead his men with his own fangs drawn, but his firepower had dropped from seventeen to thirteen before the group had so much as sighted the enemy. But he could still direct his men and perhaps get in some good licks with his guns.

At around 0945, Leslie flew directly over VT-3 and six of VF-

3's fighters. He "continued to 'S' turn and follow VT-3." About fifteen minutes later, he asked Massey, in code, if he had spotted the enemy. According to Lt. D. W. Shumway, leader of the Third Division, Massey "replied in the affirmative," but Leslie did not receive it.

At 1005 Leslie's gunner, ARM 1/C. W. E. Gallagher, spotted the Mobile Force almost dead ahead about thirty-five miles away. In a few minutes, Leslie heard "considerable discussion over the radio regarding VT-3 being attacked by fighters."

Leslie had no difficulty in choosing his target:

> The carrier was a large one with a full deck painted dark red, a forward elevator, a relatively small superstructure located about ⅓ of the length of the ship aft from the bow on the starboard side, vertical smoke stacks which were inboard from the starboard side and adjoining the superstructure. It could fit the description of the KAGA except for the vertical smoke stacks. The latest model I have seen of the KAGA shows its smoke stacks encased as one protruding horizontally from the starboard side and aft of the superstructure. [Capitals in original.]

To the westward, Leslie saw another carrier with its superstructure on the port side. Later he deduced that this was *Akagi*. Another flattop was indeed somewhat to the westward, and she carried her bridge to port. But she was *Hiryu*, still busily dodging VT-3's torpedo attacks. Under the impression that Lt. Wallace C. Short's VS-5 was nearby, Leslie radioed Short to hit the carrier to westward. Not until much later did he learn that VS-5 had been held back.

By now, Leslie's radioman warned that his target was launching planes. Leslie made one final, unsuccessful attempt to contact VT-3 and VF-3. Then he realized that the coordinated attack so carefully crafted had come apart. It was up to him. He did not know that his group was about to become the third prong of a triple attack which could not have been better coordinated had all concerned rehearsed it for weeks.

At "about 1225" (1025 Midway time) Leslie led his men down, firing at the bridge with his fixed guns. Then further frustration—his guns jammed, so he "retired for 4½ minutes at high speed to the SE."

Thus Holmberg had the honor and responsibility of leading the actual bombing attack. Heading slightly stern to bow, he caught the large red circle on the deck in his telescopic sight. He held his dive a bit longer than usual, pulling out around 200 feet. Flames were coming from both sides of the carrier as its antiaircraft opened fire. He felt what he assumed was shrapnel hit his plane, but it did not upset his dive, which was almost schoolbook perfect. As he cleared the ship, he saw his target burst into a mass of colors—red, blue, green, and yellow—as it exploded into flame. A plane was taking off just as the bomb detonated, and it blew the aircraft off the deck and into the water. So reported Ens. R. M. Elder, following in plane 3-B-14.

"Five direct hits and three very near misses were scored immediately thereafter," according to Shumway. A bit on the exuberant side, but the results were quite enough to satisfy all but the most dedicated nitpicker. Of the three carriers struck in the attack, Soryu suffered the most prompt, intensified damage.

Commencing at 1025, three direct hits in as many minutes, neatly lined up along the port side, triggered ferocious deck fires as well as induced explosions in the bomb-storage, torpedo-storage, and ammunition rooms, plus gas tanks.

There exists the usual conflicting testimony about hits, but Holmberg believed that he had caught the carrier amidships between elevators, and Soryu's executive officer, Comdr. Hisashi Ohara, agreed. The second hit crashed through the flight deck just in front of the forward elevator, exploding in the hangar deck. The third struck either forward of the Number Three elevator, or among the armed and fueled aircraft awaiting takeoff.

In any case, "fires enveloped the whole ship in no time," Nagumo reported. As the flames roared and crackled, Capt. Ryusaku Yanagimoto placed himself on the signal tower to starboard of the bridge, shouting commands, and ordering and begging his men to save themselves. Obviously no living thing could last much longer on *Soryu*. Belowdecks, heat so infernal that it melted and warped the hangar-deck doors drove survivors topside. The anchor deck became an impromptu hospital where doctors and medical corpsmen worked like robots, ignoring the choking smoke, to give pain-relieving shots to those badly injured, bandaging and stopping bleeding where they could. Those beyond hope had to be left untended to save those who had a chance for life. A large group of sailors were massed on the forward deck with a number of officers, including Ohara, when a terrific induced explosion shot many of them, Ohara among them, into the sea.

Exactly half an hour passed from the first hit on *Soryu* at 1025 until Yanagimoto ordered, "Abandon ship." The main engines were stopped, the steering system inoperable, and the fire mains gone. Thirty short minutes had transformed *Soryu* from a smart, proud carrier to a burned-out crematorium. *Hamakaze* and *Isokaze* hovered nearby to pick up survivors, rescuing some from the water while others were fortunate enough to go over the side in good order.

During the process, someone noticed that Yanagimoto was not with them, and looking up, the men could see their captain still on the tower, shouting words of encouragement to the survivors and crying out, "Banzai!" Consternation swept the crewmen when they realized that he meant to go down with the ship. Yanagimoto was one of the best loved and most respected skippers in the Japanese or any other Navy, and the men resolved to rescue him in spite of himself. They deputized Chief Petty Officer Abe, a Navy wrestling champ, to bring him to safety, by force if necessary. Abe did his best. He climbed back up the tower, saluted his captain, and said, "Captain, I have come on behalf of all your men to take you to safety. They are waiting for you. Please come with me to the destroyer, sir."

Yanagimoto kept on staring straight ahead as if he had not

heard. Doggedly Abe advanced on him to pick the captain up bodily in his great wrestler's arms when Yanagimoto turned slowly. He did not utter a word, but his eyes stopped Abe dead in his tracks. The sailor saluted and left his captain. As he moved away, tears smarting in his eyes, he could hear Yanagimoto softly singing "Kimigayo," the national anthem.

About two hundred men had been flung over *Akagi*'s side [by the two bomb hits and the induced explosions that followed]. Masuda was frantically trying to corral everyone below deck under cover. Fuchida went to the briefing room, which was rapidly becoming an emergency hospital. He asked a rescue worker why they did not take the wounded to sick bay and learned that the entire lower levels were afire. On hearing this, Fuchida tried to reach his cabin to salvage what he could, but fire and smoke turned him back. Had he and Genda been content to relax in the comfort of their hospital beds, they would have shared the fate of the other patients, every one of whom perished.

Fuchida wandered back to the bridge, as if instinctively seeking his Eta Jima classmate with whom he had shared so much joy and now must share sorrow. By now Genda realized all too well the full measure of Japan's loss, but he was not the type to weep on anyone's shoulder. He looked at Fuchida briefly and remarked laconically, *"Shimatta* [We goofed]," which seemed to sum up the situation in a nutshell.

Meanwhile, Nagumo's chief of staff, Rear Adm. Ryunosuke Kusaka, had been adding up the score in his usual practical fashion. The radio room and antenna had been destroyed, making any communication impossible. Despite prompt flooding of forward ammunition and bomb storage rooms and activating carbon-dioxide fire-fighting apparatus, matters were rapidly getting out of hand. By 1042, the steering apparatus was out of commission, the engines stopped, and all hands were ordered to fire-fighting stations. Only two machine guns and one antiaircraft gun remained able to fire.

With all these factors in mind, Kusaka decided the time had

come to let Rear Adm. Hiroaki Abe, commander of CruDiv 8 and next senior officer to Nagumo, assume temporary command of the Mobile Force while Nagumo transferred his flag elsewhere. With the brain trust of the Mobile Force still intact, they could continue the fight with *Hiryu* as the nucleus, preferably in a night attack, the Japanese specialty. Therefore, Kusaka urged Nagumo to leave *Akagi* and reestablish his headquarters on another ship.

"But Nagumo, having a feeling heart, refused to listen to me," recalled Kusaka. "I urged him two or three times, but in vain. He firmly continued to stand by the side of a compass on the bridge." At this point Captain Aoki, an Eta Jima classmate of Kusaka's, moved close to him and said softly, "Chief of Staff, as the ship's captain I am going to take care of this ship with all responsibility, so I urge you, the commander in chief, and all other staff officers to leave this vessel as soon as possible, so that the command of the force may be continued."

Thus reinforced, Kusaka raised his voice and scolded Nagumo for letting his heart rule his head in such an important matter. Finally, Nagumo bowed to the dictates of reason and consented to be rescued. His decision almost came too late, for already the stairways from the bridge were blocked by fire, and the staff had to evacuate by shimmying down a rope. Being chunky, Kusaka nearly stuck in the window, but squeezed through with the aid of a few hearty shoves, only to fall from the middle of the rope to the flight deck, twisting both ankles and burning his hands and one leg.

Fuchida was the last man down the rope, which had already begun to smolder. One of the thundering explosions which continually rocked *Akagi* hurled him high in the air and smashed him onto the flight deck with a force that broke both legs in the ankle, arch, and heel region. He thought that this was the end of the line for him, and between pain, grief, and physical weakness, he faced the prospect with few emotions beyond an intense weariness. Little tongues of flame were licking in his direction and his uniform had actually begun to smolder when two enlisted men ran out of the smoke, picked him up, and swung him in a net aboard a lifeboat filled with Nagumo and his staff headed for the light cruiser *Nagara*. Fuchida was not officially a member of the staff, hence was not scheduled to evacuate until the rest of the flying officers did so, but he could not be left behind in that condition.

As Genda was about to enter the boat, a petty officer, noting that Genda had burned one hand, pulled off his glove and handed it over, saying, "Air Staff Officer, please use this." At almost the same moment, a sailor, Genda's "boy," rushed up and gave him a *han* (seal) and his bank deposit book. Somehow the boy had braved the flames below deck to salvage what he could of his chief's possessions. Genda was by no means certain he would live to use either item, and in any case his savings were far from princely, but the kindness of both these men, who could think of another at such a moment, touched him deeply.

Nagumo's lifeboat lurched through the water, the oars scattering liquid diamonds, glittering like the tears some of the rowers could not help shedding. The officers denied themselves this relief, in the stoic tradition of their training. Genda sat down beside Makishima, who had lost his camera, film, and everything else but his life. The photographer was inexpressibly shocked to hear Genda mutter softly, "If *Shokaku* and *Zuikaku* had been here, there wouldn't have been a calamity like this." Makishima looked around apprehensively, to see if Nagumo or Kusaka had heard that word *calamity* coming from such a one as Genda, "who had been regarded as a hope of the Japanese Navy."

Capt. Chisato Morita looked at Genda and observed without visible emotion, "The outcome will surely decide the fate of Japan." Every head in the boat flew up, but no word was spoken.

Nagumo lifted his close-cropped gray head, gazed unblinkingly at the bridge where he had commanded in glory, and lowered his head again. Makishima thought the lines in the admiral's face had already deepened, and he appeared to be praying for the souls of his dead.

Saved for Another Day

from *A Proud American*

BY JOE FOSS WITH DONNA WILD FOSS

Joe Foss has led a busy, successful life—among his many adventures are two terms as governor of South Dakota, a stint as the first commissioner of the American Football League, and a tour as president of the National Rifle Association. Somehow he also found time to become a nationwide television personality as the host of two long-running shows, The American Sportsman and The Outdoorsman: Joe Foss.

Yet before all that, Joe Foss was a fighter pilot. As a Marine aviator during World War II he received credit for twenty-six confirmed victories and was decorated with the Congressional Medal of Honor.

In the following excerpt from his autobiography, A Proud American, we join young Joe Foss on Guadalcanal in the South Pacific in the autumn of 1942. He is learning the art of leading men and staying alive while playing the deadly game of war.

IT WAS NOVEMBER 7, 1942. TO DATE OVER FIVE THOUSAND JAPA-nese soldiers had died on Guadalcanal trying to take back the Imperial outpost. The mood on the island was guardedly optimistic. Tokyo Rose's arrogant predictions, accurately reflecting the Japanese command's belief that the Americans were doomed, had gone unfulfilled. We had held our ground.

The day started quietly, but for some reason I felt a bit uneasy, anxious. Religion was something I'd always taken for granted but not on a very personal basis, although I would at times repeat the Lord's Prayer, the only way I knew how to pray. Late that afternoon I found myself repeating it more than usual before we left to strafe the group of ten Japanese destroyers and a light cruiser spotted about 150 miles north steaming in toward the island. We would act as decoys to provide cover while the torpedo planes struck the flotilla.

One reason for my anxiety was Danny Doyle. I was worried about him. Doyle's best friend, Casey Brandon, had been shot down and killed a few days earlier, and this was the first time I'd allowed Doyle to fly since then. Brandon and Doyle had been inseparable. Brandon was an opinionated and articulate Irish-Norwegian farm boy from Grand Rapids, Minnesota, who had finished high school at sixteen and gone on to graduate from the University of Minnesota with high honors. He'd been offered a postgraduate post in aeronautical engineering at Annapolis but turned it down in favor of more direct participation in the war.

Danny Doyle, two years younger than Brandon, was also from a Minnesota farm. All Irish, he was dark, wiry, full of sauce, and afraid of nothing. He had graduated from State Teachers' College in Mankato, Minnesota, and intended to teach after the war. His passion as a child had been the rare coconut his mother bought and hid from him for fear he would eat it all before the rest of the family had a share. Danny found it particularly funny that he was now camped in the middle of a coconut plantation.

I never minded the pair's irreverent wisecracks and practical jokes. They were good at what they did and were excellent for the squadron's morale. Even their nicknames reflected their friendship; Doyle's tag, the code name used when flying, was Fool, and Brandon's was Ish—the Foolish Twins.

I couldn't forget Danny's reaction the night Brandon didn't return. Doyle's plane had been grounded that day with mechanical problems, and Brandon flew into combat for the first time without his usual wingman. No one saw him die, but as the hours passed without word of the downed flier, Doyle grew from grimly pensive to raving with hatred. "Those goonies are going to pay if it's the last thing I do," he vowed.

Seeing how disturbed he was by the loss of his friend, I'd grounded him for fear he'd do something truly foolish. Finally, however, I had to let him fly again, although his despondency showed no real signs of abating.

When we sighted the Japanese flotilla, they had company—six float Zeros, equipped with pontoons for water takeoffs and landings—directly in front of and below us, in hot pursuit of another flight led by Maj. Paul Fontana.

"Don't look now, but I think we have something here," I radioed to my wingman, Boot Furlow.

We pulled up behind the Zeros, and Boot slipped right in under my wing just as I fired a short burst. The deadly spray ripped into the wing mount of one of the Zeros and blew the plane into a thousand pieces.

We peeled off in opposite directions to avoid hitting each other and the exploding wreckage. Boot trailed a second plane and shot it down in a flaming arc, while I looked to the left and saw my premonition come true. Danny Doyle was flying unswervingly toward a Zero, and I knew how the game would end. Without firing a shot, Danny flew straight through the enemy plane, demolishing both planes and ending his own life.

Later it would take me some time to get over Danny's death. I took all our losses hard—all the men were very close to me—but Danny's death hit me harder because I had let him fly when he was still upset. For now, however, in the heat of battle, I had to grit my teeth and let him go.

I whipped into a quick wingover and accelerated toward the buzzing swarm, looking around for another shot. But it was over; all six had been blasted out of the sky, leaving only a few pieces of falling debris and five blossoming parachutes with empty harnesses. When I spotted the sixth it was about two thousand feet above me, and the Japanese pilot was struggling out of the harness. Pulling free, he plunged past my plane, falling headfirst into the sea. Apparently the other five had committed suicide in the same way, and I wondered what strange vow they had taken.

With the Zeros out of the way we went after the ships, our original target, who were already peppering the air with AA fire. I signaled my flight to join with Fontana's squadron in reverse order, leaving me to fly the tail-end position. As I lined up to dive for a strafing run, I swiveled my head for one of my habitual cloud scans. Lucky I did, because I spotted the float of a Japanese plane, like an inverted shark fin, protruding through the bottom of a cloud. *Better get rid of this baby so he doesn't follow us down*, I thought.

Circling away from the group, I flew upward to get above the bogey, still cloaked by the clouds. When he emerged from the mists I made a diving run for my prey, figuring this was duck soup, but I'd overestimated my adversary. The plane I was stalking was not the swift and nimble Zero but a scout ship with a rear gunner. The slow-moving plane seemed to be standing almost stationary in the clouds.

I dove in too fast and had to roll on my side to avoid crashing into the rear of the plane. The quick-thinking pilot of the scout plane rolled as well, giving his tail gunner a perfect shot at me, at nearly point-blank range. That little squeak in the backseat just riveted me with that *putt-putt-putt* gun, and several of the .29-caliber shells pierced the left side of my engine cowling and shattered on through the side of the canopy three or four inches from my face—right across and out the other side. That really got my attention, I can tell you. I glanced around at the wings and tail, then checked my instruments. Despite the shrieking wind roaring through the holes in the canopy, it appeared there was no serious damage.

"This is Red Leader," I radioed. "Continue your attack."

When we came in view of the enemy fleet, Oscar Bate was in a perfect position, so he led the attack. Because of the condition of my canopy, I was unable to dive, but on my second pass I made a belly shot into the scout, sending a stream of shells into the base of the plane's right wing. It burst into flame almost at once. As the smoking plane spiraled toward the sea, I spotted a second scout, its pilot apparently unaware that his companion had been knocked out of the clouds. Circling behind him, I pulled up for an unhurried belly shot and sent my nineteenth victim to join his buddy in the drink.

Leveling off, I looked for my squadron. Then I spotted the

rest of the flight, maybe a mile and a half away, streaking out of range of the ships' guns to regroup and head back to base.

I tried to call the rest of my flight, but couldn't raise anyone. Apparently my radio was dead, which wasn't unusual. The radios in the Wildcats were inclined to frequent failure, especially mine. Bad radios plagued me. Probably this time one of the Japanese shells had damaged my aerial, but I continued calling for help just in case my radio was transmitting and I was being heard.

Just then my plane started to miss and backfire, burping out puffs of white smoke. Heading for the rendezvous point, I throttled back repeatedly to prevent the engine from conking out or vibrating off its mounts. A few moments later it quit again. I pulled back and shoved her on; it quit and started again.

At this point I started getting nervous. The other planes had long since regrouped and headed back, and I was alone in the clouds without friends—a dangerous predicament. The wind screamed through my shattered canopy as the speed increased. It sounded like the canopy was going to come off.

Suddenly I sighted a lone Wildcat. It was Jake Stub, who was having engine trouble, too. He was flying even slower than I was, and we were both losing altitude. Then we ran into some rain squalls and heavy clouds, which separated us.

Breaking out of the clouds in heavy rain, with Stub nowhere in sight, I could make out the silhouette of two islands up ahead and steered for them.[1] Flying on feeling instead of watching my compass, I mistook them for the gateway to Guadalcanal.

I was gaining and losing altitude sporadically as my engine cut out and recovered. Soon the stops got closer than the starts, and I realized I wasn't going to make it back to Henderson. Checking my compass, I saw that I was thirty degrees off course, with nightfall rapidly approaching.

Viscous sheets of another squall appeared dead ahead, and I

---

1. Later I would learn that Jake got shot down shortly after I had seen him. It took him five days to get back to home base. Jake had spotted Zeros chasing me that I had not seen, but apparently they lost me when I went into the clouds.

flew left to circumvent it. Just as I came abreast of the storm, a plume of smoke swirled out of my motor, and the engine stopped cold. No amount of urgent manipulation of the throttle would bring it back to life. Now all I could hear was the whistling of the wind rushing over the plane's outer skin and through the holes in the canopy.

The storm was growing, and if I landed in the water, my chances of being spotted from the air were minimal if not nonexistent. Suddenly I keenly lamented the fact that I had never learned to swim!

I began rocking to and fro in the cockpit in the motion a child uses to move a kiddie car forward foot by foot, as though I could propel the plane physically. Bathed in sweat, I felt like my hair was standing up so straight it would raise the helmet right off my head.

I spotted an island off to my left and set a glide path for it. Fortunately I was at about 13,000 feet; I figured I should have plenty of altitude to make the distance. I'd ditch the plane in the water directly offshore and paddle to land with the aid of my Mae West, the bulky life vests we wore at all times when we flew.

As I circled in over the deserted shoreline, looking for a smooth, sandy beach on which to land, I miscalculated. The maneuver had cost me considerable altitude, and when I circled back out to sea to make another landing approach, I rapidly ran out of elevation and speed. Now I had no choice. I was going down in the water almost five miles from land.

The thought of having to swim five miles was terrifying; the single test I'd failed during flight training was the basic swimming test. Adding to my woes was the storm, now in full force, whipping up the sea and ruining my visibility.

I opened the canopy and pushed it back so I could climb out when I hit the surface. As the water rose to meet me, I pulled the plane's nose up, intending to skip the machine like a rock on a pond, but the tail section bashed against the water and bounced up above the front of the plane. When I hit the water a second time, I nosed into the Pacific like a torpedo from a dive bomber. The impact threw the canopy forward and slammed it shut. Water poured through the rents in the canopy with the force of a wave breaking on a beach.

The Grumman manual promised that the plane would float at least thirty seconds, but the heavily armored machine sank immediately. Gliding into the depths, I found myself in utter darkness with water gushing into the cockpit through the fist-sized punctures in the canopy. Only then did I remember my training. Even when every precaution is taken, a water landing is a dangerous maneuver—and in my excitement and panic I had neglected two precautions. I forgot that I was supposed to jettison the canopy entirely before hitting the water, and I forgot to release the snaps on the leg straps of my parachute harness.

Trapped in the dark plane, numb with fear and cold, I forced myself to act. *Listen, dope,* I told myself. *If you don't quiet down, you're going to spend a long time inside this bird on the bottom of the ocean!*

Water filled the cockpit as I felt for the latches that held the canopy, unfastened them, and pushed it open with all my strength. I fought to maintain consciousness, but momentarily blacked out and sucked in brackish seawater.

Just like the old story goes, my whole life passed before my eyes as I lost track of the real world. I saw my buddies gathered around the Short Snorters table, sorting and distributing my personal belongings among themselves and talking about what a fine fellow old Joe had been. I had a lot of things I loved, like my sewing kit, and I could just see those punks sitting around there having a good time with it. It irritated the daylights out of me and snapped me back to reality.

Forcing myself to action was agony, and I restrained my gagging cough, a reaction to the ingested seawater, through sheer force of will. I had no idea how long I'd been under the water, but my body was screaming for oxygen. Reaching down, I unhooked my leg straps, swallowing more seawater in the process.

No longer locked to the plane, I was pulled upward toward

the surface by the current streaming past the rapidly sinking Wildcat and by my buoyant parachute pack and life preserver. Fortunately I had remembered to crack the air cylinders on my Mae West, and the life jacket's buoyancy, along with my floatable parachute pack, began to pull me toward the surface— fanny up.

Suddenly my left foot caught and wedged under the cockpit seat, trapping me and holding me fast as the Wildcat continued its descent into the deep. For a moment I thrashed helplessly in the water. Then, using the fabric of my flight suit for a grip, I pulled my way, hand over hand, toward my captured foot. The need to breathe was almost uncontrollable, but I tapped the last of my strength to free my foot. Finally, disengaged from the airplane, I felt the crushing pressure of the cold water as I shot upward.

The passage seemed an eternity. My craving for air was pure pain. When I finally reached the surface, it was backside first, the parachute pack on my back pushing my face underwater. The boxing matches of my youth were child's play compared with the fight I waged with my own safety gear as I struggled to undo the stubborn straps of the parachute harness that had twisted with the fastenings of the Mae West, all the time swallowing more seawater.

I got one strap unbuckled and twisted the chute around under my stomach. At least now I could keep my head above water. Then at last I unsnapped the remaining strap, only to have the loose-fitting Mae West float up over my ears. I pulled the adjustment straps tighter, and all of a sudden I was floating peacefully.

Now all I had to do was swim five miles to shore through a raging storm!

Gasping and coughing and shaking, I remembered the instructions: relax and try to swim calmly. Thinking I should get rid of all excess weight, I unlaced my boots and let them sink. Instantly I regretted doing this. *I know I'm going to need them on that island; the coral will tear my feet to shreds.* I didn't scuttle my parachute, figuring I could use it as a cover after reaching shore.

But the odds of making it to the island were slight, and I knew it. Between the storm and the rapidly approaching darkness, it was difficult to see clearly. Also, it seemed like the current was carrying me out to sea.

I started thrashing my arms and doing some kind of ridiculous bicycle-pedaling motion with my legs, which all amounted to a crazy kind of jig with a lot of splashing and little progress. *Sure glad nobody's here to see this*, I thought.

Suddenly a stone's throw away something caught my eye. "Shark fins!" I think I yelled it out loud. *What a way to go. After all I've been through, I'm going to check out as a hunk of shark bait.*

Now, trying to swim became doubly fearful. Every time I reached an arm out to paddle I was afraid I'd draw back a stub. Though sharks normally don't bother humans, many in the area had developed a taste for human flesh because of the numerous naval and aerial battles that left men bleeding in the waters of the slot. Men from both sides had fallen prey to the carnivorous sea creatures, and I was terrified.

Then I remembered the chlorine. My flight suit was equipped with little capsules of chlorine shark repellent. (It's a good thing I didn't know, as would later be proven, that chlorine doesn't protect swimmers from shark attacks.)

I broke one open, hoping the sharks disliked the smell as much as I did. Then I started praying harder than I'd ever prayed in my life. I confessed every sin I could remember and kept praying, "God help me!"

I had never felt more alone or more helpless.

Four or five hours drifted by, and I was growing weaker struggling against the sea. Then, through the black night around me, I heard something. *Voices!* I turned my head in the direction of the sounds. *Canoe paddles?*

Two flickers of light moved in an odd pattern across the water. *Japs!* I thought. *They saw me hit the drink!*

I stopped swimming and floated silently as the splashing of oars grew louder and louder. It appeared there were two boats traveling toward me. The boatmen were carrying on a mumbled conversation, but I couldn't make out any words or accents.

When the light was only yards away, I could see that they were outrigger canoes, heading straight at me. I held my breath, afraid the noisy thumping of my wildly beating heart would give me away.

The clumsy Mae West made it impossible to duck underwater, so I desperately tried to push myself silently to one side. The canoes skimmed by, too close for comfort, but even then I couldn't discern the nationality of the murmurs and low-pitched conversation.

The searchers combed the waters, back and forth, but somehow I escaped their notice. Finally someone yelled, "Let's look over 'ere."

It was an Australian accent and the most welcome sound I'd ever heard.

"Hey!" I yelled. "Over here!"

The lights headed toward me immediately and circled. When I finally saw the faces of the men, they were grotesquely highlighted by the lanterns. Almost all were natives, and they were armed with war clubs.

"Hey, get me out of here!" I yelled. "I'm an American . . . friend . . . birdman . . . flier . . . pilot . . . I got shot down."

A hand reached out of the darkness to pull me into the outrigger. It was the hand of Father Dan Stuyvenberg, a Catholic priest.

My parachute was waterlogged and weighed a ton.

"You must be a superman to drag anything like that along with you," said the other white man. Later I would learn that he was Tommy Mason Robertson, a sawmill owner from the island of Malaita.

As the natives paddled back to shore, Robertson held his lantern higher to get a better look at me. In a flash something struck the lantern from his hand and sent it clanking across the bottom of the boat. The something that had knocked the lamp from his grip was flipping in the bottom of the boat: a slender garlike fish, about twenty inches long, with a sharp, pointed nose.

"I should've kept the lantern down," Tommy apologized. "Guess I got careless in all the excitement. Plenty of men have lost their eyes at night doing that. These jumping fish go toward light. Even the reflection of your eyes will attract them."

That was enough to convince me, and until we landed, I kept my hands over my face and peeked through my fingers.

The men also pointed out that the jut of land I'd been swimming toward was overpopulated with man-eating crocodiles. If somehow I'd made it to land, I'd probably have been somebody's supper. Talk about an obstacle course!

The island was Malaita, and my rescuers were from the Catholic mission there. The mission colony consisted of two compounds, one for the women and another for the men, as well as a scattering of native dwellings.

When we landed, I stumbled from the beach to a campfire where the islanders had gathered to wait for the searchers' return. The welcoming party included two bishops, four fathers, two brothers, and eight sisters. The place was a regular melting pot of nationalities. The missionaries were from France, the Netherlands, Norway, Russia, Italy, and even a brother from Emmetsburg, Iowa, and a sister from Boston. Most of them had escaped to Malaita when the Japanese invaded neighboring islands. Some of their fellow workers had not been so fortunate; the Japanese had an ugly fetish for bayoneting missionaries through the throat, and two nuns had been raped and killed by a group of Japanese soldiers.

I was exhausted and feeling sick from the seawater I'd swallowed, but my rescuers were anxious to hear what was going on in the outside world. Their only sources of news were Tommy Robertson's tiny radio aboard his scow and meager reports from natives who crossed the channel from one of the other islands. One of the sisters had been in the islands for forty years. Though she had seen the airplanes that strafed and bombed the islands, she had never seen an automobile.

Dry clothes and an excellent meal revived me. Steak—the first fresh meat I'd had in weeks—eggs, papaya, pineapple, and a delicious dark bread. No supplies had arrived on the island for months, but they gave me the best they had.

They kept me awake for some time, fascinated by my stories about the war and other progress in the outside world. When I finally hit the sack, it was a thatch mat with a pillow that felt more like a hundred-pound bag of rock salt, but I was so exhausted I could have slept on a bed of nails. And I slept well, except for one bout of nausea from all the seawater I'd swallowed.

The sound of hymns woke me the next morning. I ached from head to toe, and when I stood up, my shaky legs brought my crash landing vividly to mind. I rubbed the sleep out of my eyes and left the long, narrow one-room thatched building. Following the sound, I came upon an open-sided thatched hut, which was obviously a church; the altar was made of carved bamboo and coconut shells, and before it stood one of the priests leading a congregation of seminaked natives. Some of the older natives were a fearful sight, clad in red loincloths and savage-looking jewelry made from shells and animal teeth, their mouths stained red from chewing betel nuts, and their hair standing out like it was charged with electricity. The missionaries had told me the night before that this particular tribe had a reputation for being hostile, but here they were, singing hymns.

After the service Father Dan arranged a reception and breakfast near his living quarters so that everyone could shake hands with me. The entire village turned out. Again, though food was in short supply, they brought out their best—eggs, fresh goat's milk, papaya, and other exotic fruits I didn't recognize, and more of that delicious bread.

I had once joked with my men, "If I get shot down, don't come looking for me for a couple weeks, because I'll be fishing." With their fine hospitality and the surf fishing I could do, a couple weeks here would seem like heaven.

But there was a war on, and somehow I had to get back to

my outfit. After breakfast I stretched out my chute in a clearing, knowing that any circling American plane would recognize it as a distress signal.

The missionaries told me about an airplane that had crashed on the side of the mountain not far from the village and wanted me to go with them to investigate. They were unsure which country it belonged to. Minutes later we started up the steep trail to find the site of the crash. As we moved through the jungle, we heard an airplane approaching, and the party started to scatter.

"It's a Grumman F4F. Probably looking for me," I said, and ran into a clearing. As the plane turned, the pilot looked right down at me. I recognized Dutch Bruggeman from our squadron, and he recognized me. When he turned and headed for home, I told the priests that it wouldn't be long before someone came back for me.

After a short time, a PBY appeared on the horizon. The pilot set the flying boat down far out at sea and cruised in toward the bay, so that any enemy observers would have a hard time pinpointing where he was heading.

I hurriedly said good-bye to my new friends and gave my chute to the nuns to make vestments for the church. I understand that to this day that parachute silk adorns the altar of the Catholic church on Malaita, with the letters *U.S.* still clearly visible.

Homecoming was a raucous event—sort of like someone coming back from the dead. Someone said I came back "dressed in a pair of sailor's white trousers, smoking a cigar, and talking a mile a minute."[2] That's the way I remember it, too.

"Joe!" they shouted. "We thought for sure you were a goner!"

Once more I was kept awake telling stories, but this time I was the one catching up on what had happened while I'd been gone. Several good men and friends had died, and despite my

---

2. Thomas G. Miller Jr., *The Cactus Air Force* (New York: Harper & Row, 1969), p. 179.

fatigue, we talked for hours. I even did my popular impression of a befuddled Jap commander calling roll after we'd wiped out his entire flight.

We camouflaged our feelings with laughter, rather than think too hard about our fallen comrades and our own narrow escapes. Of the original eight in my flight, half were gone forever, and many of the guys had silently given me up for dead before word arrived that I'd been sighted on Malaita.

That night I wrote in my diary: "Glad to be back again. Thankful is the word. Yesterday I prayed more than I ever prayed in my life."

One thought kept running through my mind as I lay on my cot and stared into the darkness: *I've been saved for another day— for some reason.*

One day I landed particularly pleased with myself. While shooting down three Zeros I had escaped the melee without catching even one bullet.

That was also the day Jack Conger went down.

When I was in high school, my cousin Jake and I once sneaked in through the back door of the Dakota movie theater in Sioux Falls. We sat down quietly near the front of the house hoping no one would notice us, but we'd only been there a few minutes when an usher, a high school kid even younger than we were, walked up behind us and firmly escorted us outside. That usher was Jack Conger. Now we were fighting for our lives together.

On this particular day, eight Japanese fighters attacked Henderson, and Jack Conger was one of the four Wildcats who met them overhead. Locked in extended combat with an equally determined and capable Japanese pilot, Jack could not get in a killing shot. When he ran out of ammunition, he was so caught up in the passion of battle that he turned his Grumman straight up as the Zero flew over, intending to use his propeller as a buzz saw to take off the enemy's tail rudder.

I was only about 1,500 feet below on the ground at the time, watching as Conger misjudged and hit halfway between the tail and the cockpit, chewing at least five feet off the Zero's tail before both planes started falling toward the water off the beach we controlled. Both pilots clambered out of their cockpits and pulled their rip cords. I jumped into a nearby jeep and raced for the beach, where I found a group of sailors and Marines already going after the two pilots in a small higgins boat, a squarish rough-iron vessel with a bow that would lower to the beach when landing.

The Japanese flier was closest to the shore and the boat started for him, but he pointed out toward Conger and gestured for them to go for him first. When the rescuers got to Conger, one of the sailors laughed and said, "Your friend back there said to pick you up first."

"Well, he's a real sport," said Conger. "There is a little chivalry left in the war at that."

With Conger in the boat, they turned back toward the Japanese pilot. The Marines wanted to finish the enemy at a distance, but Conger insisted on rescuing the man. I could hear the heated argument clearly from where I stood knee-high in the surf.

Conger won the debate and personally reached down to grab the enemy airman's life vest to pull him into the boat. The pilot smiled and extended an arm up to Conger. As the two clasped hands, the Japanese pilot whipped his other arm around with a cocked 8-mm Nambu pistol, rammed the barrel between Conger's eyes, and pulled the trigger.

The gun misfired with only a wet click, but Conger threw himself backward against the other side of the boat so violently that he was plagued with back problems for the rest of his life. The Japanese pilot then turned the pistol to his own head, and the wet ammunition misfired again. Conger grabbed a five-gallon gasoline can and hit the Jap over the head with it.

As the Japanese pilot passed me, he spit at me, and I wanted to shoot that sucker.

An interesting footnote to this event would occur years later, in April 1990, when Jack Conger once again met the Japanese pilot, Shiro Ishikawa. The two veterans shook hands and talked for the first time since this incident forty-eight years earlier. After being shot down and captured, Ishikawa, a member of the Second Air Group of the Imperial Japanese Navy, spent the rest of the war in a prisoner of war camp in New Zealand.

Significant moments like this may be locked in history, but time heals and God can give us a forgiving heart. Suburo Sakai, the top surviving Japanese ace, with whom I often share platforms at university symposiums, recently told me that I am his best friend in America.

Target: Hong Kong

from *God Is My Copilot*

BY ROBERT L. SCOTT, JR.

Robert L. Scott was an old fighter pilot, thirty-four, when World War II started, but he proved, again, that if you really want it, there's always a way. He wound up in China and was soon fighting Zeros in a Curtiss P-40. He had racked up an enviable combat record—a dozen kills—and was a group commander when he was ordered back to the States—the Army Air Corps PR types wanted a hero to hype war bonds. He was elected whether he liked it or not.

Scott was as good on the stump as he was in the air. He dictated God Is My Copilot *in three days between speaking engagements in 1943. The book had everything—shooting, flying, dying, a titanic struggle against merciless villains, victory beautiful and sweet, all set in exotic China, foreign and mysterious—no wonder it became an instant best-seller. Hollywood immediately cranked out a patriotic movie, now long forgotten, but the book is today a classic of aviation literature. The selection that follows is my favorite passage.*

COL. MERIAM C. COOPER WAS THE CHIEF OF STAFF TO THE GENeral. His business was war, too. Cooper had been one of the greatest heroes of the First World War and was one of the greatest soldiers I have ever seen. I never discovered when it was he slept. At any time of night he was apt to come into my room, when he visited us in Kunming from his usual headquarters in Chungking. Or when I'd go to see him, I could find him smoking his ever-present pipe at any hour. Cooper had served in the American Air Force in the last war, and when the war was over, he had kept right on fighting. He had enlisted with the Poles in the Russian-Polish war and had been second-in-command of the

Kosciuszko Squadron. After leading many dangerous strafing raids, he was awarded Poland's highest military decorations. Later he made a reputation as an explorer in Persia, Siam, and Africa. Following an active part in the formation of Pan-American Airways, he became one of the best known moving-picture producers in America.

Cooper was a soldier through and through, one of the most intelligent men that I could hope to meet, and the perfect chief of staff for General Chennault. Through his constant attention to our espionage in eastern China, we learned of the Japanese task forces coming through Hong Kong on their way to the Solomons and Saigon, and also of the large amount of shipping in Victoria harbor.

Now Cooper was working tirelessly to plan our greatest raid against the Japanese. I remember vividly how he toiled for six days and six nights at the general's house on the logistics for our proposed attack on the largest convoy that had come through Hong Kong. Morning after morning, when I went in to breakfast, the floor around the table would be ankle deep with Walnut tobacco from Cooper's pipe, but the plans would be those of a master. General Chennault and Colonel Cooper made, in fact, the perfect tactical team. Everything was ready for the bombing raid by the middle of October, and we merely waited for word from the east that the harbor between Kowloon and Hong Kong was filled with Japs.

Toward the end of October came the word we had so long been waiting for. Victoria harbor was filled with Japanese shipping. In deepest secret we got ready to go.

Our ships would leave from Kunming, but we would of course use the intermediate bases in the Kweilin-Hengyang section, 500 miles to the east. Hong Kong, you will recall, is about 325 miles southeast of Kweilin. It is protected by surrounding enemy fighter fields at Canton and Kowloon. Our objectives would be the shipping in the harbor, the shipping at the docks in Kowloon, and the ships at the drydocks in Hong Kong.

Early on the morning of October 25 our twelve bombers took

off from Yunnan for Kweilin, and shortly afterward Hill, Alison, Holloway, and I led the fighters off. We were all to infiltrate into Kweilin, a few ships at a time, so as not to alert the coast of eastern China.

For two weeks I had worried about this attack. I thought it would come any day, and because of the tension I couldn't sleep. But now I was on the way. I could see the shark-mouths of the P-40s all around, and the whole thing was easy—just what I had wanted all the time. We sat down at Kweilin at one-minute intervals at eight o'clock. The bombers were soon in, and the Chinese were busy servicing the field full of ships. They were the happiest people I had ever seen. They'd point toward Japan and point down with their thumbs and say, "Bu-hao."

While they serviced the ships, we hurried to the alert cave and were briefed by the general. We had to work fast, for we were so close to Japanese bases that we could have been caught on the ground with our Air Force if we hadn't been careful. In fifty minutes we were away, the fighters first, then the bombers. Making our assembly over the designated point, we were off on our greatest mission to date.

All of us were proud to be going. But as I looked at those seven P-40s escorting ten bombers, I could not help feeling apologetic for that greatest country in the world that we were representing. Oh, God, if the day could soon come when we could go against this enemy with a thousand bombers, even a hundred bombers!

Now I had the familiar "wind-up" feeling that precedes combat. The palms of my hands perspired freely. As I wiped them on the legs of my trousers, I saw that the sweat was like mud; it had mixed with the red dust of Kweilin Field through which we had taken off.

Our altitude kept increasing to 20,000 feet, while down below at 17,000 were the medium bombers in javelin formation: two V's of three, and the last element a diamond of four. We passed one of the river junction checkpoints that enabled me to compute our ground speed. In fifty minutes I could see the glint of the sun on the Pacific Ocean. As I saw the bomber formation again, I felt proud of the crews of those perfectly spaced ships. This really was like a football game: the bombers were carrying the ball while we in the peashooters ran the interference.

Now I could even smell the freshness of the Pacific. The sky had never been so blue. The beauty of the day and the beauty of those weapons flying so smoothly under us made me forget the scratching of the oxygen mask on my sunburned neck. It was a joy to look back and see the six shark-mouths on the other P-40s grinning at me.

As we got closer to the target, we split our formation of fighters automatically. Tex Hill, Hampshire, and Sher stayed with me; Marks took the other three on the opposite flank of the bombers. The country below had become lower in elevation but was green and still hilly. Over the radio, as we reached the point north of Macao, came the jabbering of Japanese voices on our frequency, and we knew from its ominous sound that they were warning of our attack.

I tensed a little and looked about for enemy planes. Far to my left I could see the three rivers meeting at Canton, could see two fields from which I knew Zeros were taking off to intercept us. We had bypassed Canton purposely by thirty miles. I saw the bombers changing course: we were around Canton now and were going to steer straight for the north of Kowloon peninsula. The blue Pacific looked friendly, reminding me of the southern-California coast. The old, familiar fog banks that should have been covering San Clemente and Catalina were shrouding instead the Ladrones Islands, with only their hilltops visible, sticking out from the fog on the China Sea.

We were turning over Macao, where the Clippers used to land. To the south I could see another Jap field, Sanchau Island. Now to the right was Hong Kong Island, shaped like a kidney and mountainous, just about nine miles long and three or four miles across. I could make out the indentations of the romantic-sounding bays whose names I knew—Sandy, Telegraph, Kellet, and Repulse. There were points of land jutting toward the mainland—Quarry Point, with its naval drydock, and Shek Tong Tsui, the point over which we would fight our aerial battle. Reaching toward the island like a finger was Kowloon Peninsula, separated from it by the blue waters of Victoria harbor. Near the end of the spit of land closest to Hong Kong, I saw the large modern Peninsular Hotel. All of us knew that Japanese generals and staff officers slept there.

We came across the Great West Channel, passed north of Stonecutters Island, and came to our turning point, seven miles north of Kowloon. The bombers were turning south now for the bombing run. This was the crucial moment.

I crossed around and over General Haynes and his formation, watching vigilantly. Far below I saw dust on Kai Tak airdrome and knew that enemy ships were taking off to attack us. My throat felt dry and I had trouble swallowing; I turned my gun switch off and on nervously.

Now I saw the bomb-bay doors opening, and I couldn't keep the tears of excitement from burning my eyes. Antiaircraft was beginning to dot the sky with black and white puffs. As I dove almost to the level of the bombers, I could feel the ack-ack rock my fighter ship. I kept S-ing to watch for the enemy fighters that must be coming. The white stars on the upper wings of the bombers below were like an American flag waving, and it gave me the same feeling that I get when I see home after a long absence. As loud as I could against the roar of the engine, I shouted, "Come up, you devils!"

I saw the yellow bombs begin to fall in long strings, imposed on the dark green of the world below. They got smaller and smaller as the noses pointed slowly down. Remembering my movie camera, I tried to take pictures of the explosions. The bombs seemed to take years to fall, and I began to think they were all duds. The ack-ack burst closer as the Japs got the range while we went straight in. I know I was never more excited in all my life. I yelled, "Okay, Hirohito—we have lots more where those came from!" I kept looking behind and under us for the bombs to burst.

And then I saw the first white explosion—right on the docks of Kowloon. After that they came so fast you couldn't count them. I let my camera run as the explosions turned from white to black—there were oil fires now. I could see the flash of the antiaircraft guns from the north shore of Hong Kong Island as we continued across Victoria harbor. I risked another look at the target; it was covered with smoke from one end to the other. Then I got my eyes back to searching for enemy interceptors—we had to be extra careful now.

Why didn't the bombers turn for home? They had dropped the bombs, but they were still going on endlessly toward that point of Shek Tong Tsui. All of us were keyed up. But then the long javelin of B-25s began to turn to the right. Mission accomplished—now they had the downhill run to base, and I began to get that old feeling of relief. Then, somehow, I felt cheated. Where were the enemy fighters? I raised my camera, sighted again, and took the formation as it swung over the burning docks.

Then, as I glanced about, I saw them, silhouette after silhouette, climbing terribly steeply toward the bombers. I know now that they had got there from Kai Tak below in four minutes; they had made the 16,000 feet in that short time. I felt my camera drop to my lap, hit my knee, then drop to the metal floor of the fighter. I was fumbling now for the mike button on the throttle; then I was calling, "Bandits ahead—Zerooooos! At eleven o'clock." Fumbling again for the throttle quadrant, shoving everything as far forward as I could, I marveled at the steepness of the climb the enemy ships were maintaining. I called, "Zeros at twelve o'clock," to designate their direction clockfashion from us. I heard Tex Hill reply, "Yes, I see 'em." I could hear the jabber of the Japs still trying to block our frequency.

I was diving now, aiming for the lead Zero, turning my gunsight on and off, a little nervously checking again and again to see that the gun switch was at ON. I jerked the belly-tank release and felt the underslung fifty-gallon bamboo tank drop off. We rolled to our backs to gain speed for the attack and went straight for the Zeros. I kept the first Zero right in the lighted sight and began to fire from over a thousand yards, for he was too close to the bombers. Orange tracers were coming from the B-25s, too, as the turret gunners went to work.

Five hundred yards before I got to the Zero, I saw another P-40 bearing the number 151 speed in and take it. That was Tex Hill. He followed the Zero as it tried to turn sharply into the bombers and shot it down. Tex spun from his tight turn as the Jap burst into flames. I took the next Zero—they seemed to be all over the sky now. I went so close that I could see the pilot's head through the glass canopy and the little tail wheel that was not retracted, and I knew it was a Navy Zero—the little wheel was built for the arresting gear of a carrier. My tracers entered the cockpit and smoke poured back, hiding the canopy, and I went by.

As I turned to take another ship below me, I saw four airplanes falling in flames toward the waters of Victoria harbor. I half-rolled again and skidded in my dive to shake any Zero that might be on my tail. I saw another P-40 shooting at a Jap, but there was a Zero right on his tail. I dove for this one. He grew in my sights, and as my tracers crossed in front of him, he turned into me. I shot him down as his ship seemed to stand still in the vertical bank. The ship was three or four hundred yards from me, and it fell toward the water for a time that seemed ages. An explosion came, and there was only black smoke; then I could see the ship again, falling, turning in a slow spin, down—down—down.

I shot at everything I saw. Sometimes it was just a short burst as the Jap went in for our bombers. Sometimes I fired at one that was turning, and as I'd keep reefing back on my stick, my ship would spin, and I'd recover far below. I shot down another ship that didn't see me. I got it with one short burst from directly astern, a no-deflection shot. In this attack I could see the Japanese ship vibrate as my burst of six 50-caliber guns hit it. First it just shook, then one wing went up. I saw the canopy shot completely off; then I went across it. Turning back in a dive to keep my speed, I watched the enemy ship, as it dove straight down, stream flames for a distance the length of the airplane behind.

As I looked around now, the bombers were gone, but climbing up from the south I saw four twin-engine ships that I thought were I-45s; later we decided they were Japanese Messerschmitts. I had plenty of altitude on the leader and started shooting at him from long range, concentrating on his right engine. He turned to dive, and I followed him straight for the water. I remember grinning, for he had made the usual mistake of diving instead of climbing. But as I drew up on the twin-engine ship, I began to believe that I had hit him from the long range. His ship was losing altitude rapidly in a power glide, but he was making no effort to turn. I came up to within fifty yards and fired into him until he burned. I saw the ship hit the water and continue to burn. We had been going toward the fog bank in the direction of the Philippines, and I wondered if the Jap had been running for Manila.

I shot at two of the other twin-engine ships from long range but couldn't climb up to them. Then I passed over Hong Kong Island, flying at a thousand feet, as I was too low but didn't want to waste any time climbing. And I saw something that gripped my heart—a fenced-in enclosure which I knew was Fort Stanley, the British and American prison camp. There was a large group standing in the camp and waving at my ship. My saddest feeling of the war came over me then. Here were soldiers who had been prisoners of the Japanese for nearly a year. Month after month they had waited for the sight of Allied airplanes attacking Hong Kong—and at last it had come. Even in their suffering they were waving a cheer to the few United States planes that had finally come, and I swore to myself I'd come back again and again.

Then I saw above me the crisscrossing vapor paths of an area where fighter ships have sped through an air attack. They almost covered the sky in a cloud. Here and there were darker lines that could have been smoke paths where ships had burned and gone down to destruction.

I was rudely jerked back to attention by a slow voice that yet was sharp: "If that's a P-40 in front of me, waggle your wings." I rocked my wings before I looked. Then I saw the other ship, a P-40 nearly a mile away. I think from the voice it was Tex Hill. I went over toward him and together we dove toward home.

The presence of the other P-40 made me feel very arrogant and egotistical, for I had shot down four enemy ships and had damaged others. So I looped above Victoria harbor and dove for the Peninsular Hotel. My tracers ripped into the shining plate glass of the penthouses on its top, and I saw the broken windows cascade like snow to the streets, many floors below. I laughed, for I knew that behind those windows were Japanese high officers, enjoying that modern hotel. When I got closer, I could see uniformed figures going down the fire escapes, and I shot at them. In the smoke of Kowloon I could smell oil and rubber. I turned for one more run on the packed fire escapes filled with Jap soldiers, but my next burst ended very suddenly. I was out of ammunition. Then, right into the smoke and through it right down to the treetop levels, I headed northwest to get out of Japanese territory sooner and went as fast as I could for Kweilin.

I was the last ship in, and the general was anxiously waiting for me, scanning the sky for ships to come in. He knew I had shot down an enemy, for I had come in with my low-altitude roll of victory. But when I jumped from my cramped seat and said, "General, I got four definitely," he shook my hand and looked very happy. "That makes nineteen then," he said, "for the fighters and the bombers."

We had lost a fighter and a bomber. The bomber had become a straggler when one engine was hit by antiaircraft; then it was shot to pieces by one of the twin-engined Jap fighters. The pilot had managed even then to get it down, but he had remained in the ship to destroy the bombsight and had been shot through the foot by a Jap cannon. Two of the bomber crew had bailed out and were captured. The other two carried the injured pilot until he had begged them to leave him alone and escape. They had bandaged his foot tightly, but had refused to go without him.

As they moved on through the enemy lines that night, they stopped to rest, and the wounded pilot crawled away from them to insure their getting away to the guerrilla lines. They escaped, and later we received a letter signed by the other two crewmen, which said that the pilot had been captured and was then in a Japanese hospital. The letter was a Japanese propaganda leaflet that the Japs had dropped near Kweilin, but being properly signed, it gave us hope for the remainder of the crew, and for the heroic pilot, Lieutenant Allers.

Long Flight Home

from *Thunderbolt!*

BY ROBERT S. JOHNSON WITH MARTIN CAIDIN

P-47 Thunderbolt pilot Robert S. Johnson was the U.S. Army Air Force's fourth-highest-scoring ace in World War II with twenty-eight confirmed victories, all in Europe. Only Francis S. Gabreski shot down more Germans, thirty-one.

In his autobiography, written with well-known aviation writer Martin Caidin, Johnson relates that he had the usual troubles that most green fighter pilots experience—aerial blindness, overaggressiveness, didn't check six, etc. After his senior officers got on his case about breaking formation, he decided to stick to his leader come hell or high water. Hell came first. But we'll let him tell you about it in a passage that ranks among the best flying stories ever put on paper.

DOVER BELOW, THE CLIFFS MELTING INTO THE CHANNEL WATERS. A day of crystal clarity, scattered clouds far below us, miles between the puffy white. There is absolutely no limit to visibility; the earth stretches away forever and forever. A strange world—made for solitary flight, and yet made also, it seems, of three-dimensional movement, the gliding through space of forty-eight fighters, each alone, each linked also by the unseen thread of metallic, radio voices.

Over the Channel, only a mile or so off the French coast. Still climbing, the altimeter winding around slowly, clocking off the hundreds, the thousands, past ten thousand, reaching for twenty. The coastline drifts by, quiet and almost sleepy in the rich sun, unrevealing of gun batteries and listening posts and radar scanners already reporting of our position, number, height, and course, data flashed back to German antiaircraft batteries, to fighter fields, to command posts. From this altitude, France slumbers, beautiful and green.

Le Tréport beneath our left wings, the mouth of the Seine River clear and sharp. "Blue Flight, stay sharp. Nine zero degrees. Let's go." Blue Flight wheels, banks, and turns in unison with its squadron, the Sixty-first matching flawlessly the wheeling of its two sister squadrons. Below the formation, the Seine River, occupied territory.

"Open up, Blue Flight." Our radio call, orders to the other flights. Move out, separate into combat formation. Pilots work stick and rudder; the Thunderbolts ease away from one another. Now Blue Flight is in its combat position, each Thunderbolt 200 yards apart. Between each flight of four fighters stretches a space of 500 yards and, even farther out, holding a distance of 1,500 yards, ride the squadrons. Almost constantly I turn and look, turn and look, watching the position of my own planes, seeking out strange black specks in the sky, alert for the plunging Focke-Wulfs or Messerschmitts.

Marching in precision, the Sixty-third Squadron flies to the north, very high, in down-sun position. I turn my head and see the Sixty-second Squadron, to our south, and slightly above our own altitude. Other things to check as I divert my attention to the cockpit. Gun switch on. Gunsight on. Check the chute harness. Shoulder and leg straps tight, catches secure, the harness fastened. Don't make it easy for the Jerries—check the "elephant trunk." I inspect the oxygen tube, start to count: "Three, six, nine, twelve, fifteen, eighteen, twenty-one, twenty-four, twenty-seven, thirty." Oxygen okay; the count by threes to thirty clear and sharp, no faltering. Escape kit secured. If—that big if—I go down, I want to be sure of my equipment, my procedures, my position. It's a long walk through France and Spain, *if* luck holds.

The Thunderbolts move into the skies of Europe. A moment to myself. Alone, yet not alone, I pray. If He allows, a moment of thanks on the way home. There won't be time to pray once the black-crossed fighters rush in.

Keep looking, keep looking! It's that moment of carelessness, the second of not paying attention, when the fighters bounce. Occasionally I glance ahead, but I am in the end slot, exposed in the Blue 4 position. At all times my head swivels, my eyes scanning every inch of the sky from my right wingtip, rearward, and above, over my canopy, and down. The silk scarf around my neck isn't a hot-rock decoration; without the silk to protect my skin, my neck would by now be raw and bleeding from rubbing against the wool collar of my shirt.

Out of the corner of my eye—a speck. There, far to the right! I catch my heart with my teeth, swallow, snap my head to the right. I squint, study the sky. A speck of oil on the windshield, not a fighter. Gratefully, my heart drops back where it belongs.

Fifteen miles inland, the Thunderbolt phalanx due north of Rouen, still over the sparkling Seine. My head continues to swivel, my roving gaze stops short as I notice a formation of sixteen fighters, directly behind and slightly above us. They're coming in fast, flying a duplicate of our own formation. Thunderbolts? I look to the left; the sixteen fighters of the Sixty-third Squadron are rock steady. To the right; there, the sixteen fighters of the Sixty-second Squadron. Who the hell are these other people? For several seconds I stare at their silhouettes—they're Focke-Wulfs!

Slow, Johnson, take it slow, and be clear. I press the radio mike button on the throttle and make an effort to speak slowly and distinctly. "Sixteen bandits, six o'clock, coming in fast, this is Keyworth Blue Four, over." No one replies, no one makes a move. The Thunderbolts drone on, utterly oblivious of the sixteen fighters streaking in. Am I the *only* man in the group who sees these planes? I keep my eyes glued to the fighters, increasing in size with every second, trailing thin streaks of black exhaust smoke as they rush toward us under full power.

"Sixteen bandits, six o'clock, coming in fast—this is Keyworth Blue Four—*over!*" Now I see the enemy fighters clearly—Focke-Wulfs, still closing the gap. Again I call in—I'm nearly frantic now. My entire body seems to quiver. I'm shaking; I want to rip the Thunderbolt around and tear directly into the teeth of the

German formation. It's the only thing to do; break into them. For a moment, a second of indecision, I lift the P-47 up on one wing and start the turn—no, dammit! I swore I wouldn't break formation; I would act only on orders and not on my own. I jab down again on the button, this time fairly shouting the warning of enemy fighters.

What the hell's the matter with them? I glance quickly at the other Thunderbolts, expecting the leader's big fighter to swing around and meet the attack. The P-47 drones on, unconcerned, her pilot apparently oblivious to the enemy. My finger goes down on the button and I call, again, "Sixteen bandits, six o'clock, coming in f—"

A terrific explosion! A split second later, another. And yet another! Crashing, thundering sounds. *Wham! Wham! Wham!* One after the other, an avalanche smashing into my fighter, heavy boulders hurtling out of nowhere and plunging with devastating force into the airplane. A blinding flash. Before my eyes the canopy glass erupts in an explosion, dissolves in a gleaming shower. Tiny particles of glass rip through the air. The Thunderbolt shudders through her length, bucks wildly as explosions flip her out of control. Still the boulders rain against the fighter, a continuing series of crashing explosions, each roaring, each terrifying. My first instinct is to bail out; I have a frantic urge to leave the airplane.

Concussion smashes my ears, loud, pounding; the blasts dig into my brain. A new sound now, barely noticed over the crashing explosions. A sound of hail, rapid, light, unceasing. Thirty-caliber bullets, pouring in a stream against and into the Thunderbolt. Barely noticed as they tear through metal, flash brilliantly as tracers. The Thunderbolt goes berserk, jarring heavily every time another 20-mm cannon shell shears metal, tears open the skin, races inside, and explodes with steel-ripping force.

Each explosion is a personal blow, a fist thudding into my body. My head rings, my muscles protest as the explosions snap my body into the restraining straps, whip my head back against the rest. I am through! This is it! I'm absolutely helpless, at the mercy of the fighters pouring fire and steel into the Thunderbolt. Squeezed back in my seat against the armor plating—my head snaps right and left as I see the disintegration of my '47. A blow spins my head to the left as a bullet creases my nose. Behind me I can feel the steel being flayed apart by the unending rain of cannon shells.

I notice no pain. I have only a frantic feeling—an explosive urge to get out!

I am not frightened; I am beyond any such gentle emotion. I am terrified, clutched in a constricting terror that engulfs me. Without conscious volition my finger stabs down the radio button and I hear a voice, loud and piercing, screaming, *"Mayday! Mayday! Mayday!"* The words blur into a continuous stream. The voice goes on and on, shouting the distress call, and not until I have shrieked for help six times or more do I recognize my own voice.

I have no time to think, almost no time to act. Moving by sheer force of habit, by practice become instinct, my hands fly over my body. Without conscious thought, without even realizing what I am doing, I wriggle free of the shoulder harness and jerk open the seat belt.

Another explosion. A hand smashes me against the side of the cockpit; for a moment acceleration pins me helplessly. The Thunderbolt breaks away completely from my control. Earth and sky whirl crazily. I'm suddenly aware that the fighter has been thrown nose down, plunging out of control. The smashing explosions, the staccato beating of the bullets, blurs into a continuous din. A sudden lunge, the fighter snaps to the right, nose almost vertical. The Thunderbolt's wild motions flip me back and forth in the cockpit. . . .

Fire! A gleaming tongue of flame licks my forehead. It flickers, disappears. Instantly it is here again, this time a searing fire sheet, erupting into the cockpit. The fire dances and swirls, disappears within a thick, choking cloud of smoke. Intense, blinding, sucked through the shattered canopy. The draft is terror. The draft of air is Death, carrying the fire from the bottom of the cockpit, over me, crackling before my face, leaping up and out through the smashed canopy.

The terror is eternity. Burn to death!

GET OUT!

I grab the canopy bar, gasping for breath, jerk it back with maniacal strength. The canopy jerks open, slides back six inches, and jams.

Trapped! The fire blossoms, roars ominously. Frantic, I reach up with both hands, pulling with every bit of strength I can command. The canopy won't budge.

Realization. The fighter burning. Flames and smoke in the cockpit. Oxygen flow cut off. Out of control, plunging. Fighters behind. Helpless.

New sounds. Grinding, rumbling noises. In front of me, the engine. Thumping, banging. Bullets, cannon shells in the engine; maybe it's on fire!

I can't see. I rub my eyes. No good. Then I notice the oil, spraying out from the damaged engine, a sheet of oil robbing me of sight, covering the front windscreen, cutting off my vision. I look to the side, barely able to look out.

Great, dark shapes. Reeling, rushing past me. No! The Thunderbolt plunges, flips crazily earthward. The shapes—the bombers! The bomber formations, unable to evade my hurtling fighter. How did I miss them? The shapes disappear as the Thunderbolt, trailing flame and smoke, tumbles through the bombers, escaping total disaster by scant feet. Maybe less!

GET OUT!

I try, oh, God, how I try! Both feet against the instrument panel, brace myself, grasp the canopy bar with both hands. Pull—pull harder! Useless. It won't budge.

Still falling. Got to pull out of the dive. I drop my hands to the stick, my feet to the rudders. Left rudder to level the wings, back pressure on the stick to bring her out of the dive. There is still wind bursting with explosive force through the shattered canopy, but it is less demoniacal with the fighter level, flying at less speed.

Still the flame. Now the fire touches, sears. I have become snared in a trap hurtling through space, a trap of vicious flames and choking smoke! I release the controls. Feet firmly against the instruments, both hands grasping the canopy bar. It won't move. *Pull harder!*

The Thunderbolt rears wildly, engine thumping. Smoke inside, oil spewing from the battered engine, a spray whipping back, almost blinding me to the outside world. It doesn't matter. The world is nothingness, only space, forever and ever down to the earth below. Up here, fire, smoke.

I've got to get out! Terror and choking increases, becomes frenzied desperation. Several times I jerk the Thunderbolt from her careening drops toward the earth, several more times I kick against the panel, pull with both hands. The canopy will not move. Six inches. Not a fraction more. I can't get out!

A miracle. Somehow, incredibly, flame disappears. The fire . . . *the fire's out!* Smoke boils into the cockpit, swirls around before it answers the shrieking call of wind through the shattered glass. But there is no flame to knife into flesh, no flame. . . . Settle down! *Think!* I'm *still* alive!

The terror ebbs, then vanishes. At one moment I am beset with fear and frenzy, with the uncontrollable urge to hurl my body through the restraining metal, anything, just to escape the fire. Terror grips me, chokes my breathing and thinking, and, in an instant, a moment of wonder, it is banished. I no longer think of other aircraft—enemy or friendly. My mind races over my predicament; what I must do. I begin to relax.

The cessation of struggle, physically and within the mind, is so incredibly absolute that for long seconds I ponder. I do not comprehend this amazing self-control. It may be simply that I am overwhelmed by the miracle of still being alive. Perhaps it is the loss of oxygen at five miles above the earth. The precious seconds of relief flee all too quickly. I must still get out of the stricken airplane if I am to live.

Feet on the instrument panel, hands on the bar. Pull. I pull with all my strength until I am fairly blue in the face. I feel my muscles knotting with the strength of desperation, my body quivers with the effort. Not even this renewed struggle avails me. Cannon shells have burst against the canopy, twisted and curled metal.

The fighter heels sickeningly over on her side, skids through the air, flips for earth. I barely pay attention to the controls; my feet and hands move almost of their own accord, coordinating smoothly, easing the airplane from her plunge. Out of the dive again, the desire to survive becoming more intense.

I *must* get out. I hunch up in the cockpit, desperation once again rising about me like a flood. The canopy, the canopy. Life or death imbedded within that blackened, twisted metal. C'mon, you! I hunch my shoulder, lunge at the metal. Again, and again! Hard blows that hurt. Steel slams into my shoulder, hard, un-yielding. I cry out in frustration, a wordless profanity. My hands ball into fists and I beat at the canopy, throwing punches, hard, strong blows. But I am not in the ring, not striking at flesh and bone. The steel mocks me, unyielding, triumphant. I sit back for a moment, level the P-47 and wonder.

There is another way out. The canopy is shattered, atop me, to both sides. I stand up in the seat, poke my head and shoulders through the broken canopy. I hardly notice the heavy force of the wind and cold. I ignore it. My shoulders are through, I stand to my waist—I can get out!

Despair floods my mind. The parachute snags against the ripped canopy. It can't clear; there's not enough space between the shattered cockpit for both my body and the chute. I'm not going without it! I crawl back to the seat, right the spiraling airplane, and think.

All through the struggle to escape the fighter, I have been talking to myself. Over and over again I have been repeating, "You can get out, you can. If you have to, you can get out!" Again and again the words formed, until finally reality ruled. And after each attempt: "You just must not have to."

I settle back in the seat, the terror and desperation vanished, caught by the wind shrieking through the cockpit, whisked away and scattered forever. I relax, a deliberate move to enable me to think clearly, to study my problem and to seek the solutions. My mind is clear, my thoughts spinning through my brain. I think of everything, a torrent of thoughts that refuse to be clouded, thoughts of everything imaginable.

I am absolutely unconcerned at the moment about enemy aircraft. I know the sky about me is filled with the black-crossed fighters, with pilots eager to find so helpless a target as a crippled Thunderbolt, trailing a greasy plume of smoke as it struggles through the sky, descending. There is no fear of death or of capture. The terror and desperation which so recently assailed me have been born of fire, of the horror of being burned alive. Now the fire is gone, the terror flung away with its disappearance. Solve the problems, Johnson, find the answers. You can't bail out.

A sound of danger snaps me back to full awareness. The engine is running very rough. Any moment, it seems, the giant power plant will tear itself free of its mounts to tumble through space, trapping me in an airplane unbalanced and uncontrollable. I turn my attention fully to flying, realizing that the Thunderbolt is badly crippled, almost on the verge of falling out of my control. Oil still bursts from the holes and tears in the cowling, a thin spray smearing itself against the windscreen, making vision forward almost impossible.

I cannot get out; I must ride this potential bomb to the very ground. My left hand moves almost automatically, easing the throttle back, a move made to keep the engine from exploding. Again—good fortune! The grinding, throbbing noise subsides; much smoother now. My chances are getting better.

I keep thinking of all the intelligence lectures we have sat through, buttocks sore on benches, about how to avoid capture, how to escape to Spain, to return to England. Intelligence officers, reading reports, after a while dull with repetition. Then the actual escapees, pilots who bailed out or crashed, who hid and ran and survived by their wits, who *did* walk out of France, aided by the underground to reach Spain and, eventually, to return to England. It could be done; it had been done. I could do it as well as any. My mind wanders; strangely, I seem to be looking forward to the challenge. It is a thought wholly ridiculous: to anticipate and savor the struggle to escape a land swarming with quick-fingered troops.

One entire B-17 crew had been shot down and lost not a moment in hustling their way out through France and into Spain. In just three weeks from the moment they bailed out of their burning Fortress and fell into space, they were in England. A record. *I* can do that—three weeks and I'll be back. Each time I dwell on the matter my mind tricks me, returns to me pictures of Barbara and my family.

What am I doing! I have been flying toward England, an instinctive move to fly toward the Channel. I remember words, lectures. "If you're going down, if you can't make the Channel, far out into the Channel, turn south. The coast is thick with Germans, and you won't have a chance if you go down there. Head south, head south, south . . ."

The words flash by in my mind. Obediently, I work the controls, change my course. I look down. Twenty thousand feet to the earth. There—I can see them. They're so clear and sharp. In my oxygen-starved brain, I *see* the Germans. They are like ants, hordes of ants, each carrying a gun and a sharp, glittering bayonet. For twenty miles inland the horde is thick, impenetrable, inescapable. I can't land *there;* I can *see* the German soldiers.

The Thunderbolt turns, heads for Paris. I will fly over the sprawling city, continue flying south, try to get as close as possible to the Spanish border.

This means a crash landing, evasion, escape. I think about procedures once I am on the ground, the Thunderbolt stopped. My plans are clear—I'll belly the crippled Thunderbolt in, slide the fighter wheels up along an open field. I will land as far south in France as the crippled airplane will take me in the continuing descent. I plan to make the walk through Spain as short as possible, to get out quickly. I will *not* be captured. I'll evade them; others have—*I will!* The thought races through my mind; it stays with me through all the moments of considering the crash, the evasion, the escape back to England.

There, clipped to the right side of the cockpit near my knee, an incendiary grenade. Check it! Procedure! Words and method are habit by now. I hold the bomb, grip it tightly. This is the way you do it. The moment the ship stops its sliding across the ground ... get out. Fling the bomb into the cockpit. Turn the fighter into flames and smoke and ashes.

My mind begins to wander; there is still clarity, but now there is less concentration. The thoughts flit in and out, they appear and flee of their own volition. One instant I think of escape procedures, then my mind dwells on the pilots after they return to Manston. I picture them in my mind, talking about my missing airplane, listing me as missing, probably dead, victim of the sudden bounce by the sixteen determined German fliers. I think about Dick Allison, victim of a fatal crash caused by vertigo. Dick was married, and my thoughts hover about his wife. I remember her, pretty, wonderful; I think of her holding their newborn child. I think of her, never again seeing Dick; the child never to know the father.

I cannot escape the thoughts. Dick's face looms before me, a face dissolving into a Thunderbolt spinning through clouds, a gout of flame, mushrooming smoke. His widow, the child. Then it disappears, the pictures are gone. Barbara. Thoughts only of her. That last sight of my wife, tearful, trying so bravely to smile as the train carried her away. How many months since I've seen Barbara? Seen home? Barbara back home, at Lawton, learning that I was missing. She knew enough of fighters, knew enough to realize the odds were that I would not survive.

In brief seconds the pictures flash into being, a kaleidoscope of people and thoughts and emotions, a world marching in accelerated time before my vision. I can't do this to them; I can't go down. I've *got* to get back!

My mind reels drunkenly; for several moments I think of the Thunderbolt burning while I flee. I do not realize the truth. Hypoxia is upon me. My body and brain clamor for oxygen, desire, covet the life-giving substance. The hypoxia becomes worse as I stagger through the air, thin and cold at 19,000 feet. The symptoms are drunkenness, a hypoxic intoxication, giddy in its effects, lethal if it is sustained. And yet, through this dangerous moment, I plan with all seriousness my crash landing, plan to shed the parachute and escape through the shattered canopy.

Barbara. My folks. Again I think of them. Again their presence invades the fog of hypoxia, struggles to the fore. Visions of loved ones; my concern for them forcing upward through the mists, the false sense of confidence. Again the thoughts are safety, are mental clarity, are the key to survival. The thoughts of their pain, their anguish. Sharp, clear. I *can't* go down.

My head is clearing. The fog is breaking up, dissolving. All this time I have been convinced that the fighter is incapable of flight, that it can only glide. I have been flying in a shallow glide, descending gently, losing altitude, at 170 miles per hour. Go for the Channel. Fly over the water, far enough out from the French coast to avoid detection by the Germans. Fly as close as possible to England, ditch the ship in the water, crawl through the hole. Air-Sea Rescue will pick me up, will race out to the scene of the ditching in boats or in planes, to rescue me, bring me back to England. Barbara and the folks may never even know that I've been in trouble.

Stick and rudder, still descending gently. The fighter wheels around in a graceful turn, almost ludicrous for a smoking, badly shot-up machine. But the Thunderbolt is still true, still responsive. She obeys my commands. I head for England, a goal, a place to fly, a home to return to.

I stare at the instrument panel. A shambles. Smashed glass, many of the instruments broken. The Thunderbolt descends, nose slightly down, settling gradually, at about 170 miles per hour. I have no airspeed indicator, but I know this fighter, know her feel.

My mask seems to choke me. Strapped to my face, it had been, unknown to me, useless, unable to supply oxygen from a source shot away. I bank the fighter, stare down. At a height I estimate to be ten thousand feet, I unhook the mask from one side of my face, suck deeply the good clean air, air now richer with oxygen, oxygen to clear my head, to return to me my full senses.

With the newly returned clarity comes soberness, a critical evaluation of my predicament. I am in trouble, in serious, dangerous difficulty. Not until this moment do I realize that I have been flying almost blinded. My eyes burn, a stinging sensation that increases every moment in pain.

I touch my face with my hands. No goggles, and memory comes to me. Yesterday I broke a lens, I turned the goggles in for repair. This morning I took off on the only combat mission I ever flew or was to fly without goggles. It was a foolish move, and now, over occupied France in a crippled, smoking fighter, I am paying the penalty for my own stupidity.

In the opening moments of attack a 20-mm cannon shell had ripped through the left side of the cockpit, exploded with a deafening roar near my left hand, and wreaked havoc with the hydraulic system. The blast sheared the flap handle and severed the hydraulic lines. Since that moment the fluid had poured into the cockpit. Then several more shells exploded, blasted apart the canopy. Wind entered at tremendous speed and, without respite, whipped the fluid into a fine, stinging spray.

Now the wind continues its devastating work. The fluid sprays into my eyes, burning and stinging. I fail to realize during the flight through thin air the effect on my eyes of the fluid.

My hand raises to my face, and I flinch. The pain is real, the source is evident. My eyes are swollen, puffed. Around them the skin is raised, almost as if I have been beaten with fists. It's hard to see. Not until now, not until this moment, do I realize that I am seeing through slits, that if my face swells any more, the skin will close over my eyes.

The moment this happens, I am finished. Half the time I fly with my eyes closed, feeling out the struggling crippled fighter. It is now that my sense of balance, my sense of flight, comes to my aid. I can *feel* the Thunderbolt when she begins to skid, to slip through the air. I can feel a wing lowering, feel the sudden change of wind draft in the cockpit. I listen carefully, strain with eyes closed to note labor in the engine, to hear the increase in propeller revolutions, in engine tone, when the nose drops. This is how I fly, half-blinded, eyes burning.

When I open my eyes to see, I must stick my head through the hole in the cockpit in order to look ahead. For the windscreen is obscured by oil. I do this several times. The wind stabs my eyes with ice picks, and the pain soars.

My attempts to clean my face, to rub away the fluid from my eyes, are pitifully hopeless. I pull a handkerchief from a pocket, wipe at my burning eyes. The first time I find relief. But the cockpit is filled with spray. My hands, my face, my clothes, are bathed, soaked in hydraulic fluid. In a moment the handkerchief, too, is drenched. Each time I rub my eyes I rub blood from my nose and the fluid deeper into my skin, irritating the eyes.

And yet, incredibly, I am calm and resolved. A succession of miracles has kept me alive, and I am not about to fret anxiously when only calmness will continue my survival. The pain in my eyes is nothing to the pain I have felt; certainly nothing against the past few minutes. Each time I open my eyes to check my flight, I scan the entire sky. My head swivels, I stare through burning eyes all about me. I am over enemy territory, heavily defended country, alone, in a crippled, smoking airplane, half-blind. I have no company, and I do not savor the sight of other aircraft. I wish only to be left alone, to continue my slow, plodding pace through the air. I've got to get as far out over that Channel as possible.

Again I look around. My head freezes, I stare. My heart again is in my throat. A fighter, alone. I am close to the Channel, *so* close, as I stare at the approaching machine. Slightly behind the Thunderbolt, from four o'clock at about 8,000 feet, the fighter closes in. I squint my eyes, trying to make out details. The fighter slides still closer.

Never have I seen so beautiful an airplane. A rich, dappled

blue, from a dark, threatening thunderstorm to a light sky blue. The cowling is a brilliant, gleaming yellow. Beautiful, and Death on the wing. A Focke-Wulf 190, one of Goering's Boys on the prowl after the raging air battle from which I have been blasted, and slicing through the air—at me. I stare at the airplane, noting the wax coating gleaming on the wings and body.

What can I do? I think of waving my handkerchief at him, then realize the absurdity of such a move. That's silly! I'll rock my wings. But what good will this do? I'm at a loss as to my next move—for I don't dare to fight in the disabled Thunderbolt. I've got to get out over the Channel, continue my flight toward the water and a chance at safety and survival.

I simply stare at the Focke-Wulf. My eyes follow the yellow nose as it closes the distance. The moment the nose swings on a line that points ahead of the Thunderbolt—all hell will break loose. That can only be the German's move to lead my fighter with his guns—the moment before he fires.

All I can do is to sit and watch. Closer and closer slides the sleek fighter. I begin to fidget, waiting for the yellow flashes to appear from his guns and cannon. Nothing. The guns remain silent, dark. The Focke-Wulf nose is glued on a line to the Thunderbolt. Damn—I'll bet he's taking pictures of me! Rare photographs of a crippled American fighter completely at his mercy.

The yellow-and-blue fighter glides in, still closer. I wonder what he has in mind, even as the Focke-Wulf comes to barely fifty yards away. I think of what *I* have always wanted to do, to close in to point-blank range, to stick my four right guns almost in his cockpit and the four left guns against his tail—and fire. That would really scatter him! And that's just what this bastard wants to do—to *me!*

He's too close. I shove the stick forward and to the right, swerving the Thunderbolt beneath the Focke-Wulf. I've got to get to the Channel; every move, every maneuver leads to that destination—the Channel water. As the fighter drops earthward, I bank and turn back to my left, heading directly out toward the coast. I glance up as the Focke-Wulf passes over me to my left, swings beautifully in an easy curve, and slides on my tail.

Thoughts race through my mind. I know he's going to work me over, just the second he feels he is in perfect position. I can't stop him, I can't fight in the crippled Thunderbolt; I don't even know if the airplane will stay together through any maneuvers. Every moment of flight since I was shot up has been in a long and gradual descent, a glide, easy enough even for a disabled airplane. But now ... I can't slug it out with this Focke-Wulf.

I look the Thunderbolt over. For the first time I realize just how severe a battering the airplane has sustained. The fighter is a flying wreck, a sieve. Let the bastard shoot! He can't hurt me any more than I've been hurt!

I push back in the seat, hunching my shoulders, bringing my arms in close to my body. I pull the seat adjuster, dropping the seat to the full protection of the armor plate. And here I wait.

The German takes his time. He's having a ball, with a helpless pigeon lined up before his guns. When will he shoot? C'mon, let's have it! He waits. I don't dare move away from the armor plating. The solid metal behind me is my only chance for life.

Pellets stinging against the wings, the fuselage, thudding into the armor plate. A steady, pelting rain of hailstones. *And* he's not missing! The .30-caliber bullets pour out in a stream, a rain of lead splashing all over the Thunderbolt. And all I can do is to sit there, crouched behind the armor plating, helpless, taking everything the Kraut has to dish out.

For several seconds the incredible turkey shoot continues, my Thunderbolt droning sluggishly through the air, a sitting duck for the Focke-Wulf. How the P-47 stays together is a mystery, for the bullets continue to pour into it.

I don't move an inch. I sit, anger building up. The bullets tear metal, rip into spars, grinding away, chopping up the Thunderbolt. My nerves grate as if both hands hold a charge of electricity. Sharp jolts against my back. Less than an inch away, bullets crash against the armor.

To hell with this! My feet kick right and left on the rudder

pedals, yawing the P-47 from side to side. The sudden movement slows the fighter to a crawl, and in that second the Focke-
Wulf overruns me and bursts ahead.

My turn. I may be almost helpless, but there are bullets in
the guns! Damn him—I can't see the Focke-Wulf. I stick my
head out of the window, wince from the pain of wind stabbing
my swollen eyes. There the bastard is, banking away. I kick right
rudder, skid the Thunderbolt, squeeze the trigger in anguish.
Eight heavy guns roar; my ship shudders as steel spits through
the air. The moment of firing is more gesture than battle, for I
cannot use my sights, I can barely see. The bullets flash in his
direction, but I hold no hope that the Focke-Wulf will falter.

It doesn't. The sleek fighter circles lazily to the right, out of
range. I watch him closely. Blue wings flash, the FW-190 swoops
up, sweeps down in a wide turn. He's boss of the situation, and
I simply fly straight and level as the German fighter slides into
a perfect, tight formation with me! This is ridiculous, but I'm
happier with the Jerry playing tag off my wing than sitting behind me and blazing away at the Thunderbolt.

The Focke-Wulf inches in closer, gleaming blue wing sitting
over mine, the top so close that I can almost lean out of the
cockpit and touch the waxed metal. I stare across the scant feet
separating our two planes. Our eyes lock, then his gaze travels
over the Thunderbolt, studying the fighter from nose to tail. No
need to wonder what he is thinking. He is amazed that my
airplane still flies; I know his astonishment that I am in the air.
Each time his gaze scans the Thunderbolt he shakes his head,
mystified. For at such close range he can see the tears and holes,
the blackened and scorched metal from the fire, the oily film
covering the nose and windscreen, the shattered canopy.

The Kraut stares directly at me and lifts his left hand. He
waves, his eyes expressionless. A wing lifts, the Focke-Wulf
slides away. A long-held breath explodes from my lungs, and
relief floods my mind. I watch the yellow-nosed fighter as he
turns to fly away. But . . . he doesn't! The German plane keeps
turning . . . he's on my tail again! "That son of a bitch!" I duck.

I cower again behind the armor plate. The Focke-Wulf is directly behind me, .30-caliber guns hammering. Still the bullets come, perfectly aimed. He doesn't miss, not a single bullet misses. I *know* they don't! Frantic, I kick rudder, jerk the heavy Thunderbolt from side to side, cutting my speed. The German waits for the maneuver; this time he's not sucked in. He holds back as the P-47 skids from side to side, and then I see the yellow nose drawing closer to me.

He pulls alongside tight to the P-47. Perfect formation, one battered, shot-up Thunderbolt and the gleaming new Focke-Wulf. By now we are down to 4,000 feet, passing directly over Dieppe, our speed still 170 miles per hour. Over Dieppe! The realization makes me shudder, for below my wings lie the most intense antiaircraft concentrations along the entire coast.

They don't fire! Of course! The Focke-Wulf pilot is saving my life! *He* doesn't see Dieppe as a horror of flak. This is, to him, friendly territory, an area over which to fly with impunity. Unknowingly, he gives me yet another lease on life, is the unwitting party to the succession of miracles which, through one cumulative disaster after the other, are keeping me alive. Even his presence, his attacks, are in a way miraculous. For the German has laced me over with his .30-caliber guns, and it is only the smile of fortune that he found me after his four heavy cannon had expended their explosive shells.

Water below . . . the Channel beneath my wings! Still in perfect formation, the dappled blue FW-190 glides slowly downward with me. Then we are at 3,000 feet. The coast two miles from me, and hope flares anew. There is a chance now, an excellent chance to make it into the Channel where I can be rescued! I stare at the German pilot. His left hand raises slowly to his forehead in an informal salute; he waves, and his fighter lifts a wing as he slides off to the right.

Relief, the gasp of pent-up breath. Oh, no! Here he comes again! Nothing to do but to crouch within that armor plating. The enemy fighter sits behind me, perfectly in the slot. He's extra careful this time. A series of sharp bursts ripple from his guns. Again the hailstones pelting the tin roof, the bullets smashing into the fighter. Shuddering and helpless, the P-47 takes the punishment, absorbs the terrible beating. I have long given up hope of understanding why this machine continues to stay in the air. The German is whipsawing his bursts, kicking rudder gently as he fires. A stream of bullets, swinging from left to right, from right to left, a buzzsaw flinging bullets from one wingtip across the plane, into the armor plate, straight across. The firing stops.

Here he comes again. The yellow nose inching alongside, the gleaming Focke-Wulf. The German pilot again slides into formation, undesired company in the sky. For several minutes he remains alongside, staring at the wreck I am flying. He shakes his head in wonder. Below my wings the Channel is only a thousand feet away. A blue wing lifts, snaps down. I watch the salute, the rocking of wings. The sleek fighter accelerates suddenly and turns, flying away in a long climbing turn back to the coast.

Free! England ahead, the Channel lifting to meet the crippled P-47. How far, how far can I drag the Thunderbolt with her smashed and laboring engine before she drops into the waves?

All this time I have been so tense that my hand gripped the throttle and held down the mike button, transmitting all the things I had called the Jerry pilot, as well as the gunfire and the smashing of bullets into the Thunderbolt. And again, an inadvertent move comes to my aid. The moment the Focke-Wulf disappears, I release the throttle knob and begin my preparations for ditching. My plan is to belly into the Channel, nose high, tail down. As the fighter slews to a stop in the water, I will crawl out through the shattered canopy, dragging my folded dinghy life raft with me. Then, inflate the raft, move away from the sinking plane, and pray that Air-Sea Rescue will find me before the Jerries do, or before I drift long enough to starve. I am ready for all this, calm and prepared for the impact into the water.

And then . . . a voice! The moment my finger lifts from the mike button, I hear a voice calling urgently. "Climb if you can, you're getting very faint, climb if you can, you're getting very faint!" It's the Air-Sea Rescue radio—homing on me and giving instructions. At this instant I realize that it really is true—I'm still alive! The rugged old 'bolt, she'll fly, she'll bring me home yet!

I call back, exultation and laughter in my voice, nearly shouting. "Okay, out there! I'll try. I'll do everything I can, but I'm not sure what I can do. I'm down to less than a thousand feet now." And finally I discover that the battered and crippled Thunderbolt really *can* fly! I have been in a steady glide, convinced all this time the fighter is on the verge of falling out of control, and now—only now—I discover that she'll fly. It is too good to be true, and I shout with glee.

I ease back on the stick. The Thunderbolt answers at once, nose lifting, and hauls upward in a zoom climb. I hold the fighter with her nose high until the speed drops to just above stalling.

Now, level out. Hold it, increase speed to at least 170 miles per hour, back on the stick again. And climb! Again I repeat the maneuver, a crippled series of upward zooms, each bringing me higher and higher. Each zoom—a terrific boost to my morale. Clouds above me, a scattered overcast at 5,000 feet. Just below the cloud deck, nose level, more speed, and back on the stick. She goes! The big fighter rears upward into the clouds. Another leveling out, another zoom, and I'm on top. From less than 1,000 feet to more than 8,000! I'm shouting happily to myself, so cocky and confident and joyous that I'm nearly drunk from the sensation. Everything is wonderful! *Nothing* is going to stop me now! I nurse the fighter, baby the controls, and the crippled airplane responds, slides through the air, closer and closer to safety.

"Blue Four, Blue Four." The voice is clearer, sharper. "We have you loud and clear, Blue Four. Steer three four five degrees, Blue Four, steer three four five degrees."

"Hello, Control, hello, Control, this is Blue Four. I can't steer your heading. Most of my instruments are shot out. I have a general idea of my direction, but I cannot follow your exact heading. Direct me either left or right. Direct me either left or right. I will correct in this manner. Over."

Mayday Control stays with me every moment, sending flight corrections. I think the Channel is only forty miles across, but I am far south, and long miles stretch ahead of me. At my laboring speed, it seems I'll never get across the water! The minutes drag. How long can this airplane keep flying? I listen for any change in engine sound, for a faltering of the thunder ahead of me. But the engine sings true, maintaining power, and at 170 miles per hour we drone our way above the clouds, guided by an invisible voice through space, drawn inexorably toward home.

Time drags. Thirty minutes. Below the clouds, only the Channel. Thirty-five minutes, forty minutes. And then, a break in the clouds, the overcast becomes broken white cumulus, and there . . . directly below me, the stark white cliffs of Dover! I'm too happy to keep radio silence, I whoop joyously. "Control, this is Blue Four. Those white cliffs sure look wonderful from up here!" No one can imagine just how wonderful they look!

The controller seems to share my joy. In the next several minutes he guides me unerringly through the clouds and steers me to the Hawkinge air base. I can't find the field. The controller tells me I am directly over the base, but this doesn't help. My eyes are too swollen, the field too well camouflaged. I pass directly over the hidden airfield, circle the field under the direction of the Mayday controller, but cannot see a thing.

I check the fuel gauges: about a hundred gallons left. I call the controller. "Hello, Mayday Control; hello, Mayday Control, this is Keyworth Blue Four. I'm okay now. I'm going to fly to Manston. I'd like to land back at my outfit. Blue Four, out."

Immediately a call comes back. "Roger, Blue Four. If you're sure you can make it, go to B channel and give them a call. Mayday Control, out." He signs off. I switch radio control and call Manston. The field is less than forty miles away, almost in sight. The Thunderbolt chews up the miles, and soon I begin to descend, heading directly for the field.

"Hello, Manston Tower, this is Keyworth Blue Four, Pancake,

over." The reply comes at once. "Hello, Blue Four, hello, Blue Four, this is Manston, Pancake number one, zero six zero, over."

"Hello, Manston. Blue Four here. I'm shot up. I will have to make a belly landing. I do not know the condition of my landing gear. I have no hydraulics for flaps or brakes. Over."

"Blue Four from Manston. Make a wheels-down landing if you possibly can. Repeat, make a wheels-down landing if you possibly can. We are very crowded and have other crippled airplanes coming in. Over."

"Okay, Manston, from Blue Four. I'll try it. Check my wheels as I come over the tower. I cannot bail out, repeat, I cannot bail out. I have no hydraulic system to pull the wheels back up, no brakes, no flaps. Over."

I move the landing gear control to DOWN position. Fate still smiles on me. The wheels drop down, lock into position. With all the holes and gaping tears in the Thunderbolt, the wheels and tires have come through unscathed. I circle the field with my eyes almost closed, at 500 feet and less than 150 miles per hour.

This is it; now or never. I descend, turn into a long gliding turn for the runway so that I can see my point of touchdown. I cannot see through the oil-covered windscreen. Carefully, carefully, not enough power for an emergency go-around. I fly every inch toward the runway, nursing the Thunderbolt down. Over the very end of the field, just above stalling speed, I chop the throttle, drop the heavy fighter to the grass. It is one of the best landings I have ever made!

The fighter rolls down the hill to the center of the Manston field. On the rough, grassy landing strip I fight to keep her headed straight. Without flaps or brakes the big fighter rolls freely, barely losing speed. In the center of the field the strip slopes upward and the Thunderbolt charges along the grass. Ahead of me is a line of parked Spitfires and Typhoons; if I don't stop, I'm going to slam into them!

At the last moment I kick left rudder, letting the ship turn freely with the wind. The wing tilts, the heavy machine slews

violently about, slides backward into a slot between two Typhoons almost as if I'd planned it that way.

The Thunderbolt has brought me home. Battered into a flying,
wrecked cripple, she fought her way back, brought me home.
It's almost too much to believe! I feel a great wonder settling
about me. My hand moves of its own accord. Engine off,
switches off. My hands move over my body. Chute harness undone, straps free.

I crawl out through the hole in the canopy, dragging my parachute behind me. A grin stretches from ear to ear as I stand on
the wing, stretch gratefully.

I jump to the ground, kneel down, and plant a great big kiss
on terra firma. Oh, how good that solid earth feels!

The meat wagon is on hand, and the medics rush to me. I
imagine I'm quite a sight, with blood from my nose smeared
over my face, mixed with the hydraulic fluid. The doctor shakes
his head in wonder, and I don't blame him.

A .30-caliber bullet has nicked my nose. Splinters from 20-
mm cannon shells are embedded deeply in both hands. A bullet
has shot away the wristwatch from my arm; only the strap and
face rim remain. Burns streak the skin on my forehead. My eyes
are swollen, burning, and the flesh starting to blister. And on
my right thigh they discover two flesh wounds from .30-caliber
bullets that I hadn't even known about.

They insist on taking me to the hospital at once. Not yet; I
want to look over the Jug. And this airplane is not a pretty sight.
My awe and respect for the fighter increase as I walk around the
battered machine.

There are twenty-one gaping holes and jagged tears in the
metal from exploding 20-mm cannon shells. I'm still standing in
one place when my count of the bullet holes reaches past a
hundred; there's no use even trying to add them all. The Thunderbolt is literally a sieve, holes through the wings, nose, fuselage, and tail. Every square foot, it seems, is covered with holes.
There are five holes in the propeller. Three 20-mm cannon shells
burst against the armor plate, a scant inch away from my head.

Five cannon-shell holes in the right wing, four in the left wing. Two cannon shells blasted away the lower half of my rudder. One shell exploded in the cockpit, next to my left hand; this is the blast that ripped away the flap handle. More holes appear along the fuselage and in the tail. Behind the cockpit the metal is twisted and curled; this had jammed the canopy, trapping me inside.

The airplane had done her best. Needless to say, she would never fly again.

The doctors hustle me into the meat wagon and roar off to the hospital for a thorough checkup and repair job. They look at me with misgivings and cannot understand why I am not shaking and quivering. Not anymore—all that is behind me! I'm the happiest man on earth, bubbling over with joy. I'm back, *alive*. A dozen times I thought I'd had it, thought the end had come. And now that I am back—with wounds and injuries that will heal quickly—I'm too happy to react physically.

I feel like a man who had been strapped into the electric chair, condemned to die. The switch is thrown, the current surges. Then, miraculously, it stops. Again the switch closes, the current. . . . Then, another reprieve. Several more times the closing of the switch, the imminence of death, and the reprieve, the final freedom.

A Fighter Pilot's Christmas

from *Baa Baa Black Sheep*

BY GREGORY "PAPPY" BOYINGTON

A new generation of Americans learned of Gregory "Pappy" Boyington when his autobiography, Baa Baa Black Sheep, *inspired a television series. The book was better.*

Pappy was a unique character, an alcoholic from a troubled youth who sooner or later would have been booted out of the peacetime military. Indeed, it is impossible to imagine him today among the ranks of the technocrats who fly the hot jets—he wouldn't make it through ground school.

World War II was Boyington's salvation. He learned combat flying in Burma and China with the American Volunteer Group, the Flying Tigers, where he shot down six Japanese planes. In April of 1942 he decided to return to the States and rejoin the Marines. Suave, tactful diplomat that he was, Boyington managed to orchestrate his departure in such a way that an infuriated Gen. Claire Chennault fired a dishonorable discharge into his wake and pulled strings to ensure he would not receive military transportation in India. Still bilious, Chennault also tried to induce the Army Air Corps in India to draft Boyington as a second lieutenant. This was the ultimate insult to a Marine fighter pilot. Somehow our hero avoided the Army's tentacles and used his own money to buy passage on a ship.

Back in the States the Marines welcomed the prodigal son with open arms. Too old for fighters, Boyington wormed his way into one anyway and was ultimately credited with twenty-eight victories, two more than Rickenbacker. Yet on the January 3, 1944, flight in which he scored victories number twenty-seven and twenty-eight, he was himself shot down and miraculously survived a low-altitude bailout. He spent the rest of the war as a prisoner of the Japanese.

The story of Christmas Day, 1943, that follows is a little gem that lets us meet the man who flew the plane. And we find that we like Pappy—like him a lot—a revelation that would come as no surprise to those who knew him as a comrade.

DON'T ASK ME WHY IT HAD TO BE ON A CHRISTMAS DAY, FOR HE who can answer such a question can also answer why there have to be wars, and who starts them, and why men in machines kill other men in machines. I had not started this war, and if it were possible to write a different sort of Christmas story I would prefer to record it, or at least to have had it occur on a different day.

Come to think of it, there was undoubtedly some basis for my feelings this day, for as far back as I could remember, Christmas Day was repulsive to me. Ever since my childhood, it had always been the same. Relatives were forever coming to our house and kissing my brother and me with those real wet kisses children dread so much, and making a number of well-wishing compliments that none of them ever seemed to believe.

And then it started after everybody had a snoutful of firewater, fighting and speaking their true thoughts. All Christmases were alike, my brother Bill and I ending up by going to a movie. And even after I was old enough to protect myself, I did the same damn thing, leaving the house and celebrating the occasion with people I didn't know, in some bar.

I was leading a fighter patrol that was intended to intercept any enemy fighters that followed our bombers, which had preceded us to Rabaul. We saw them returning from their strike at a distance and saw that Maj. Marion Carl's squadron was very capably warding off some Zeros, and before we got within range I witnessed three go up in flames from the .50-calibers triggered by Carl's pilots.

We caught a dozen or so of these fighters that had been heckling our bombers, B-24s. The Nips dove away and ran for home, Rabaul, for they must have been short of gasoline. They had been fighting some distance from their base, with no extra fuel because they wore no belly tanks. They had not expected us to follow, but we were not escort planes and didn't have to stay with our bombers.

Nosing over after one of these homebound Nips, I closed the distance between us gradually, keeping directly behind his tail, first a thousand yards, then five hundred, finally closing in directly behind to fifty feet. Knowing the little rascal couldn't have any idea he was being followed, I was going to make certain this one didn't get away. Never before had I been so deliberate and cold about what I was doing. He was on his way home, but already I knew he would not get there.

Nonchalantly I trimmed my rudder and stabilizer tabs. Nonchalantly I checked my gun chargers. As long as he could not see me, as long as he didn't even know I was following him, I was going to take my time. I knew that my shot would be no-deflection and slowly wavered my gunsight until it rested directly upon the cross formed by his vertical tail and horizontal wings. The little Nip was a doomed man even before I fired. I knew it and could feel it, and it was I who condemned him from ever reaching home—and it was Christmas.

One short burst was all that was needed. With this short burst flames flew from the cockpit, a yellow chute opened, and down the pilot glided into the Pacific. I saw the splash.

Using my diving speed with additional power, I climbed, and as I climbed, I could see off to my right two more enemy planes heading for Rabaul. One was throwing smoke. I closed in on the wounded plane, and it dove. His mate pulled off to one side to maneuver against me, but I let the smoker have it—one burst that set the plane on fire—and again the pilot bailed out.

His mate then dove in from above and to the side upon my own tail to get me, but it was simple to nose down and dive away temporarily from him. From a new position I watched the pilot from the burning plane drift slowly down to the water, the same as the other had done. This time his flying mate slowly circled him as he descended, possibly as a needless protection.

I remember the whole picture with a harsh distinction—and on Christmas—one Japanese pilot descending while his pal kept circling him. And then, after the pilot landed in the water, I went after the circling pal. I closed in on him from the sun side and nailed him about a hundred feet over the water. His Zero made a half-roll and plunked out of sight into the sea. No doubt his swimming comrade saw me coming but could only watch.

This low altitude certainly was no place for me to be in enemy territory, so I climbed, but after searching for a half hour I saw no more of the little fellows in this vicinity.

I next decided, since I was so close, to circle the harbor of Rabaul so that I could make a report on our recent bombings there. Smoke was coming from two ships. Another had only the bow protruding from the water, and there were numerous circles all around that had been created by exploding bombs.

While I was looking at all this, and preparing mental notes, I happened to see far below a nine-plane Nip patrol coming up in sections of threes. Maneuvering my plane so that I would be flying at them from the sun side again, I eased toward the rear and fired at the tail-end Charlie in the third V. The fire chopped him to bits, and apparently the surprise was so great in the rest of the patrol that the eight planes appeared to jump all over the sky. They happened to be Tonys, the only Nip planes that could outdive us. One of them started after my tail and began closing in on it slowly, but he gave up the chase after a few minutes. The others had gotten reorganized, and it was time for me to be getting home.

On the way back I saw something on the surface of the water that made me curious. At first I thought it was one boat towing another, but it wasn't. It was a Japanese submarine surfacing. Nosing my Corsair over a little steeper, I made a run at the submarine and sent a long burst into her conning tower. Almost immediately it disappeared, but I saw no oil streaks or anything else that is supposed to happen when one is destroyed, so I knew that I had not sunk her.

My only thought at this time was what a hell of a thing for one guy to do to another guy on Christmas.

The Stars Still Shine

from *Bomber Pilot*

BY PHILIP ARDREY

If war is nothing else to the men who fight it, it is a loss of innocence. No one goes through the fires unscathed. B-24 Liberator pilot Philip Ardrey documents that change very well in his book Bomber Pilot, *another classic about war in the air. Here is his description of a minor raid you won't find in history books, a description written by a man who has already seen too much.*

WE HEARD A RUMOR THAT WE MIGHT BOMB WIENER NEUSTADT again. It hadn't been bombed since that day back in August when we hit it from Bengasi. From Tunis the raid wouldn't be as long as the first one was, which was one real advantage. When we first heard that we might be going back, many thought that it would be a long but easy mission. The idea behind that was that we'd been there before and met only meager opposition, and so we should find it easy to go there again. I disagreed. I knew from the intelligence reports that we had on the importance of the installations there that the Nazis must have bolstered their defenses a great deal. I felt it would be the same old story told about many heavy bomber units hitting an important target the second time. The second time you usually get your pants shot off.

Then too, I had heard stories about flak guns—that only brand-new flak guns are extremely accurate. After firing even a comparatively few rounds the carriages loosen up, so that the guns are much less accurate firing on a formation flying at twenty-three or twenty-four thousand feet. When we were over Wiener Neustadt before, there was no heavy flak. Whatever guns they had there now, I reasoned, would probably be new ones, since they certainly wouldn't bring in used guns to a place as important as that. In addition to my reasoned ideas, I had a host of unexplainable suspicions that the second raid on Wiener Neustadt, if run now by us, would be a very rough raid.

After a few days of rumors I got word that we really would run the raid. There was no particular pressure on me to go. In any case, I wouldn't be allowed to lead the group or even be deputy leader. Thus if I went, it would be merely to lead my squadron. But one thing entered the picture to make it a little different. That was that Gen. Jimmie Hodges, our division commander, would be in the lead ship of our group, and with us he would be leading the three groups flying that day. When the general rode, the bars were down for other subordinate unit commanders. That is, though I might generally be limited to fly on those missions where I might be group leader or deputy group leader, if the general flew, I could fly in any capacity I could fit into.

I set up Ed Fowble to lead my squadron of six ships flying the low left position on the group lead. Ed and I had seen some rough ones together. We rode over Messina together in the old days before the Sicilian invasion began and saw the best flak the Jerries had to offer in Sicily; we ran the gauntlet at Ploesti together, and we'd damn well take a second look at Wiener Neustadt together.

The raid was held up a day or two after the first briefing because the runway, which had no hard surface, was too muddy to bear our loaded airplanes. It is a bad thing to hold up a mission after it has been briefed. Somehow we felt that it was evident there were leaks in our security, and we were continually afraid the enemy intelligence knew in advance where we were going. After a couple of days without rain we got up just before dawn one morning to hear that this was the day. We got another hurried briefing chiefly on the weather, ate one meal and took another in the form of K rations with us to the ships.

We took off and assembled our group over the field and

headed out on the long course. We were going across the Italian peninsula, then up the Adriatic Sea to the hip of the boot and on into Austria. We would turn left when abreast of our target and make a bombing run from east to west. After leaving the target we would let down a thousand feet or so to facilitate regrouping of the formation, turn left again, and come home.

The mission went about as planned. One surprise was that over Italy on the way in we flew over a town where we got a good deal of unexpected flak. We swore at our intelligence for not warning us about the guns there. There had been absolutely nothing said about them at briefing. But then the Germans were withdrawing in Italy, and it was likely the guns had just been moved in from a point farther south. It was a good excuse, but little consolation to us. We were a long way from the target to be running any risk of flak damage. We felt bursts all around our ship, but we suffered no apparent damage, and on we went.

We turned up the Adriatic and progressed on into Austria. We made our turn and started from the IP—the initial point— into the target. A few minutes later we were on the bombing run. Just as we started, and even when there were long minutes to go before we reached our bomb release line, huge black flak bursts suddenly puffed up all around us. It was a clear day, we were at about fifteen thousand feet, which was a moderately easy range for heavy guns. One thing proved the type of fire being directed at us—there was no cloud of flak ahead of us to fly into. The very first shells that went off broke almost between our engine nacelles. That let us know it was aimed fire, and not a barrage. The guns were brand-new—they had to be to shoot like that. They were not the 88-mm type; they were 105s.

Here I would like to correct a frequent fallacy made by writers describing bombing raids. The noise a bomber pilot hears is awful, but that noise isn't the loud noise of shells bursting. The pilot is encased in many thicknesses of clothing—even his head is almost completely covered. Tightly clamped against his ears are his headphones, built into his helmet. Out of these head-phones comes most of the noise he hears. The horrible screaming is the noise of the enemy radio-jamming apparatus. It is like a death cry of the banshees of all the ages. On our missions it usually started faintly in our headphones as we neared the enemy coast and grew louder and louder. A pilot had to keep the volume of his receiver turned up high in order to hear commands over the air through the bedlam of jamming. After a few hours of it I felt that I would go crazy if I didn't turn the volume down. I would turn it down when I was out of the target area, but I knew when I did that I might be missing an important radio order or a call from another ship asking for help or direction in one way or another.

We could hear the firing of our own guns. Chiefly we could hear the top turret. In addition to the noise of the top turret we could hear the nose guns, the waist guns, the ball turret, and finally the tail turret. We really couldn't hear the tail turret, but after we had ridden in our bombers for a while there was a peculiar faint vibration that would run down the skin of the ship and up the seats to let us know little Pete Peterson of Fowble's crew was warming up his guns. When Pete's guns chattered, some Nazi always regretted it. And when I felt the vibrations of his guns coming through the seat of my pants, it was like someone scratching a mosquito bite in the middle of my back.

But then about the flak. You could hear it—faintly. When flak was very, very near, you could see the angry red fire as the shells exploded before the black smoke formed. You could hear the bursts sounding like *wuff-wuff-wuff* under your wings. You could see the nose of the ship plowing through the smoke clouds where the bursts had been. You could hear the sprinkle of slivers of shrapnel go through the sides of the ship if they were hitting close to you. I always said that if you hear the flak—if you get the *wuff-wuff-wuff*—and really hear it over the screaming of the radio and other sounds, then it is deadly close. You don't realize the terror it strikes into some airmen's hearts until you've had your own plane shot to hell a few times. I laughed at Franco's flak coming through Gibraltar. It wasn't much flak, but I wouldn't laugh six months later when I had seen more of it.

And yet with the increasing terror came a greater understanding that there was little a heavy-bomber pilot in the midst of a large formation could do about flak. There came a determined calm to contain one's terror. The leader of a large group or a larger combat-wing formation knew that attempts at "evasive action" simply could not be made anywhere that enemy fighters were active. Usually the worst flak we saw was while we were on or closely approaching the bombing run, when we could not afford to make turns for any reason, except to put the bombardier over the target. After the bombs were away, if the formation was one of medium or larger size—that is, twenty-four ships or more—the wisdom of turns, except as briefed, was questionable. If fighters were about, such turns might loosen the formation. Loosening the formation meant greater vulnerability to fighter attacks. The way we were flying there was really nothing you could do when the flak started breaking around your ship but sit and look at it—and pray. If we knew some localities on the route in or out were heavily defended, we would try to fly around them. But once in flak, we just had to look at it.

That was certainly the way it was our second trip over Wiener Neustadt. The shells broke on all sides of us as we went in. We heard the angry *wuff-wuff-wuff* of the bursts above the maniac's ball of noise coming over the radio. We could see the flare of fire in the bursts of the shells. I was looking out to the right of the ship. The formation was good and tight in spite of the flak, and to the high right of my ship was the lead squadron and the ship in which General Jimmie was flying. Just under his left wing was an airplane flown by a Lieutenant Matson of Paul Burton's squadron. General Hodges's plane was piloted by the indefatigable Capt. Ken Caldwell, the group first pilot in whom Colonel Wood and Major Brooks had the greatest confidence.

As I looked out on that hell of shellfire, I think I felt as much terror as I have ever felt in an airplane. For some reason I think I was more frightened than I had been over Ploesti. I can't explain it unless it had seemed to me this was a raid that would be costly without reasonable results to compensate. Somehow we had no adequate purpose on this raid to bolster up our courage. I felt it was just a "big raid" to give bomber command some satisfaction for having sent us to Africa.

As I was looking out watching the group leader and wondering how any of us could get through the fire, I saw a direct burst of a shell center the bomber directly to my right front—Matson's ship. It was in the low left element of the lead squadron, and almost in front of me—a little high and to the right. Matson's Lib was perhaps a little more in line with the ship of Mac McLaughlin than with my own. Mac was flying his beloved *Ole Irish* on my right wing. But the hit Lib was so close in front of both of us that I wondered how we were going to get by. When the shell went off inside the bomber, the sides of it seemed to puff out momentarily. It didn't blow to bits, but big chunks of it flew off and tongues of flame licked out of its spread seams in all directions. The stricken plane pulled up right in front of us. We nosed our ship down, and so did Mac. The flaming Lib then pulled up high and out to the left, pieces falling off of it all the way. As we went by and under it, we could see it glowing like the inside of a furnace.

The next moment our bombs were away. Then in another moment Sergeant Le Jeune, our Louisiana Cajun flight engineer, was trying to get the bomb-bay doors closed. The bombardier hadn't been able to close them from the nose compartment. Communication with our crew stations in the rear was cut off. Flak had evidently cut the interphone lines. It had also cut several of the hydraulic lines in the bomb bay, and consequently the bomb doors wouldn't go closed. With the bomb doors open our ship wouldn't fly as fast as the others without use of excessive power. That meant one of two things: either we would drop behind and run the danger of being hit by enemy fighters, or we would stay up with the formation by using added power and run the danger of giving out of gas before we got back across the Mediterranean. It seemed a long way home at that point.

Sergeant Le Jeune went out on the catwalk and hung between the gaping doors, the icy wind blowing through, and the whole inside of the bomb bay including the precarious point of his footing covered with slippery hydraulic fluid. He tried to pull or kick the doors closed. Finally he decided to cut in the last reserve of hydraulic fluid to get the doors closed. The hydraulic lines would be temporarily charged and the doors might close before all the reserve supply of fluid ran out. If so, that would mean that when we got back we would have to use the emergency manual procedures to get the landing gear and the flaps down, and we would probably be without brakes. Le Jeune had done his best—even hanging head down in the open bomb bay and pulling at the doors—so this seemed to be the only other thing to do. He crept aft on the catwalk and cut in the reserve supply. Then I moved the lever to the Close-doors position and the doors slammed shut as the remaining fluid poured out like blood from open veins into the bomb bay.

Later Le Jeune made another checkup inside the bomb bay. He found one serious fuel leak that had already filled the inside of the ship with heavy gas fumes, but he managed to get this patched well enough so that, though the fumes were heavy, the additional loss of fuel was slight. With that job completed, I asked him to go aft again and check particularly to see if the crew members were all right. I had not been able to use the interphone to any of the rear stations, and I thought it likely that someone might have been hit in the midst of that flak storm. Then I took stock of the ship and was happy to see that all the engines were apparently functioning okay. Ed and I could tell quite easily that the cables to the control trim were cut, but with both of us on the main controls we managed to keep the ship steady without too much difficulty.

The formation had loosened during the last minute of the bomb run and now began to close up again. We were clear of the target and at last out of the field of fire of the guns below. We were not at that moment under enemy fighter attack, but we could hear many distress calls over our radio coming from other ships and other formations in the rear not as lucky as us. We held a tight formation and evidently that sufficed to render us at least temporarily immune. On such missions it always became a contest in formation flying. The Jerries jumped the loosest formation and shot it to pieces. It behooved us to fly better formation than some other group in order not to be elected.

In a few minutes Sergeant Le Jeune came forward and reported that all personnel in the rear were okay, though there were holes in the ship by the score, big and small. Our trim tab cables were beyond repair, and one of the main aileron cables was partly cut through. It might give way, but there were enough strands holding so that if we handled the ship gingerly we stood a good chance of getting home. I knew it was by the grace of God and nothing else that we could have so much flak damage and yet none of it critical.

We kept our place in the formation and after two endless hours found ourselves a long way out on the way home. We were almost beyond the point where fighter attack was likely. As we passed north of Rome, we saw a great flak barrage thrown up, but we flew around it. The flight across the Mediterranean seemed almost interminable. I was wondering all the time about the difficulties we might have in landing our ship. Finally, just about as our navigator, Sollie, predicted, we saw the misty coast of Africa ahead. The formation, which had loosened up a bit on the flight across the water, tightened up again to get in proper shape for the peel off to land.

There were many other ships that had obviously suffered flak damage, but we seemed to be in worse shape than any of those that had made it back from the target. I called the formation lead plane to say that we would pull out of formation and wait until all the other ships had landed before we came in. We had enough fuel left to risk the wait, and we didn't want to take a chance on blocking a runway when there were others behind still to land. We got acknowledgment of our message and pulled out of the formation in a gentle diving turn to the left. We had had about four and a half hours of anxiety.

The group was lined up in tight formation going over the field in the direction for landing. Now the peel-off was beginning, and one after another of the big ships banked sharply to the left and swung around the traffic circle, putting landing gear and flaps down to land in rapid succession. We hovered above and waited. Finally the last ship cleared the runway. We called in for our landing and started the arduous process of getting the landing gear down by the manual emergency procedure. Sergeant Le Jeune went through it as though he had to do it every day. Finally he got the big wheels cranked down after cranking the winch back in the bomb bay until his back almost broke. He checked the gear and announced to us in the cockpit, "Gear down and locked."

We turned on the base leg, putting it far back from the field. I started the manual system of working the flaps, broke the safetying wire, and began vigorously pumping the hand pump. I was afraid that the pump wouldn't work because I watched the flap indicator for about the first fifty pumps and saw nothing happen. But finally the pressure built up enough so that the flaps started slowly down. I managed to get them down about halfway as we were on the final approach to the runway and I left them there. Sergeant Le Jeune had ordered the waist gunners to go as far to the rear as possible so that they would weigh the tail of the plane down. We would probably want to drag the tail on landing, because it was obvious we would have little or no brake pressure. As a rule the accumulators hold brake pressure up pretty well even though the rest of the hydraulic system is gone. But once the brakes are applied, they must be held in the on position. If the central hydraulic system is out when they are let up, the accumulator pressure goes out.

We touched down easily, nose higher than usual. Ed pulled back on the wheel and I helped him on my wheel, so that the nose rose even higher until we could hear the tail skid touch and drag down the rough runway. Dragging might buckle a rear bulkhead, but that would be all right. It would slow us down and prevent going off the end of the runway with a possible landing-gear failure on the uneven ground beyond.

The ship slowed down more and more until it became necessary to let the nose down. It wouldn't stay up any longer. The nosewheel came down pretty hard and we were wondering if the nose strut would fail, leaving us down by the bow. It held. "Brake her, Ed," I said. "We'll see what we've got." Ed applied the pressure and the brakes took hold. He held his pressure on them until the ship stopped. Then he tried them again, but the pressure gauges showed his last pressure gone. We cut the engines and left the hulk that had flown like an airplane to be towed in by tugs. It wasn't safe to taxi without brakes.

The landing and general handling of the ship had been a tribute to Ed Fowble and his crew. Sergeant Le Jeune and Ed had done everything the way the Consolidated handbook prescribes handling emergencies. The result was that the crew was safe and sound, and the ship had only battle damage. We got out of it and looked it over. Holes were poked through it in every direction. A couple of the members of the crew had been hit by flak, which had failed to puncture their flak suits. Besides the myriad of holes in the wings and fuselage, we noticed the sad old ship dismally leaked gas out of several of her self-sealing fuel cells, which had been punctured. They were going to have to be replaced, but the self-sealing feature of their construction had worked well enough to slow the fuel leaks so that the amount of fuel lost coming home was not critical. Here was old *I* for *item*, the second one Fowble had had, in which he had taken no less pride than the first. She would fly again, but not until a great deal of work had been put in on her. I said a prayer of thanks that we all got home.

I felt this would probably be my last raid in Africa—a happy thought. At least rumors had it that this would be the last. After this we should be ready to go back to England for good. And yet I felt some melancholy mixed with happiness that this was probably the end of Africa. I had seen a good number of our boys go down that day, which was not easy to forget.

When I went to dinner, I found the great Murph there. He had prepared for my return by bartering for a bottle of red

Tunisian wine and a loaf of good French bread. I drank almost the whole bottle of wine and ate several big chunks of bread and then curled up on the cot and went to sleep.

The next day the squadron commanders were called over to Colonel Wood's headquarters. We were told to bend every effort toward getting our ships ready. The rains would soon set in for good, and he wanted to lose no time in getting out. That was the best news I had had in ages.

As I came out of the tent I saw the smiling face of Mac McLaughlin waiting for me. Mac had some pieces of metal in his hand. "Thought you might like some of these," he said.

"What are they?"

"Pieces of Matson's ship. They lodged in my number one engine nacelle. Pieces of that ship hit both of us. I guess I got most of them, though. You might want these and you might not. Anyway, here they are if you do." And, of course, I did.

I went to the area where my ships were parked and told Sergeant Peterson, my line chief, to turn on full steam to get the ships ready. Those boys on the line already had the rumor about leaving and were working like beavers. They got news by some medium that is faster than two-way radio.

I walked from ship to ship noting the damage. Much of it could be repaired in England. Jobs of patching holes in most cases, if they were just holes in the airplane skin, wouldn't be done here. New fuel cells had to be put in several ships because the Wiener Neustadt guns had let too much sun into the old ones.

In a very few days we had the first ships ready to go. The rest were just about ready. This time I decided to fly with Wright on the trip back. Sergeant Peterson told me Ed Fowble's ship would probably be ready to go the same day as the rest of them, but for a later takeoff. If not, it would be no more than a day late. And so we planned takeoff of the first ships for early one morning about a week after the trip to Austria. We were given a forecast of good weather to Marrakesh. The moment seemed propitious, and with the sharp edge of dawn we were warming up engines. I had said good-bye to Ed and received his unnecessary assurances that he would not be far behind. No one would ever leave Ed far behind. When I got into our ship I didn't even look back at the field where we had been so singularly uncomfortable for the month past. We didn't circle, we just turned on course to Marrakesh and kept going.

Arriving in Marrakesh, I was suffering from a virulent case of dysentery. I had had a touch of it at the time of takeoff, but upon landing my tummy was sending signals one right after the other which were unmistakable. My intestines were writhing like a basketful of snakes, and occasional flashes of pain made me think of hara-kiri. I reported directly to the infirmary where I found a doctor busying himself with a patient. He looked at me, and without even asking me what the trouble was, he said, "I'll be with you in just a minute; I've got just the stuff to fix you up." He put a bottle of white liquid and some pills in my hand. "Take these according to direction," he said. I must have looked decidedly green to make diagnosis so simple because I hadn't said a word. After that I lay on a cot I found in one of the buildings kept for transient officers until the time for the briefing for the night takeoff.

I must have slept an hour or so before Bob Wright came in to wake me. We walked over to the briefing room together. I was weak but happy and confident that in a few hours I would shake the dust of Africa from my shoes for the last time. I sat in the briefing not listening to much that was said. Then Lt. Col. Bob Miller, our group air executive, wormed his way through the seated crewmen to my chair. "I want to see you," he said, and walked out. I followed him.

Outside he turned and said, "Did you hear about Fowble?"

"What is it?"

"He just crashed. A few miles north of the field. Out of gas. Men in the tower saw his landing lights go on and saw him glide in trying to make a dead-stick landing. The ship burned. All of them were killed instantly except Sergeant Mike and Sergeant

Le Jeune. They are in a serious condition but have been able to tell a little bit of the story."

Ed had been unable to get properly gassed up at Tunis. He also had a slight fuel leak in addition to the ones that had been discovered and repaired after the ship's last mission. Being given a good weather report, he had taken off with less than a full load of fuel. He would not be left behind, and waiting for more fuel made a difference of enough hours so that his flight would have been delayed until the next day. Bad weather, plus a slight variation from course, plus the slight fuel leak, combined to make the plane run out of gas within a mile or two of the field. And now, except for two, they were all dead. I thought of Ed and Byrd, his copilot, and Phifer and Sollie, the bombardier and navigator, and little Pete, the tail gunner, and all the others. I prayed that Sergeants Le Jeune and Mike might live, but the later news was that they lingered only a short while and died.

The news of this incident hit me with soul-shaking impact. "Please tell Wright I'll wait for him in the ship," I said. I left the building where the briefing was going on and wandered through the desert darkness the mile or so out to where our plane was parked. I crawled into it and curled up on the flight deck. I don't think I really went to sleep. I think I sank into a kind of morose stupor.

When next I remembered anything, we were winging our way out over the ocean. Someone had thrown an Army blanket over me. I could hear the drone of the engines and the noise of the radio man at my feet pecking out his message to Casablanca Radio hundreds of miles to the rear. And I could see a star out the little bit of window visible from where I lay.

The Runner

from *Stuka Pilot*

BY HANS ULRICH RUDEL

*The most decorated German soldier of World War II was Hans
Ulrich Rudel, who somehow survived six extraordinary years
of air combat. He spent most of his career flying Stuka dive
bombers, lost a leg, then returned to flying status and finished
the war in an FW-190. Rudel's 2,530 combat sorties is a record
you can set in concrete—no one will ever surpass it.*

*How did he survive six years of combat? Well, he was very
lucky. In addition, he was a damn good pilot and an extremely
tough, determined man. Perhaps his iron will was the critical
factor. Here is one of his adventures.*

ON 20 MARCH 1944, AFTER SEVEN SORTIES IN THE NIKOLAYEV AND
Balta area, I take off with my squadron on the eighth of the
day, our first mission for five days against the bridge at Jampol.
The sky is a brilliant blue and it can be taken for granted that
after this prolonged respite the defense will have been considerably strengthened by flak and fighter protection.

As my airfield and Rauchowka itself is a quagmire, our fighter
squadron has moved to the concrete airfield at Odessa. We, with
our broad tires, are better able to cope with the mud and do
not immediately become bogged down in it. We fix a rendezvous
by telephone for a certain time about thirty miles from the target
at 7,500 feet above a conspicuous loop of the river Dniester.
But apparently difficulties have also cropped up at Odessa. My
escort is not at the rendezvous.

The target is clearly visible, so naturally we attack. There are
several new crews in my squadron. Their quality is not as good
as it used to be. The really good men have by this time been

long since at the front, and petrol for training purposes has been strictly rationed to so many gallons per man. I firmly believe that I, had I been restricted to so small an allowance, could not have done any better than the new trainees.

We are still about twelve miles from our objective when I give the warning: "Enemy fighters." More than twenty Soviet Lag 5s are approaching. Our bomb load hampers our maneuverability. I fly in defensive ellipses so as to be able at any moment to come in myself behind the fighters, for their purpose is to shoot down my rear aircraft. In spite of the air battle I gradually work round to my objective. Individual Russians who try to shoot me down by a frontal pass I disappoint by extremely mobile tactics, then at the last moment dive through the midst of them and pull out into a climb. If the new crews can bring it off today, they will have learned a lot.

"Prepare for attack, stick together—close up—attack!"

And I come in for the attack on the bridge. As I dive, I see the flash of a host of flak emplacements. The shells scream past my aircraft. Henschel says the sky is a mass of cotton wool, his name for the bursting flak. Our formation is losing its cohesion, confound it, making us more vulnerable to the fighters. I warn those lagging behind:

"Fly on, catch up, we are just as scared as you are."

Not a few swear words slip past my tongue. I bank round and at 1,200 feet see my bomb nearly miss the bridge. So there is a wind blowing.

"Wind from port, correct to port."

A direct hit from our No. 3 finishes off the bridge. Circling round, I locate the gun sites of the still-aggressive flak and give the order to attack them.

"They are getting hell very nicely today," opines Henschel.

Unfortunately two new crews have lagged slightly behind when diving. Lags cut them off. One of them is completely riddled and zooms past me in the direction of enemy territory. I try to catch up with him, but I cannot leave my whole squadron in the lurch on his account. I yell at him over the R/T, I curse him; it is no use. He flies on to the Russian bank of the Dniester. Only a thin ribbon of smoke rises from his aircraft. He surely could have flown on for another few minutes, as the other does, and so reached our own lines.

"He lost his nerve completely, the idiot," comments Fickel over the R/T. At the moment I cannot bother about him anymore, for I must try to keep my ragged formation together and maneuver back eastward in ellipses. After a quarter of an hour the Red fighters turn off defeated, and we head in regular formation for our base. I order the skipper of the seventh flight to lead the formation home. With Pilot Officer Fischer, flying the other staff aircraft, I bank round and fly back at low level, skimming the surface of the Dniester, the steep banks on either side. A short distance ahead in the direction of the bridge I discern the Russian fighters at 3,000 to 9,000 feet. But here in the bed of the river I am difficult to see, and above all my presence is not expected. As I climb abruptly over the scrub on the riverbank, I spot our aircraft two or three miles to the right. It has made a forced landing in a field. The crew is standing near it and they gesticulate wildly as I fly over at a lower level.

"If only you had paid as much attention to me before, this delicate operation would not have been necessary," I mutter to myself as I bank round to see whether the field is suitable for a landing. It is. I encourage myself with a breathed: "All right then . . . get going. This lot today will be the seventh crew I shall have picked up under the noses of the Russians."

I tell Pilot Officer Fischer to stay in the air and interfere with the fighters in case they attack. I know the direction of the wind from the bombing of the bridge. Flaps down, throttle back, I'll be down in a jiffy. What is happening? I have overshot—must open up and go round again. This has never happened to me before at such a moment. Is it an omen not to land? You are very close to the target which has just been attacked, far behind the Soviet lines! Cowardice?

Once again throttle back, flaps down—I am down . . . and instantly notice that the ground is very soft; I do not even need to brake. My aircraft comes to a stop exactly in front of my two colleagues. They are a new crew, a corporal and a LAC. Henschel lifts the canopy and I give them a sign to hop in and be quick about it. The engine is running; they climb in behind with Henschel. Red Falcons are circling overhead; they have not yet spotted us.

"Ready, Henschel?"

"Yes." I open the throttle, left brake—intending to taxi back so as to take off again in exactly the same way as I landed. My starboard wheel sticks deep in the ground. The more I open my throttle, the more my wheel eats into it. My aircraft refuses to budge from the spot. Perhaps it is only that a lot of mud is jammed between the mudguard and the wheel.

"Henschel, get out and take off the mudguard, perhaps then we can make it."

The fastening stud breaks, the wheel casing stays on; but even without it we could not take off, we are stuck in the mud. I pull the stick into my stomach, ease it, and go at full throttle into reverse. Nothing is of the very slightest use. Perhaps it might be possible to pancake, but that does not help us either. Pilot Officer Fischer flies lower above us and asks over the R/T:

"Shall I land?"

After a momentary hesitation I tell myself that if he lands, he, too, will not be able to take off again and reply:

"No, you are not to land. You are to fly home."

I take a look round. There come the Ivans, in droves, four hundred yards away. Out we must get. "Follow me," I shout— and already we are sprinting southward as fast as our legs can carry us. When flying over, I have seen that we are about four miles from the Dniester. We must get across the river whatever we do, or else we shall fall an easy prey to the pursuing Reds. Running is not a simple matter; I am wearing high fur boots and a fur coat. Sweat is not the word! None of us need any spurring on; we have no mind to end up in a Soviet prison camp, which has already meant instant death to so many dive-bomber pilots.

We have been running for half an hour. We are putting up a

pretty good show; the Ivans are a good half a mile behind. Suddenly we find ourselves on the edge of almost perpendicular cliffs at the foot of which flows the river. We rush hither and thither, looking for some way of getting down them . . . impossible! The Ivans are at our heels. Then suddenly a boyhood recollection gives me an idea. We used to slide down from bough to bough from the tops of fir trees, and by braking our fall in this way we got to the bottom safely. There are plenty of large thorny bushes, like our dog rose, growing out of the stone face of the cliff. One after the other we slide down and land on the riverbank at the bottom, lacerated in every limb and with our clothes in ribbons. Henschel gets rather jittery. He shouts:

"Dive in at once. Better to be drowned than captured by the Russians."

I advise common sense. We are aglow from running. A short breather and then strip off as many garments as we can. The Ivans have meanwhile arrived panting at the top. They cannot see us because we are in a blind angle of their field of vision. They rush up and down unable to imagine where we have disappeared to. It is a cinch they think it impossible that we have leapt over the precipice. The Dniester is in flood; the snows are thawing out, and here and there a lump of ice drifts past. We calculate the breadth of the river as six hundred yards, the temperature as three to four degrees above freezing. The three others are already getting into the water; I am just divesting myself of my fur boots and fur jacket. Now I follow them, clad only in shirt and trousers; under my shirt my map, in my trousers pockets my medals and my compass. As I touch the water, I say to myself, "You are never going in here"—then I think of the alternative and am already striking out.

In a very short while the cold is paralyzing. I gasp for breath, I no longer feel that I am swimming. Concentrate hard, think of the swimming strokes and carry out the motions! Only imperceptibly the far bank draws nearer. The others are ahead of me. I think of Henschel. He passed his swimming test with me when we were with the reserve flight at Graz, but if he goes all out today under more difficult conditions, he will be able to repeat that record time, or perhaps get very near it. In midstream I am level with him, a few yards behind the gunner of the other aircraft; the corporal is a good distance in front, he seems to be an excellent swimmer.

Gradually one becomes dead to all sensation save the instinct of self-preservation, which gives one strength; it is bend or break. I am amazed at the others' stamina, for I as a former athlete am used to overexertion. My mind travels back. I always used to finish with the 1,500 meters, often glowing with heat after trying to put up the best possible performance in nine other disciplinary exercises. This hard training pays me now. In sporting terms, my actual exertion does not exceed 90 percent of my capability.

The corporal climbs out of the water and throws himself down on the bank. Somewhat later I reach the safety of the shore with the LAC close after me. Henschel has still another 150 yards to go. The other two lie rigid, frozen to the bone, the gunner rambling deliriously. Poor chap!

I sit down and watch Henschel struggling on. Another 80 yards. Suddenly he throws up his arms and yells, "I can't go on, I can't go on anymore!" and sinks. He comes up once, but not a second time. I jump back into the water, now drawing on the last 10 percent of energy which I hope is left me. I reach the spot where I just saw Henschel go down. I cannot dive, for to dive I need to fill my lungs, but with the cold I cannot get sufficient air. After several fruitless attempts I just manage to get back to the bank. If I had succeeded in catching hold of Henschel, I should have remained with him in the Dniester. He was very heavy and the strain would have been too much for almost anyone. Now I lie sprawled on the bank . . . limp . . . exhausted . . . and somewhere a deep-seated misery for my friend Henschel. A moment later we say a Paternoster for our comrade.

The map is sodden with water, but I have everything in my head. Only—the devil only knows how far we are behind the Russian lines. Or is there still a chance that we may bump into the Rumanians sooner or later? I check up on our arms; I have a 6.35-mm revolver with six rounds, the corporal a 7.65 with a full magazine, and the LAC has lost his revolver whilst in the water and has only Henschel's broken knife. We start walking southward with these weapons in our hands. The gently rolling country is familiar from flying over it. Contour differences of perhaps six hundred feet, few villages, thirty miles to the south a railway running east to west. I know two points on it: Balti and Floresti. Even if the Russians have made a deep penetration, we can count on this line still being free of the enemy.

The time is about 3 P.M., the sun is high in the southwest. It shines obliquely in our faces on our right. First we go into a little valley with moderately high hills on either side. We are still benumbed, the corporal still delirious. I advise caution. We must try to skirt any inhabited places. Each of us is allotted a definite sector to keep under observation.

I am famished. It suddenly strikes me that I have not had a bit to eat all day. This was the eighth time we had been out, and there had not been time for a meal between sorties. A report had to be written out and dispatched to the group on our return from every mission, and instructions for the next one taken down over the telephone. Meanwhile our aircraft were refueled and rearmed, bombs loaded and off again. The crews were able to rest between whiles and even snatch a meal, but in this respect I did not count as one of them.

I guess we must now have been going for an hour; the sun is beginning to lose its strength and our clothes are starting to freeze. Do I really see something ahead of us or am I mistaken? No, it is real enough. Advancing in our direction out of the glare of the sun—it is hard to see clearly—are three figures three hundred yards away. They have certainly seen us. Perhaps they were lying on their stomachs behind this ridge of hills. They are big chaps, doubtless Rumanians. Now I can see them better. The two on the outside of the trio have rifles slung over their shoulders, the one in the middle carries a tommy gun. He is a young man, the other two are about forty, probably reservists. They approach us in no unfriendly manner in their brown-green uniforms. It suddenly occurs to me that we are no longer wearing uniforms and that consequently our nationality is not immediately evident. I hastily advise the corporal to hide his revolver while I do likewise in case the Rumanians become jittery and open fire on us. The trio now halts a yard in front of us and looks us over curiously. I start explaining to our allies that we are Germans who have made a forced landing and beg them to help us with clothing and food, telling them that we want to get back to our unit as quickly as possible.

I say, "We are German airmen who have made a forced landing," whereupon their faces darken and at the same moment I have the three muzzles of their weapons pointing at my chest. The young one instantly grabs my holster and pulls out my 6.35. They have been standing with their backs to the sun. I have had it in my eyes. Now I take a good look at them. Hammer and sickle—ergo Russians. I do not contemplate for a second being taken prisoner, I think only of escape. There is a hundred-to-one chance of pulling it off. There is probably a good price on my head in Russia, my capture is likely to be even better rewarded. To blow my brains out is not a practical consideration. I am disarmed. Slowly I turn my head round to see if the coast is clear. They guess my intention and one of them shouts, "*Stoy!*" (Halt!) I duck as I make a double turn and run for it, crouching low and swerving to right and left. Three shots crack out; they are followed by an uninterrupted rattle of quick fire. A stinging pain in my shoulder. The chap with the tommy gun has hit me at close range through the shoulder, the other two have missed me.

I sprint like a hare, zigzagging up the slope, bullets whistling above and below me, to right and to left. The Ivans run after me, halt, fire, run, fire, run, fire, run. Only a short while ago I believed I could hardly put one leg in front of the other, so stiff was I with cold, but now I am doing the sprint of my life. I have never done the four hundred yards in faster time. Blood spurts from my shoulder and it is an effort to fight off the blackness before my eyes. I have gained fifty or sixty yards on my pursuers; the bullets whistle incessantly. My only thought: "Only he is lost who gives himself up for lost." The hill seems interminable. My main direction is still into the sun in order to make it more difficult for the Ivans to hit me. I am dazzled by the glare of the sun and it is easy to miscalculate. I have just had a lesson of that. Now I reach a kind of crest, but my strength is giving out and in order to stretch it still further, I decide to keep to the top of the ridge; I shall never manage any more up and down hill. So away at the double southward along the ridge.

I cannot believe my eyes: on the hilltop twenty Ivans are running toward me. Apparently they have seen everything and now mean to round up their exhausted and wounded quarry. My faith in God wavers. Why did He first allow me to believe in the possible success of my escape? For I did get out of the first absolutely hopeless corner with my life. And will He now turn me over unarmed, deprived of my last weapon, my physical strength? My determination to escape and live suddenly revives. I dash straight downhill, that is, down the opposite slope to that by which I came up.

Behind me, two or three hundred yards away, my original pursuers, the fresh pack to one side of me. The first trio has been reduced to two; at the moment they cannot see me, for I am on the far side of the hill. One of them has stayed behind to bring in my two comrades, who stood still when I took to my heels. The hounds on my left are now keeping a parallel course, also running downhill, to cut me off.

Now comes a ploughed field; I stumble and for an instant have to take my eyes off the Ivans. I am dead tired, I trip over a clod of earth and lie where I have fallen. The end cannot be far off. I mutter one more curse that I have no revolver and therefore not even the chance to rob the Ivans of their triumph in taking me prisoner. My eyes are turned toward the Reds. They are now running over the same ploughland and have to watch their step. They run on for another fifteen yards before they look up and glance to the right where I am lying. They are now level with me, then diagonally in front, as they move forward on a line 250 yards away. They stop and look about them, unable to make out where I can have got to.

I lie flat on the slightly frozen earth and scratch myself with my fingers into the soil. It is a tough proposition; everything is so hard. The miserable bits of earth I manage to scrape loose I throw on top of me, building up a foxhole. My wound is bleeding, I have nothing to bandage it with; I lie prone on the ice-cold earth in my soaking-wet clothes; inside me I am hot with excitement at the prospect of being caught at any moment. Again the odds are a hundred to one on my being discovered and captured in less than no time. But is that a reason to give up hope in the almost impossible, when only by believing that the almost impossible is possible can it become so?

There now, the Russians are coming in my direction, continually lessening the distance between us, each of them searching the field on his own, but not yet methodically. Some of them are looking in quite the wrong direction; they do not bother me. But there is one coming straight toward me. The suspense is terrible. Twenty paces from me he stops. Is he looking at me? Is he? He is unmistakably staring in my direction. Is he not coming on? What is he waiting for? He hesitates for several minutes; it seems an eternity to me. From time to time he turns his head a wee bit to the right, a wee bit to the left; actually he is looking well beyond me. I gain a momentary confidence, but then I perceive the danger once more looming large in front of me, and my hopes deflate. Meanwhile the silhouettes of my first pursuers appear on the ridge; apparently, now that so many hounds are on the scent, they have ceased to take their task seriously.

Suddenly at an angle behind me I hear the roar of an airplane and look up over my shoulder. My Stuka squadron is flying over the Dniester with a strong fighter escort and two Fieseler Storches. That means that Flight Officer Fischer has given the alarm and they are searching for me to get me out of this mess. Up there they have no suspicion that they are searching in quite the wrong direction, that I have long since been six miles farther south on this side of the river. At this distance I cannot even attract their attention; I dare not so much as lift my little finger. They make one circuit after another at different levels. Then they disappear heading east, and many of them will be thinking, "This time even he has had it." They fly away—home. Longingly I follow them with my eyes. You at least know that tonight you will sleep under shelter and will still be alive, whereas I cannot guess how many minutes more of life will be granted me. So I lie there shivering. The sun slowly sets. Why have I not yet been discovered?

Over the brow of the hill comes a column of Ivans, in Indian file, with horses and dogs. Once again I doubt God's justice, for now the gathering darkness should have given me protection. I can feel the earth tremble under their feet. My nerves are at snapping point. I squint behind me. At a distance of a hundred yards the men and animals file past me. Why does no dog pick up my scent? Why does no one find me? Shortly after passing me they deploy at two-yard intervals. If they had done this fifty yards sooner, they would have trodden on me. They vanish in the slowly falling dusk.

The last glow of evening yields to blue; feebly twinkling stars appear. My compass has no phosphorescent dial, but there is still light enough to read it. My general direction must remain the south. I see in that quarter of the sky a conspicuous and easily recognizable star with a little neighbor. I decide to adopt it as my lodestar. What constellation in the Russian firmament can it be? It is growing dark and I can no longer see anybody. I stand up, stiff, aching, hungry, thirsty. I remember my chocolate—but I left it in my fur jacket on the bank of the Dniester. Avoiding all roads, footpaths, villages, as Ivan is sure to have sentries posted there, I simply follow my star across country, up hill and down dale, over streams, bogs, marshes, and stubbly harvested maize fields. My bare feet are cut to ribbons. Again and again in the open fields I stub my toes against big stones. Gradually I lose all feeling in my feet. The will to live, to keep

my freedom, urges me on; they are indivisible; life without freedom is a hollow fruit. How deep is Ivan's penetration of our
front? How far have I still to travel? Wherever I hear a dog bark,
I make a detour, for the hamlets hereabouts are certainly not
inhabited by friends. Every now and again I can see gun flashes
on the distant horizon and hear a dull rumble; evidently our
boys have started an artillery bombardment. But that means the
Russian breakthrough has gone far. In the gullies which cut
through the occasionally rising ground, I often lose my footing
in the darkness and slump into a ditch where the gluey mud
stands knee-deep. It sucks me in so tightly that I no longer have
the strength to pull myself out and flop with the upper part of
my body sprawled on the bank of the ditch—my legs deep in
slime. Thus I lie exhausted, feeling like a battery gone dead.
After lying there for five minutes I am faintly recharged and
summon up the strength to crawl up the sloping bank. But re-
morselessly the same mishap is repeated very soon, at latest at
the next uneven ground. So it goes on till 9 P.M. Now I am done
in. Even after longish rests I cannot recover my strength. Without water and food and a pause for sleep it is impossible to carry
on. I decide to look for an isolated house.

I hear a dog barking in the distance and follow the sound.
Presumably I am not too far from a village. So after a while I
come to a lonely farmhouse and have considerable difficulty in
evading the yelping dog. I do not like its barking at all as I am
afraid it will alarm some picket in the nearby village. No one
opens the door to my knocking; perhaps there is no one there.
The same thing happens at a second farmhouse. I go on to a
third. When again nobody answers, impatience overcomes me
and I break a window in order to climb in. At this moment an
old woman carrying a smoky oil lamp opens the door. I am
already halfway through the window, but now I jump out again
and put my foot in the door. The old woman tries to shove me
out. I push resolutely past her. Turning round, I point in the
direction of the village and ask, *"Bolshewisti?"* She nods. Therefore I conclude that Ivan has occupied the village. The dim

lamplight only vaguely illumines the room: a table, a bench, an ancient cupboard. In the corner a gray-headed man is snoring on a rather lopsided trestle bed. He must be seventy. The couple share this wooden couch. In silence I cross the room and lay myself down on it. What can I say? I know no Russian. Meanwhile they have probably seen that I mean no harm. Barefoot and in rags, the tatters of my shirt sticky with coagulated blood, I am more likely to be a hunted quarry than a burglar. So I lie there. The old woman has gone back to bed beside me. Above our heads the feeble glimmer of the lamp. It does not occur to me to ask them whether they have anything to dress my shoulder or my lacerated feet. All I want is rest.

Now again I am tortured by thirst and hunger. I sit up on the bed and put my palms together in a begging gesture to the woman, at the same time making a dumb show of drinking and eating. After a brief hesitation she brings me a jug of water and a chunk of corn bread, slightly mildewed. Nothing ever tasted so good in all my life. With every swallow and bite I feel my strength reviving, as if the will to live and initiative has been restored to me. At first I eat ravenously, then munching thoughtfully, I review my situation and evolve a plan for the next hours. I have finished the bread and water.

I will rest till one o'clock. It is 9:20 P.M. Rest is essential. So I lie back again on the wooden boards between the old couple, half-awake and half-asleep. I wake up every quarter of an hour with the punctuality of a clock and check the time. In no event must I waste too much of the sheltering dark in sleep; I must put as many miles as possible behind me on my journey south. Nine forty-five, 10 o'clock, 10:15, and so on; 12:45, 1 o'clock—getting-up time! I steal out; the old woman shuts the door behind me. I have already stumbled down a step. Is it the drunkenness of sleep, the pitch-dark night, or the wet step?

It is raining. I cannot see my hand before my face. My star has disappeared. Now how am I to find my bearings? Then I remember that I was previously running with the wind behind me. I must again keep it in my back to reach the south. Or has it veered? I am still among isolated farm buildings; here I am sheltered from the wind. As it blows from a constantly changing direction, I am afraid of moving in a circle. Inky darkness, obstacles; I barge into something and hurt my shins again. There is a chorus of barking dogs, therefore still houses, the village. I can only pray I do not run into a Russian sentry the next minute. At last I am out in the open again where I can turn my back to the wind with certainty. I am also rid of the curs. I plod on as before, up hill, down dale, up, down, maize fields, stones, and woods where it is more difficult to keep direction because you can hardly feel the wind among the trees. On the horizon I see the incessant flash of guns and hear their steady rumble. They serve to guide me on my course. Shortly after 3 A.M. there is a gray light on my left—the day is breaking. A good check, for now I am sure that the wind has not veered and I have been moving south all right.

I have now covered at least six miles. I guess I must have done ten or twelve yesterday, so that I should be sixteen or eighteen miles south of the Dniester.

In front of me rises a hill of about seven hundred feet. I climb it. Perhaps from the top I shall have a panorama and shall be able to make out some conspicuous points. It is now daylight, but I can discover no particular landmarks from the top; three tiny villages below me several miles away to my right and left. What interests me is to find that my hill is the beginning of a ridge running north to south, so I am keeping my direction. The slopes are smooth and bare of timber so that it is easy to keep a lookout for anyone coming up them. It must be possible to descry any movement from up here; pursuers would have to climb the hill and that would be a substantial handicap. Who at the moment suspects my presence here? My heart is light because although it is day, I feel confident I shall be able to push on south for a good few miles. I would like to put as many as possible behind me with the least delay.

I estimate the length of the ridge as about six miles; that is interminably long. But—is it really so long? After all, I encourage myself, you have run a six-mile race—how often?—and with a time of forty minutes. What you were able to do then in forty minutes, you must now be able to do in sixty—for the prize is your liberty. So just imagine you are running a marathon race!

I must be a fit subject for a crazy artist as I plod on with my marathon stride along the crest of the ridge—in rags—on bare, bleeding feet—my arm hugged stiffly to my side to ease the pain of my aching shoulder.

You must make it . . . keep your mind on the race . . . and run . . . and keep on running.

Every now and again I have to change to a jog-trot and drop into a walk for perhaps a hundred yards. Then I start running again . . . it should not take more than an hour . . .

Now unfortunately I have to leave the protective heights, for the way leads downhill. Ahead of me stretches a broad plain, a slight depression in exactly the same direction continues the line of the ridge. Dangerous because here I can be more suddenly surprised. Besides, the time is getting on for seven o'clock, and therefore unpleasant encounters are more likely.

Once again my battery is exhausted. I must drink . . . eat . . . rest. Up to now I have not seen a living soul. Take precautions? What can I do? I am unarmed; I am only thirsty and hungry. Prudence? Prudence is a virtue, but thirst and hunger are an elemental urge. Need makes one careless. Two farmhouses appear on the horizon out of the morning mist. I must effect an entry. . . .

I stop for a moment at the door of a barn and poke my head round the corner to investigate; the building yawns in my face. Nothing but emptiness. The place is stripped bare, no harness, no farm implements, no living creature—stay!—a rat darts from one corner to another. A large heap of maize leaves lies rotting in the barnyard. I grub amongst them with greedy fingers. If only I could find a couple of corncobs . . . or only a few grains of corn. . . . But I find nothing . . . I grub and grub and grub . . . not a thing!

Suddenly I am aware of a rustling noise behind me. Some figures are creeping stealthily past the door of another barn: Russians, or refugees as famished as I am and on the self-same quest? Or are they looters in search of further booty? I fare the same at the next farm. Here I go through the maize heaps with the greatest care—nothing. Disappointedly I reflect, if all the food is gone, I must at least make up for it by resting. I scrape myself a hole in the pile of maize leaves and am just about to lie down in it when I hear a fresh noise: a farm wagon is rumbling past along a lane; on the box a man in a tall fur cap, beside him a girl. When there is a girl, there can be nothing untoward, so I go up to them. From the black fur cap I guess the man is a Rumanian peasant.

I ask the girl, "Have you anything to eat?"

"If you care to eat this . . ." She pulls some stale cakes out of her bag. The peasant stops the horse. Not until then does it occur to me that I have put my question in German and have received a German answer.

"How do you come to know German?"

The girl tells me that she has come with the German soldiers from Dnepropetrovsk and that she learned it there. Now she wants to stay with the Rumanian peasant sitting beside her. They are fleeing from the Russians.

"But you are going straight in their direction." I can see by their faces that they do not believe me. "Have the Ruskis already reached the town over there?"

"No, that is Floresti."

This unexpected reply is like a tonic. The town must lie on the Balti-Floresti railway line, which I know.

"Can you tell me, girl, if there are still any German soldiers there?"

"No, the Germans have left, but there may be Rumanian soldiers."

"Thank you and God speed."

I wave to the disappearing wagon. Now I can already hear myself being asking later why I did not "requisition" the wagon . . . the idea never entered my mind. For are the pair not fugitives like me? And must I not offer thanks to God that I have so far escaped from danger?

After my excitement has died down, a brief exhaustion overcomes me. For those last six miles I have been conscious of violent pain; all of a sudden the feeling returns to my lacerated feet, my shoulder hurts with every step I take. I meet a stream of refugees with handcarts and the bare necessities they have salvaged, all in panic-stricken haste.

On the outskirts of Floresti two soldiers are standing on the scarp of a sandpit; German uniforms? Another few yards and my hope is confirmed. An unforgettable sight!

I call up to them, "Come here!"

They call down, "What do you mean: come here! Who are you anyway, fellow?"

"I am Squadron Leader Rudel."

"Nah! No squadron leader ever looked like you do."

I have no identification papers, but I have in my pocket the Knight's Cross with Oak Leaves and Swords. I pull it out of my pocket and show it to them. On seeing it the corporal says:

"Then we'll take your word for it."

"Is there a German *Kommandantur*?"

"No, only the rear-guard HQ of a dressing station."

That is where I will go. They fall in on either side of me and take me there. I am now crawling rather than walking. A doctor separates my shirt and trousers from my body with a pair of scissors, the rags are sticking to my skin; he paints the raw wounds of my feet with iodine and dresses my shoulder. During this treatment I devour the sausage of my life.

"What clothes do you intend to wear?" the doctor asks me. All my garments have been cut to ribbons. "We have none to lend you." They wrap me naked in a blanket and off we go in an automobile to Balti. We drive up in front of the control hut on the airfield. But what is this? My squadron officer, Pilot Officer Ebersbach, opens the door of the car:

"Pilot Officer Ebersbach, in command of the Third Squadron advance party moving to Jassy."

A soldier follows him out carrying some clothes for me. This means that my naked trip from Floresti has already been reported to Balti from there by telephone, and Ebersbach happened to be in the control hut when the message came through. He has been informed that his colleague who has been given up for dead will shortly arrive in his birthday suit. I climb into a Ju-52 and fly to Rauchowka to rejoin the squadron. Here the telephone has been buzzing, the news has spread like wildfire, and the wing cook, Runkel, already has a cake in the oven. I look into grinning faces, the squadron is on parade. I feel reborn, as if a miracle had happened. Life has been restored to me, and this reunion with my comrades is the most glorious prize for the hardest race of my life.

The Greatest Ace

from *The Blond Knight of Germany*

BY RAYMOND F. TOLIVER AND TREVOR J. CONSTABLE

The Luftwaffe's Erich Hartmann was the most successful fighter pilot in the history of aerial warfare. In his two and a half years of combat during World War II, he flew 1,405 combat missions and engaged the enemy 825 times. He shot down 91 twin-engined aircraft and 261 fighters—a total of 352 confirmed kills. Ten of his victims were P-51 Mustangs flown by Americans—the rest of his kills were flown by Soviet pilots. In our era of ever-smaller air forces flying ever more expensive aircraft, it is inconceivable that a future fighter pilot could break Erich Hartmann's record.

Although Hartmann was shot down many times, he survived the war and was captured by an American tank unit. He was just twenty-three years old. The Americans turned Hartmann over to the Soviets, who staged a kangaroo political trial for the dreaded "Black Devil of the South" and imprisoned him in a slave-labor camp for ten and a half years. Released in 1955, he resumed his career in the new Luftwaffe and finally retired as a colonel in 1970.

Hartmann was the consummate professional aerial killer. Dogfights were not his style. He preferred to single out an unwary adversary, get in very close and shoot, then retire. Wars cannot be won in a day. Hartmann once explained, "Every day kill just one, rather than today five, tomorrow ten . . . that is enough for you. Then your nerves are calm and you can sleep good, you have your drink in the evening and the next morning you are fit again."

In the excerpt that follows, we meet the master learning his trade.

ERICH HARTMANN DID NOT SCORE HIS SECOND VICTORY UNTIL 27 February 1943. Soon afterward, a new and dynamic personality appeared on the Seventh Squadron scene, an officer who was destined to give Erich solid impetus toward the top—1st Lt. Walter Krupinski. Appointed to replace Captain Sommer, Krupinski was the same smiling tiger who had so narrowly escaped from his crash-landed Me-109 the day Erich arrived at the front at Maykop. The new CO of Seventh Squadron took over his command in typical fashion, earning Erich's immediate respect and awe.

Krupinski arrived at Taman Kuban, introduced himself as the new squadron commander, and asked immediately for a serviceable fighter. He went up, was promptly shot down, and bailed out. Brought back to the field by car, he demanded another Me-109, took off again immediately, and this time scored two kills, returning intact to the airfield. There was no doubt about this squadron commander: he was a tiger, and he obviously didn't need any tightly ordered discipline in leading his soldiers. Erich liked Krupinski immediately.

The new squadron commander's next request was for a wingman to be assigned to him. His hell-for-leather reputation had preceded him, and the NCO pilots were reluctant to assume the responsibility of protecting him. Paule Rossmann came to Erich as a representative of the sergeants.

"Would you please fly as First Lieutenant Krupinski's wingman, Erich?"

"Why? Don't the sergeants want the job?"

Rossmann appeared a little embarrassed.

"The old-timers say that he is a sharp officer," said Paule, "but he can't fly. They think it is better all around if an officer is his wingman. Will you do it?"

Erich found Rossmann hard to refuse. He agreed to see Krupinski. Erich was unhappy about the whole thing when he offered himself to the new squadron commander, because many of the sergeants were decorated veterans and usually knew a good fighter pilot from a bad one. Erich felt a little like a lamb going to the slaughter. Krupinski's bullish bluntness did little to ease Erich's mind.

A strapping, five-foot-nine-inch dynamo, Krupinski was already famous in the Luftwaffe by the spring of 1943 as one of its outstanding characters and playboys. Walter Krupinski was a ripe, mature personality who looked and acted—on the military side of his life at least—far beyond his years. After six months' duty in the Reich Labor Service he was drafted as a *Fahnenjunker* (cadet) in the Luftwaffe on 1 September 1939.

He had been flying as a senior cadet, and later as a commissioned officer, since the end of 1941 and had once flown as the great "Macky" Steinhoff's wingman. He was a successful and famous JG-52 ace with over seventy victories at the time Erich Hartmann offered his services as a wingman. Krupinski was destined to end the war as the fifteenth-ranked fighter ace of the world with 197 victories, and at the surrender he was a member of Adolf Galland's elite Squadron of Experts in JV-44, flying the Me-262 jet fighter.

Krupinski's exploits through the years had earned him a reputation for toughness that preceded him to Taman. He had a penchant for getting himself into impossible situations, and for wounds, bailouts, and crash landings. He once belly-landed near the Kuban River, coming down in a meadow which the German infantry had mined. As his shattered kite slid along the grass, it tripped a series of mines, and Krupinski immediately concluded that he was being bombarded by artillery.

Krupinski's first impulse was to jump out of the plane and bolt for cover. His life was saved by a German infantry sergeant who bawled out the explosive facts about the field to him as he clambered clear of the cockpit. The soldiers took two hours to extricate him, walking out to him and testing the ground with sticks as they came. His career was a skein of similar incidents, culminating in the last months of the war when he was enjoying himself on recuperation leave at the Fighter Pilots' Home in Bad Wiessee. At Steinhoff's urging, he took reluctant leave of a big barrel of cognac provided for the pilots and flew the ME-262 in Galland's JV-44. Krupinski's crash arrival at Maykop, with the burning fighter spewing live ammunition in all directions, was fresh in Erich's mind as he confronted this formidable personality.

"Sir, my name is Hartmann. I am to be your wingman."

"Been out here long?"

"No, sir. About three months."

"Any victories?"

"Two, sir."

"Who have you been flying with?"

"Rossmann mainly, but also with Dammers, Zwernemann, and Grislawski."

"They're all good men. We'll get along all right. That's all for now."

Walter Krupinski retired as a lieutenant general and is living in Neunkirchen-Seelscheid in West Germany. His only recollection of his first meeting with Erich Hartmann is an indelible impression of Erich's extreme youth.

"He appeared not much more than a mere baby. So young and full of life. As he walked away from me that first day, I thought to myself, 'Such a young face.' "

This same impression of Erich was shared at this time by Capt. Guenther Rall, who had become *Gruppenkommandeur* of III/JG-52 in place of von Bonin, in the same shuffle that brought Krupinski to command No. 7 Squadron. Later we will make fuller contact with Guenther Rall as one of the JG-52's greatest aces, but his recollection of Erich at this time parallels that of Krupinski.

"I saw him [Erich] first in the Seventh Squadron mess, and I thought only, 'What a young boy—a baby.' He stood out first for his extreme youth, but quickly came to everyone's attention because he was a good marksman."

Erich and Krupinski took to the air the following day with disturbing initial impressions of each other. Erich was sure that he was flying with a wild tiger who could not fly, and Krupinski was sure he was flying with a baby on his wing. The first mission was sufficient to change Erich's mind about his new leader.

The new squadron commander waded into the enemy like a barroom brawler, a batteringly aggressive and fearless pilot who not only flew like a demon, but also kept a clear tactical head. Krupinski's purported inability to fly was obviously a yarn without foundation. Nevertheless, Krupinski could not shoot straight and most of his ammunition went wide.* Krupinski's weakness was therefore supplemented by Erich's strength as a marksman, for Erich had been a natural sharpshooter from the day he riddled his first drogue in training. Together, Krupinski and Erich formed a winning combat team.

Erich began by sticking close to Krupinski and, as they entered shooting range, decreased his airspeed and went to his leader's reverse as he pulled up or broke. This gave Erich a few seconds to shoot, "filling in the holes Kruppi had left." A couple of additional victories came this way. Soon they realized that they could depend on each other, and as Krupinski coached Erich, they began to read each other's mind in combat, as have all the great fighter teams in history.

When Krupinski went into an attack, Erich would stay "on the perch," watching his leader's back and telling him what to do if another enemy aircraft intervened. During Erich's attacks, Krupinski stayed on the perch and called out instructions to Erich to improve his attack or take evasive action. Erich heard Krupinski's voice on the R/T rasping the same order over and over again:

"Hey, Bubi! Get in closer. You're opening fire too far out."

Erich was emulating Rossmann, with long-range attacks. He was hitting well every time he fired, which impressed the poorer-shooting Krupinski, but it was obvious he would do even better if he closed in on his targets. As Krupinski later said, "We had so many young pilots come to us who could not hit anything

---

*Straight shot or not, the indomitable Krupinski shot down 197 enemy aircraft in slightly over 1,100 sorties.

in the air that Erich stood out immediately with his accurate long-range gunnery."

From Krupinski's constantly calling him Bubi in the air came Erich's nickname, which he has retained to this day. The whole squadron was soon calling him Bubi, and the name stuck.

Krupinski's steady urgings, "Hey, Bubi, get in closer," encouraged Erich to close his ranges. The closer he got to his foe, the more devastating the effect when he fired. Few shots went wide. Often the other aircraft could be seen to stagger under the multigun blast at close range. Even more often, there was an explosion in the air as the other machine disintegrated. When they went down that way, they would never come back up again.

Soon Erich had fully developed the tactics of air fighting from which he would never subsequently depart. The magical four steps were: "See—Decide—Attack—Reverse, or 'Coffee Break.' " In lay terms, spot the enemy, decide if he can be attacked and surprised, attack him, and break away immediately after striking; or if he spots you before you strike, take a "coffee break"— wait—pull off the enemy and don't get into a turning battle with a foe who knows you are there. The rigid observance of this tactical sequence carried Erich Hartmann to the top.

Air battles brought Erich into contact with every conceivable situation in air-to-air combat. He was not only confident of his abilities—without which no fighter pilot could ever succeed— but also extended his skills through experience. He could spot aircraft at phenomenal distances, sometimes minutes before anyone else airborne with him, and often intuit his foe's intentions. He avoided the dogfight in favor of the lethal efficiency of hit and run. The "See—Decide—Attack—Break" was a sequence never to be broken. Following it meant success, departing from it meant failure and even doom.

For joining and breaking combat Erich developed practical rules that kept him alive and unwounded while the Russian aircraft continued to fall. Under blue-sky conditions, he found the best mode of attack the high and fast approach. Where overcast

prevailed, he made his strike low and fast. He waited whenever
and wherever possible for this one fast blow rather than make
his attack under less than ideal conditions. This was his "coffee
break." Surprise was the crucial element of the successful
bounce.

In winter, with Karaya One camouflaged white and the sky
overcast, the low-to-high attack pass proved extremely successful. He conquered his earlier tendency to slacken speed when
closing in, going right to his foe at the shortest possible distance
before firing. From fifty yards the power of Karaya One's arma-
ment was devastating. Kills were scored with minimum
ammunition.

The traditional tactic of turning with an enemy was something
Erich had abandoned. Dogfighters could do it their way, and
most of them loved the dogfight. Erich preferred his own methods. After his brief and violent attack, he would roll over wing
deep and dive about two thousand feet under his foe if altitude
permitted, pulling up from behind and below for a second attack. In this position, he could stay with any turn the enemy
might attempt, and after firing, the Blond Knight was on his way
upstairs for a third pass should his foe survive the second assault.
Each pass was a repetition of the "See—Decide—Attack—
Break" cycle.

In the Eastern Front air battles, the Germans were almost
always heavily outnumbered. Consequently, Erich himself was
often bounced by Russian fighters. In the same way as he evolved
his deadly attack tactics, he developed a set of defensive rules.
Just as his attack methods rolled up his score past all the old
dogfighters, so did his defense tactics keep him from being
wounded. The two sets of tactics went hand in hand and led to
his being consistently in action. Luck was almost always with
him, but his penetrant analytical ability was ever Lady Luck's
bridegroom. Physical survival and a high score were the children
of the union.

When a Russian bounced him from behind, to one side, and
above—from "the perch"—Erich would go into a hard climbing

turn, turning *into* his enemy's firing pass. Where a Red pilot came from below and behind, Erich would go hard left or right and down, again breaking into his enemy's pass, then immediately using negative g's to lose the enemy.

Erich's coolness soon became a legend among all who flew with him. He learned to observe his Russian foes as they came in to the attack and meet their thrusts with appropriate parries. Resisting the urge to turn while an attacking Russian pilot was still outside firing range required coolness. The concept of simply sitting there while an enemy aircraft rushed in with a battery of guns charged was hard to accept in theory—and even tougher to execute in actual combat. Flying straight and level, using the rudder for slight slip, and waiting for the enemy to commit himself soon convinced the Blond Knight that he could avoid being hit under these circumstances. Vital information could often be gleaned in the split seconds before the attacking Russian opened fire.

Inexperienced or inferior pilots always gave themselves away by opening fire too early. Erich discovered that in such instances he could soon change his role from defender to attacker, but if the Red pilot held his fire and kept closing in, then it was certain that an old-timer was at the controls. A battle was then in the offing.

Erich developed only one rule for breaking away as a last-ditch maneuver, and that was to execute a movement where possible with negative g's. An attacking pilot expects his quarry to turn tighter and try to outturn him—the classic dogfight. The attacking pilot must turn even tighter in order to pull firing lead on his quarry. As a result, his quarry disappears under the nose of the attacker. At that moment the quarry can escape by shoving forward on the stick and kicking bottom rudder. The forces on his aircraft change from plus 5 g's to minus one or minus one and a half g's. This escape maneuver is almost impossible for the attacker to see or follow until it is too late. Erich made good use of this escape tactic, which threw the attacker instantly from advantage to complex disadvantage.

The attacker was first of all placed at the psychological disadvantage imposed by negative g's—weightlessness. Physically he was disadvantaged, being lifted from his seat to hang against his belt—an impossible situation in which to track a target, due to the higher negative attack angle. Finally, the erstwhile attacker lost his overview of the area, and steering the aircraft in the right direction for continued pursuit became guesswork.

Erich reserved these tactics for last-ditch situations. In all other attacks, his rule was to turn into his assailant's turn, using positive g's. He called these "My Personal Twist Regulations," and he taught them to his young wingmen to help keep them alive. His tactical skill in attack and defense took him through more than eight hundred aerial battles without a scratch—too stunning an achievement to be attributed to blind luck.

Once he clarified his tactics and got some experience, Erich's kill tally rose so quickly that he became a subject of discussion among other pilots. His consistent string of victories and seemingly charmed life made him a focus of competitive attention as 1943 wore on. There were even some pilots who thought that there must be some trickery involved in Erich's success.

Sgt. Carl Junger of the Seventh Squadron, who had flown as Erich's wingman, was invited with two other pilots to visit the nearby Eighth Squadron mess. This social gathering had a noteworthy sequel, arising out of squadron rivalry. During festivities, Junger heard Erich Hartmann's name mentioned in some of the noisy conversation. Second Lt. Friedrich "Fritz" Obleser, who had come to JG-52 about the same time as Erich, had scored well at the outset of his career, while Erich was conquering his buck fever and learning the tricks of Rossmann and the dogfighters. Once Erich settled down to lead his own elements, he rocketed past Obleser in the scoring. Fritz was expressing his skepticism about Erich's consistent skein of kills.

Junger as Erich's wingman had been witness to many of Erich's kills. He was annoyed by the implication in Obleser's remarks. The next day, Junger told the Blond Knight what Obleser had said. Erich thanked Junger and made up his mind in a flash about what should be done. He went straight to Maj. Guenther Rall, the *Gruppenkommandeur*, under whose command both the Seventh and Eighth Squadrons were operating.

"Fritz Obleser of the Eighth Squadron has been saying to other pilots that he doesn't believe my kills are genuine."

Rall's eyebrows went up. "Well, I *know* they are genuine. I see the witness reports and all the details. What do you want me to do about it?"

"I would like to have Obleser fly as wingman on a few operations, sir. That is, if it can be arranged."

Rall nodded. Pilots locking horns was nothing new to him. "Of course, I'll issue the orders. He can come down tomorrow."

A somewhat embarrassed Obleser duly reported the following day for duty as Erich's wingman. Since his temporary transfer was for observational purposes, he was assigned to the better vantage point offered by the second element in Erich's *Schwarm*. He flew two missions and saw two of Erich's devastating close-in downings, in which the Blond Knight blew up his opponents' aircraft.

On the ground, the convinced Obleser signed the two kill confirmation claims as the official witness. Fritz apologized in manly fashion for his earlier criticism and was allowed to return to the Eighth Squadron with his story. No further expressions of skepticism about Bubi Hartmann's victories came from any neighboring unit.

Cross of Lead

from *The First and the Last*

BY ADOLF GALLAND

*You met Adolf Galland earlier in this book on a bad day in
which he was shot down twice in an excerpt from* The Greatest
Aces *by Edward H. Sims. Here Galland tells of flying jet fighters, Me-262s, in the final days of the war in what he well
knew was a hopeless cause, and of being bagged again, this
time by an American in a P-51 Mustang.*

THE LAST AIR BATTLE OF THIS WAR OVER GERMANY IN WHICH THE
Americans suffered impressive losses was delivered by the German fighter arm on March 18, 1945, over Berlin. The capital of
the Reich was attacked by twelve hundred bombers that had an
escort of fourteen fighter squadrons of P-51s. Although many
flak batteries had already been removed to the nearby Eastern
Front, sixteen bombers were so heavily hit that they had to make
emergency landings behind the Soviet front line. The enemy
suffered much greater losses at the hands of the jet fighters of
the JG-7. From American flight reports one can see that the
Me-262 broke again and again with ease through the American
fighter screen and shot down one bomber after the other from
the tightly closed formations despite an inferiority of one hundred to one. Besides those shot down by flak, the Americans
had to report a loss of twenty-five bombers and five fighter
planes. The next day the Americans again suffered losses from
German jet fighters, while our piston-engined fighters could
achieve nothing against the mass of the Allied fighter escort.
Doolittle and Tedder now demanded decisive measures to prevent the operation of German jet fighters, without stating what
these measures should be.

In January 1945 we started on the formation of my unit that Hitler had ordered. It spread quickly through the fighter arm that our Forty-fourth Squadron was taking shape at Brandenburg-Briest. Our official nomination was a JV-44.

Steinhoff was in charge of retraining the pilots. Lützow came to us from Italy. Barkhorn, who had scored more than three hundred kills in the east, Hohagen, Schnell, and Krupinski were coaxed out of hospital. Many reported without consent or transfer orders. Most of them had been in action since the first day of the war, and all of them had been wounded. All of them bore the scars of war and displayed the highest medals. The Knight's Cross was, so to speak, the badge of our unit. Now, after a long period of technical and numerical inferiority, they wanted once more to experience the feeling of air superiority. They wanted to be known as the first jet boys of the last fighter pilots of the Luftwaffe. For this they were ready once more to chance sacrificing their lives.

Soon after receiving the first planes we were stationed at Munich-Riem. In the early hours of the morning of March 31, 1945, the JV-44 took off in close formation, and forty-two minutes later the planes landed in Munich. They had covered the distance of about three hundred miles in record time.

Here in Munich the unit took on its final shape. The Squadron of Experts, as we were called, had as pilots one lieutenant general, two colonels, one lieutenant colonel, three majors, five captains, eight lieutenants, and about the same number of second lieutenants. None of us imagined that we were able to give to the war the much-quoted "turn." The magic word *jet* had brought us together to experience once more *"die grosse Fliegerei."* Our last operation was anything but a fresh and gay hunting. We not only battled against technical, tactical, and supply difficulties, we also lacked a clear picture of the air situation of the floods coming from the west—a picture absolutely necessary for the success of an operation. Every day the fronts moved in closer from three sides. But worst of all our field was under continuous observation by an overwhelming majority of American fighters. During one raid we were hit three times very heavily. Thousands of workers had to be mobilized to keep open a landing strip between the bomb craters.

Surprisingly I was called by Göring to the Obersalzberg: it must have been somewhere around April 10. To my amazement he received me with the greatest civility, inquired after the progress of our initial actions, and gave me a restricted confirmation that my prediction concerning the use of bombers with the Me-262 in the defense of the Reich had been correct. This indicated that the Reichsmarshal had begun to realize that after all I had been right throughout all those sharp clashes of opinion of the last months. This was the last time I saw Göring.

Four weeks before the collapse of the armed forces the fighter arm was still in a position to represent a factor that could not be overlooked. Operations from Riem started despite all resistance and difficulties. Naturally we were able to send up only small units. On landing, the aircraft had to be towed immediately off the field. They were dispersed over the countryside and had to be completely camouflaged. Bringing the aircraft onto the field and taking off became more and more difficult: eventually it was a matter of luck. One raid followed another.

In this situation the safety of the personnel was paramount and came before any orders to clear the airfield. Each pilot was responsible for his own cover on the airfield and had to dig his own foxhole. When it came to physical work, you cannot imagine anything more lazy than a fighter pilot in his sixth year of service. My pilots moaned terribly about the stony ground at Riem. Returning from a mission, I was standing with them on our western airstrip, watching the bombers attacking railway stations in Munich in single waves. Suddenly someone called, *"Achtung! Bombenangriff!"* Already the ugly finger of death, as we called the markers of the daylight raiders, were groping for our aerodrome. I chased after one of my pilots, who slithered into a nearby hole he had dug for himself. Hellishly narrow, I thought . . . oh, a single foxhole. It was very shallow. Then the first carpet of bombs roared down, passed over our heads. Nauseating, the whistle, the explosion, the blast, the tremor of the ground. A brief pause occurred after the attack of the first formation. I was lying on top of a sergeant. It was Knier. He was shaking, but in answer to my question he insisted that he was no more afraid than I was.

Our hole had a cover. A few splinters had struck this lid with a loud metallic clang. My back was pressed against it. "Knier, what's this on my back?"

"One-hundred-pound bomb, Herr General," was the prompt reply.

I certainly began to shake. Another five salvos followed at short intervals. Outside there was smoke, debris, craters, fire, and destruction. All Germans had experienced this during the last years of the war—in the cities, in the factories, on the battlefield, on ships and U-boats: bombs, bombs, bombs! But it was an awkward feeling to be in the middle of a raid and, what is more, to be sheltered by one's own bombs.

During these last weeks of the war we were able to fit out some aircraft with additional weapons, which gave a greater firing power to the Me-262: R4M rockets of 3-cm caliber, and 500-g explosives. A single hit from these was enough to bring down a multiengined bomber. They were fixed beneath the wing in two racks that carried twenty-four rockets. In a feverish hurry our mechanics and servicing crew loaded up a few jet fighters. I took off in one of them.

In the district of Landsberg on the Lech I met a formation of about sixteen Marauders. We called these twin-engined bombers *Halbstarke*. I opened from a distance of about six hundred yards, firing in half a second a salvo of twenty-four rockets into the close-flying formation. I observed two certain hits. One bomber immediately caught fire and exploded; a second lost large parts of its right tail unit and wing and began to spiral earthward. In the meantime the three other planes that had taken off with me had also successfully attacked. My accompanying pilot, Edward Schallnoser, who once over Riem had rammed a Lightning because in his excitement he could not fire, waded into the Marauders with all his rockets. That evening he reported back to his quarters, parachute under his arm and a twisted leg.

Our impression of the efficiency of this new weapon was indescribable. The rockets could be fired outside the effective range of the defensive fire of the bombers. A well-aimed salvo would probably hit several bombers simultaneously. That was the way to break up formations. But this was the end of April 1945! In the middle of our breakup, at the beginning of our collapse! It does not bear thinking about what we could have done had we had those jet fighters, 3-cm quick-firing cannons, and 5-cm rockets years ago—before our war potential had been smashed, before indescribable misery had come over Germany through the raids. We dared not think about it. Now we could do nothing but fly and fight and do our duty as fighter pilots to the last.

Service in action still demanded heavy and grievous losses. On April 18, Steinhoff crashed on a takeoff but managed to free himself from the burning wreckage of his jet plane with very severe burns. A few days later Günther Lützow did not return from his mission. Long after the end of the war we were still hoping that this splendid officer might not have left us forever. In the same spirit and with the same devotion many more young pilots of our unit fell.

But the fate of Germany was sealed. On April 25 the American and the Soviet soldiers shook hands at Torgau on the Elbe. The last defensive ring of Berlin was soon penetrated. The Red flag was flying over the Ballhausplatz in Vienna. The German front in Italy collapsed. On Pilsen fell the last bomb of the 2,755,000 tons which the Western Allies had dropped on Europe during five years of war.

At the moment I called my pilots together and said to them, "Militarily speaking the war is lost. Even our action here cannot change anything. . . . I shall continue to fight, because operating with the Me-262 has got hold of me, because I am proud to belong to the last fighter pilots of the German Luftwaffe. . . . Only those who feel the same are to go on flying with me."

* * *

The harsh reality of the war had finally decided the question "Bomber or fighter action by Me-262?" in our favor. The leaders were completely occupied with themselves in Berlin and at other places. Numerous departments, which up to now had interfered with allocation and the operation of jet fighters, ceased to function or did not come through anymore. Commanders of the bombers, reconnaissance, combat fighters, night fighters, and sundry testing units that had been fitted out with the coveted Me-262 passed their aircraft on to us. From all sides we were presented with jet fighters. Finally we had seventy aircraft.

On April 26, I set out on my last mission of the war. I led six jet fighters of the JV-44 against a formation of Marauders. Our own little directing post brought us well into contact with the enemy. The weather: varying clouds at different altitudes, with gaps, ground visible in about only three-tenths of the operational area.

I sighted the enemy formation in the district of Neuburg on the Danube. Once again I noticed how difficult it was, with such great difference of speed and with clouds over the landmarks, to find the relative flying direction between one's own plane and that of the enemy, and how difficult it was to judge the approach. This difficulty had already driven Lützow to despair. He had discussed it repeatedly with me, and every time he missed his run-in, this most successful fighter commodore blamed his own inefficiency as a fighter pilot. Had there been any need for more confirmation as to the hopelessness of operations with the Me-262 by bomber pilots, our experiences would have sufficed.

But now there was no time for such considerations. We were flying in an almost opposite direction to the Marauder formation. Each second meant that we were three hundred yards nearer. I will not say that I fought this action ideally, but I led my formation to a fairly favorable firing position. Safety catch off the gun and rocket switch! Already at a great distance we met with considerable defensive fire. As usual in a dogfight, I was tense and excited: I forgot to release the second safety catch for the rockets. They did not go off. I was in the best firing position, I had aimed accurately and pressed my thumb flat on the release button—with no result. Maddening for any fighter pilot! Anyhow my four 3-cm cannons were working. They had so much more firing power than we had been used to so far. At that moment, close below me, Schallnoser, the jet-rammer, whizzed past. In ramming he made no distinction between friend or foe.

This engagement had lasted only a fraction of a second—an important second to be sure. One Marauder of the last string was on fire and exploded. Now I attacked another bomber in the van of the formation. It was heavily hit as I passed close above it. During this breakthrough I got a few minor hits from the defensive fire. But now I wanted to know definitely what was happening to the second bomber I had hit. I was not quite clear if it had crashed. So far I had not noticed any fighter escort.

Above the formation I had attacked last, I banked steeply to the left, and at this moment it happened: a hail of fire enveloped me. A Mustang had caught me napping. A sharp rap hit my right knee. The instrument panel with its indispensable instruments was shattered. The right engine was also hit. Its metal covering worked loose in the wind and was partly carried away. Now the left engine was hit, too. I could hardly hold her in the air.

In this embarrassing situation I had only one wish: to get out of this crate, which now apparently was only good for dying in. But then I was paralyzed by the terror of being shot while parachuting down. Experience had taught us that we jet-fighter pilots had to reckon on this. I soon discovered that my battered Me-262 could be steered again after some adjustments. After a dive through the layer of cloud I saw the autobahn below me; ahead of me lay Munich and to the left Riem. In a few seconds I was over the airfield. It was remarkably quiet and dead below. Having regained my self-confidence, I gave the customary wing wobble and started banking to come in. One engine did not react at all to the throttle. I could not reduce it. Just before the edge of the airfield I therefore had to cut out both engines. A long trail of smoke drifted behind me. Only at this moment I noticed that

Thunderbolts in a low-level attack were giving our airfield the works. Now I had no choice. I had not heard the warnings of our ground post because my wireless had faded out when I was hit. There remained only one thing to do: straight down into the fireworks! Touching down, I realized that the tire of my nosewheel was flat. It rattled horribly as the earth again received me at a speed of 150 mph on the small landing strip.

Brake! Brake! The kite would not stop! But at last I was out of the kite and into the nearest bomb crater. There were plenty of them on our runways. Bombs and rockets exploded all around; bursts of shells from the Thunderbolts whistled and banged. A new low-level attack. Out of the fastest fighter in the world into a bomb crater, that was an unutterably wretched feeling.

Through all the fireworks an armored tractor came rushing across to me. It pulled up sharply close by. One of our mechanics. Quickly I got in behind him. He turned and raced off on the shortest route away from the airfield. In silence I slapped him on the shoulder. He understood better what I wanted to say than any words about the unity between flying and ground personnel could have expressed.

The other pilots who took part in this operation were directed to neighboring airfields or came into Riem after the attack. We reported five certain kills without loss to ourselves.

I had to go to Munich to a hospital for treatment of my scratched knee. The X ray showed two splinters in the kneecap. It was put in plaster. A fine business!

The enemy, advancing from the north, had already crossed the Danube at several places. The JV-44 prepared its last transfer. Bär, who had come to us with the remnants of his Volksfighter test commando, took over the command in my place. About sixty jet fighters flew to Salzburg. Orders came from the Reichskanzlei and from the Luftwaffe staff in Berchtesgaden for an immediate transfer to Prague in order to pursue from there the completely hopeless fight for Berlin. The execution of this order was delayed until it became purposeless.

On May 3 the aircraft of the JV-44 were standing on the

aerodrome of Salzburg without any camouflage. American fighters circled overhead. They did not shoot, they did not drop any bombs; they obviously hoped soon to be flying the German jet fighters that had given them so much trouble. Salzburg prepared for the capitulation. The advanced units of Devers's army approached the town. As the rattle of the first tank was heard on the airfield, there was no other possibility left: our jet fighters went up in flames.

The Last Samurai

from *Samurai!*

BY SABURO SAKAI WITH MARTIN CAIDIN AND FRED SAITO

Saburo Sakai was the highest-scoring Japanese ace to survive World War II. In 1957 Sakai collaborated with American aviation writer Martin Caidin and Japanese journalist Fred Saito to write his autobiography, Samurai!—one of the few truly great aviation books to come out of World War II.

Sakai had been credited with fifty-seven victories against Allied planes (he would end the war credited with sixty-four kills) when he flew a Zero south from Rabaul on August 7, 1942, to contest the American landing on Guadalcanal. Twenty-seven Betty bombers and seventeen Zeros made the 550-nautical-mile trip south.

After shooting down a Wildcat and a Dauntless, Sakai closed relentlessly on the rear of a formation of eight American planes that he thought were F4F-4 Wildcat fighters. He was wrong. The planes were SBD Dauntless dive bombers, and they all contained rear gunners, each armed with twin .30-caliber machine guns.

A horrified Sakai realized his mistake when he was about fifty yards behind his intended victim and closing rapidly. Too late! At a range of less than a hundred feet Sakai squeezed the trigger of his guns, just as the Dauntless gunners opened fire.

Bullets ripped into the Zero's cockpit, and two smashed obliquely into Sakai's skull. Permanently blinded in his right eye, temporarily paralyzed on one side, Sakai somehow managed to fly his fighter the 550 nautical miles back to Rabaul.

Two years later, with the tide of war irreversibly running against Japan, the now one-eyed fighter pilot was once again allowed to fly a Zero. This time he flew from Iwo Jima. We join him now as, for the first time, he meets Hellcats aloft.

ON JUNE 24 THE QUIET LULL WHICH HAD SETTLED OVER IWO JIMA disappeared. It was about 5:20 A.M. when the air-raid alarms set up a terrific din across the island. Early-warning radar had caught several large groups of enemy aircraft less than sixty miles to the south—and coming in fast.

Every fighter plane on the island—more than eighty Zeros— thundered down the two runways and sped into the air. Mechanics dragged the remaining Bettys and Jills to shelter.

This was it! The long wait was about to be rewarded. I had a Zero under my hands again, and in another few moments I would know—by the acid test of actual combat—if I had lost my skill.

An overcast at 13,000 feet hung in the sky. The fighters divided into two groups, forty Zeros climbing above the cloud layer, and the other forty—my group—remaining below.

No sooner had I eased out of my climb than an enemy fighter spun wildly through the clouds, trailing a long plume of flame and black smoke. I had only a brief look at the fighter—it was a new type, unmistakable with its broad wings and blunt nose, the new Grumman I had heard so much about—the Hellcat. I swung into a wide turn and looked up . . . another Grumman came out of the clouds, diving vertically, smoke pluming behind.

Hard on the heels of the smoking fighter came scores of Hellcats, diving steeply. All forty Zeros turned and climbed to meet the enemy planes head-on. There was no hesitation on the part of the American pilots; the Grummans screamed in to attack. Then the planes were all over the sky, swirling from sea level to the cloud layer in wild dogfights. The formations were shredded.

I snapped into a tight loop and rolled out on the tail of a Hellcat, squeezing out a burst as soon as the plane came into the range finder. He rolled away and my bullets met only empty air. I went into a left vertical spiral and kept closing the distance, trying for a clear shot at the plane's belly. The Grumman tried to match the turn with me; for just that moment I needed, his underside filled the range finder and I squeezed out a second burst. The cannon shells exploded along the fuselage. The next second thick clouds of black smoke poured back from the airplane and it went into a wild, uncontrolled dive for the sea.

Everywhere I looked there were fighters, long trails of smoke, bursts of flame, and exploding planes. I looked too long. Flashing tracers poured directly beneath my wing, and instinctively I jerked the stick over to the left, rolling back to get on his tail and snapping out a burst. Missed. He dove out of range, faster than I could follow.

I cursed at myself for having been caught without warning, and with equal vehemence I cursed my blind eye, which left almost half of my area of vision blank. As quickly as I could, I slipped out of the parachute straps and freed my body, so I could turn around in my seat, making up for the loss of side vision.

And I looked without a second to spare. At least a half dozen Grummans were on my tail, jockeying into firing position. Their wings burst into sparkling flame as they opened fire. Another left roll—fast!—and the tracers slipped harmlessly by. The six fighters ripped past my wings and zoomed in climbing turns to the right.

Not this time! Oh, no! I slammed the throttle on overboost and rolled back to the right, turning after the six fighters with all the speed the Zero would give me. I glanced behind me—no other fighters in the back. One of these was going to be mine, I swore! The Zero closed the distance to the nearest plane rapidly. Fifty yards away I opened up with the cannon, watching the shells move up the fuselage and disappear into the cockpit. Bright flashes and smoke appeared beneath the glass; the next moment the Hellcat swerved crazily and fell off on one wing, its smoke trail growing with each second.

But there were more fighters on my tail! Suddenly I didn't want to close with them. Weariness spread over me like a smothering cloak. In the old days, at Lae, I would have wasted no time in hauling the Zero around and going for them. But now

I felt as though my stamina had been wrung dry. I didn't want to fight.

I dove and ran for it. In this condition it would have been sheer suicide to oppose the Hellcats. There would have been a slip, a second's delay in moving the stick or the rudder bar . . . and that would be all. I wanted time in which to regain my breath, to shake off the sudden dizziness. Perhaps it was the result of trying to see as much with only one eye as I had before; I knew only that I couldn't fight.

I fled to the north, using overboost to pull away. The Hellcats turned back and went after fresher game. And then I saw what was to me the most hideous of all the hundreds of air battles in which I had fought. I glanced down to my right and gaped.

A Hellcat rolled frantically, trying to escape a Zero which clung grimly to its tail, snapping out bursts from its cannon, no more than fifty yards behind. Just beyond the Zero, another Hellcat pursued the Japanese fighter. Even as I watched, a Zero plunged from above and hauled around in a tight diving turn after the Grumman. One after the other they came in, in a long snaking file! The second Zero, intent upon the pursuing Hellcat fighter, seemed entirely unaware of a third Hellcat following in its dive. And a third Zero, watching the whole proceedings, snapped around in a tight turn and caught the trailing Hellcat without warning.

It was an astonishing—and to me, a horrifying—death column which snaked along, each plane following the other before it with determination, firing at the target before its guns. Hellcat, Zero, Hellcat, Zero, Hellcat, Zero. Were they all so stupid that not one pilot, either Japanese or American, guarded his weak spot from the rear?

The lead fighter, the Grumman, skidded wildly as it hurled back smoke, then plunged toward the sea. Almost at the same moment the pursuing Zero exploded in a fireball. The Hellcat which had delivered the death blow remained in one piece less than two seconds; cannon shells from the second Zero tore its wing off, and it fell, spinning wildly. The wing had just ripped clear of the fighter when a blinding flash of light marked the explosion of the Zero. And as the third Hellcat pulled up from the explosion, the cannon shells of the third Zero tore its cockpit into a shambles.

The five planes plunged toward the sea. I watched the five splashes. The last Zero rolled, turned, and flew away, the only survivor of the melee.

I circled slowly, north of Iwo, sucking in air and trying to relax. The dizziness left me, and I turned back to the battle area. The fight was over. There were still Zeros and Hellcats in the sky, but they were well separated, and the fighters of both sides were forming into their own groups.

Ahead and to the right I saw fifteen Zeros swinging into formation, and I closed in to join the group. I came up below the formation and . . .

Hellcats! Now I understood why the surgeon, long ago, had protested my return to combat so vigorously. With only one eye my perspective was badly off, the small details were lost to me in identifying planes at a distance. Not until the white stars against the blue wings became clear did I realize my error. I wasted no time in throwing off the fear which gripped me. I rolled to the left and came around in a tight turn, diving for speed, hoping the Grummans hadn't seen me.

No such luck. The Hellcat formation broke up and the planes turned in pursuit. What could I do? My chances seemed hopeless.

No—there was still one way out, and a slim chance at that. I was almost over Iwo Jima. If I could outmaneuver the other planes—an almost impossible task, I realized—until their fuel ran low and forced them to break for home . . .

Now I appreciated the speed of these new fighters. In seconds they were closing in. They were so fast! There was no use in running any farther. . . .

I snapped back in a tight turn. The maneuver startled the enemy pilots as I climbed at them from below, swinging into a spiral. I was surprised; they didn't scatter. The lead fighter responded with an equal spiral, matching my maneuver perfectly. Again I spiraled, drawing it closer this time. The opposing fighters refused to yield a foot.

This was something new. An Airacobra or a P-40 would have been lost trying to match me in this fashion, and not even the Wildcat could hold a spiral too long against the Zero. But these new Hellcats—they were the most maneuverable enemy planes I had ever encountered. I came out of the spiral into a trap. The fifteen fighters filed out of their spirals into a long column. And the next moment I found myself circling in the center of a giant ring of fifteen Grummans. On every side of me I saw the broad wings with their white stars. If ever a pilot was surrounded in the air, I was.

I had little time in which to ponder my misfortune. Four Grummans broke out of their circle and dove at me. They were too eager. I rolled easily out of the way and the Hellcats skidded by, out of control. But what I thought was only a slight roll set me up for several other fighters. A second quartet flashed out of the ring, right on my tail.

I ran. I gunned the engine to give every last ounce of power and pulled away sufficiently to get out of their gun range for the moment. The four pursuing planes didn't worry me; it was the first quartet. How right I was! They had climbed back from their skidding plunge and were above me, diving for another firing pass.

I slammed my right foot against the rudder bar, skidding the Zero to the left. Then the stick, hard over to the left, rolling sharply. Sparkling lights flashed beneath my right wing, followed by a plummeting Hellcat.

I came out of the roll in a tight turn. The second Grumman was about seven hundred yards behind me, its wings already enveloped in yellow flame from its guns. If I hadn't known it before, I knew it now. The enemy pilots were as green as my own inexperienced fliers . . . and that could be a factor which would save my life.

The second fighter kept closing in, spraying tracers all over the sky, tracers which fell short of my own plane. Keep it up! I yelled, keep it up! Go ahead, waste all your ammunition; you'll be one less to worry about. I turned again and fled, the Hellcat closing in rapidly. When he was about three hundred yards behind, I rolled away to the left. The Grumman passed below me, still firing at empty air.

I lost my temper. Why run from such a clumsy pilot? Without thinking, I rolled back and got on his tail. From fifty yards away I snapped out a cannon burst.

Wasted. I failed to correct for the skid caused by my abrupt turn. And suddenly I didn't care what happened to the fighter in front of me . . . another Grumman was on my tail, firing steadily. Again—the left roll, a maneuver which never failed me. The Hellcat roared past, followed by the third and fourth fighters in the quartet.

Another four planes were almost directly above me, ready to dive. Sometimes, you have to attack in order to defend yourself. I went into a vertical climb, directly beneath the four fighters. The pilots banked their wings back and forth, trying to find me. I had no time to scatter them. Three Hellcats came at me from the right. I narrowly missed their tracers as I evaded with the same left roll.

The fighters were back in their wide ring. Any move I made to escape would bring several Grummans cutting at me from different directions. I circled in the middle, looking for a way out.

They had no intention of allowing that to happen. One after the other, the fighters peeled off from the circle and came at me, firing as they closed in.

I cannot remember how many times the fighters attacked nor how many times I rolled away. The perspiration rolled down my body, soaking my underclothes. My forehead was all beads of sweat, and it began to drip down onto my face. I cursed when the salty liquid trickled into my left eye . . . I couldn't take the time to rub it with my hand! All I could do was to blink, try to keep the salt away, try to see.

I was tiring much too quickly. I didn't know how I could get away from the ring. But it was very clear that these pilots weren't as good as their planes. An inner voice seemed to whisper to me. It repeated over and over the same words . . . *speed . . . keep up your speed . . . forget the engine, burn it out, keep up your speed! . . . Keep rolling . . . never stop rolling.*

My arm was beginning to go numb from the constant rolling to the left to evade the Hellcats' tracers. If I once slackened my speed in flicking away to the left, it would be my end. But how long could I keep that necessary speed in rolling away?

I must keep rolling! As long as the Grummans wanted to keep their ring intact, only one fighter at a time could jump me. And I had no fear of evading any single plane as it made its firing pass. The tracers were close, but they must hit me exactly if they were going to shoot me down. It mattered not whether the bullets passed a hundred yards or a hundred inches away, just so I could evade them.

I needed time to keep away from the fighters which raced in, one after the other, peeling off from the wide ring they maintained about me.

I rolled. Full throttle.

Stick over to the left.

Here comes another!

Hard over. The sea and horizon spinning crazily.

Skid!

Another!

That was close!

Tracers. Bright. Shining. Flashing.

Always underneath the wing.

Stick over.

Keep your speed up!

Roll to the left.

Roll.

My arm! I can hardly feel it anymore!

Had any of the Hellcat pilots chosen a different approach for his firing pass or concentrated carefully on his aim, I would surely have been shot out of the air. Not once did the enemy pilots aim at the point toward which my plane was moving. If only one fighter had spilled its tracers into the empty space leading me, toward the area where I rolled every time, I would have flown into his bullets.

But there is a peculiarity about fliers. Their psychology is strange, except for the rare few who stand out and go on to become leading aces. Ninety-nine percent of all pilots adhere to the formula they were taught in school. Train them to follow a certain pattern, and come what may, they will never consider breaking away from that pattern when they are in a battle where life and death mingle with one another.

So this contest boiled down to endurance between the time my arm gave out and I faltered in my evading roll and the fuel capacity of the Hellcats. They still had to fly back to their carriers.

I glanced at the speedometer. Nearly 350 miles an hour. The best that the Zero could do.

I needed endurance for more than my arm. The fighter also had its limits. I feared for the wings. They were bending under the repeated violence of the evading roll maneuvers. There was a chance that the metal might collapse under continued pressure and that the wing would tear off from the Zero, but that was out of my hands. I could only continue to fly. I must force the plane through the evasive rolls or die.

Roll.

Snap the stick over!

Skid.

Here comes another one.

To hell with the wings! Roll!

I could hear nothing. The sound of the Zero's engine, the roaring thunder of the Hellcats, the heavy staccato of their .50-caliber guns, all had disappeared.

My left eye stung.

The sweat streamed down.

I couldn't wipe it.

Watch out!

Stick over. Kick the bar.

There go the tracers. Missed again.

The altimeter was down to the bottom; the ocean was directly beneath my plane. Keep the wings up, Sakai, you'll slap a wave with your wingtip. Where had the dogfight started? Thirteen thousand feet. More than two and a half miles of skidding and rolling away from the tracers, lower and lower. Now I had no altitude left.

But the Hellcats couldn't make their firing runs as they had before. They couldn't dive; there was no room to pull out. Now they would try something else. I had a few moments. I held the stick with my left hand, shook the right vigorously. It hurt. Everything hurt. Dull pain, creeping numbness.

Here they come, skidding out of their ring. They're careful now, afraid of what I might do suddenly. He's rolling. A rolling pass.

It's not so hard to get out of the way. Skid to the left. Look. The tracers.

Fountains geysering up from the water. Spray. Foam.

Here comes another one.

How many times have they come at me this way now? I've lost count. When will they give up? They *must* be running low on fuel!

But I could no longer roll so effectively. My arms were going numb. I was losing my touch. Instead of coming about with a rapid, sharp rolling motion, the Zero arced around in a sloppy oval, stretching out each maneuver. The Hellcats saw it. They pressed home their attacks, more daring now. Their passes came so fast that I had barely time for a breather.

I could no longer keep this up. I must make a break! I came out of another left roll, kicked the rudder bar and swung the stick over to the right. The Zero clawed around in response and I gunned the fighter for a break in the ring. I was out, nosing down again and running for it, right over the water. The Hellcats milled around for a moment in confusion. Then they were after me again.

Half the planes formed a barricade overhead, while the others, in a cluster of spitting guns, hurtled after me. The Hellcats were too fast. In a few seconds they were in firing range. Steadily I kept working to the right, kicking the Zero over so that she jerked hard with each maneuver. To the left fountains of white foam spouted into the air from the tracers which continued narrowly to miss my plane.

They refused to give up. Now the fighters overhead were coming down after me. The Grummans immediately behind snapped out their bursts, and the Hellcats which dove tried to anticipate my moves. I could hardly move my arms or legs. There was no way out. If I continued flying low, it would only be a matter of a minute or two before I moved the stick too slowly. Why wait to die, running like a coward?

I hauled the stick back, my hands almost in my stomach. The Zero screamed back and up, and there, only a hundred yards in front of me, was a Hellcat, its startled pilot trying to find my plane.

The fighters behind him were already turning at me. I didn't care how many there were. I wanted this fighter. The Hellcat jerked wildly to escape. Now! I squeezed, the tracers snapped out. My arms were too far gone. The Zero staggered; I couldn't keep my arms steady. The Hellcat rolled steeply, went into a climb, and fled.

The loop had helped. The other fighters milled around in confusion. I climbed and ran for it again. The Grummans were right behind me. The fools in those planes were firing from a distance of five hundred yards. Waste your ammunition, waste it, waste it, I cried. But they were so fast! The tracers flashed by my wing and I rolled desperately.

Down below, Iwo suddenly appeared. I rocked my wings, hoping the gunners on the ground would see the red markings. It was a mistake. The maneuver slowed me down, and the Hellcats were all over me again.

Where was the flak? What's wrong with them down on the island? Open up, you fools, open up!

Iwo erupted in flame. Brilliant flashes swept across the island. They were firing all the guns, it seemed, spitting tracers into the air. Explosions rocked the Zero. Angry bursts of smoke appeared in the air among the Hellcats. They turned steeply and dove out of range.

I kept going at full speed. I was terrified. I kept looking behind me, fearing that they had come back, afraid that at any second the tracers wouldn't miss, that they'd stream into the cockpit, tearing away the metal, ripping into me.

I passed Iwo, banging my fist on the throttle, urging the plane to fly faster. Faster, faster! South Iwo appeared on the horizon . . . there, a cloud! A giant cumulus, rearing high above the water. I didn't care about the air currents. I wanted only to escape those fighters. At full speed I plunged into the billowy mass.

A tremendous fist seemed to seize the Zero and fling it wildly through the air. I saw nothing but livid bursts of lightning, then blackness. I had no control. The Zero plunged and reared. It was upside down, then standing on its wings, then hurtling upward tail first.

Then I was through. The storm within the cloud spit the fighter out with a violent lurch. I was upside down. I regained control at less than 1,600 feet. Far to the south I caught a glimpse of the fifteen Hellcats, going home to their carrier. It was hard to believe that it was all over and that I was still alive. I wanted desperately to get out of the air. I wanted solid ground beneath my feet.

I set down at Iwo's main strip. For a few minutes I relaxed in the cockpit, exhausted, then climbed wearily down from the Zero. All the other fighters had long since landed. A throng of pilots and mechanics ran toward the plane when it stopped, shouting and cheering. Nakajima was among them, and he threw his arms around my neck, roaring with joy. "You did it, Sakai! You did it! Fifteen against one . . . you were marvelous!" I could only lean against the plane and mumble, cursing my blind eye. It had nearly cost me my life.

An officer pounded me on the back. "We were going crazy down here," he shouted. "Every man on the island was watching you! The gunners, they couldn't wait for you to come over the island, to bring those planes into their range. Everybody had his hands on the triggers, just waiting, hoping you'd come our way. How did you do it?" he asked in amazement.

A mechanic ran up to me, saluting, "Sir! Your plane. It—it doesn't . . . I can't believe it . . . there's not a single bullet hole in your fighter!"

I couldn't believe it, either. I checked the Zero over from one end to the other. He was right. Not a single bullet had hit the fighter.

Later, back at the billet, I learned that the first group of Zeros which had flown above the clouds had fought a far easier battle than our own formation. The large Hellcat formation had climbed from the overcast directly beneath their own planes, and they had the advantage of diving, surprising the American pilots before they even knew what happened. NAP 1/C Kinsuke Muto, the Yokosuka Wing's star pilot, had a field day, shooting down four of the Grummans. The other pilots confirmed his victories. Muto flamed two Hellcats before they could even make an evasive move.

But the day's toll was staggering. Nearly forty—almost half of all our fighters—had been shot down.

The Flight of *Enola Gay*

from *Enola Gay*

BY GORDON THOMAS AND MAX MORGAN WITTS

Aerial machines that could traverse great distances and destroy whole cities were gloomily predicted by H. G. Wells while the Wright brothers were still tinkering in their bicycle shop, but he was a writer of fiction and the technology he warned against did not yet exist.

During World War I the Germans and British tried to make Wells's vision reality with both dirigibles and airplanes and failed rather dismally. They had better luck during the early years of World War II, but still the results were spotty, unpredictable. In the spring of 1945, using B-29s carrying firebombs, Curtis LeMay made the destruction of great cities a routine military operation. Within a few months the marriage of the B-29 to the atomic bomb brought absolute, indisputable success. At last, with one airplane and one bomb a huge city could be destroyed and most of its people cremated alive in one stupendous, fiery thunderclap.

Technological man triumphant, the nightmare now reality, America had the ability to obliterate cities, murder nations, exterminate entire populations. We had this awesome, end-of-the-world, Götterdämmerung capability parked right out at the air base on the edge of town, waiting. Then, predictably, someone stole the secrets and gave them to the Soviet Union, an absolute dictatorship ruled by the worst ogre of the bloody twentieth century, Joseph Stalin. Now the great terror began.

The flight of Enola Gay on August 6, 1945, changed the life of every human on this planet. Her flight was either the last blood-soaked episode in the age of total war or the first paragraph of the final chapter in the history of our species. Oh, limited wars could and did spring up after Enola Gay, but the politicians were careful lest the nuclear genie be unleashed.

226

Man had it in his power to reduce the planet to an uninhab-
itable, radioactive clinker. Everyone who lived on this tiny
planet circling this small star on the edge of this nondescript
galaxy lived with the knowledge that that power could be
used.

Let us once again fly with those men chosen by fortune to
change forever the course of human history. It is the middle
of the tropical night on the island of Tinian, in the western
Pacific. The bomb is aboard Enola Gay. *She is outside on the*
concrete now, waiting.

AT MIDNIGHT, PAUL TIBBETS WALKED TO ONE END OF THE LOUNGE
and addressed the twenty-six airmen who would be flying with
him to Japan.

Not once in the year he had commanded them had Tibbets
mentioned to anyone in the 509th the words *atomic* or *nuclear.*
Now, in this final briefing, he continued to preserve security by
merely referring to the weapon as being "very powerful" and
"having the potential to end the war."

He reminded the crews to wear their welders' goggles at the
time of the explosion. Then, in a crisp few sentences, he spelled
out the rules for a successful mission. "Do your jobs. Obey your
orders. Don't cut corners or take chances."

The weather officer stepped forward and gave the forecast:
the route to Japan would be almost cloud-free, with only moderate winds; clouds over the target cities were likely to clear at
dawn. The communications officer read out the frequencies to
be used on various stages of the mission and gave the positions
of rescue ships and planes.

Tibbets had a few final words for each of the specialists on
the mission. Navigators were reminded of the rendezvous point
above Iwo Jima where the three planes were to meet; tail gunners should check that each aircraft had its thousand rounds
of ammunition; engineers, that they were carrying seventy-four
hundred gallons of fuel (except for the strike aircraft, *Enola Gay,*
which would have four hundred gallons less to make its takeoff
easier); radiomen, that the new call sign was Dimples.

At 12:15 A.M., Tibbets beckoned to Chaplain Downey, who invited the gathering to bow their heads. Then, in a richly resonant voice, consulting the back of an envelope, Downey read the prayer he had composed for this moment.

Almighty Father, Who wilt hear the prayer of them that love Thee, we pray Thee to be with those who brave the heights of Thy heaven and who carry the battle to our enemies. Guard and protect them, we pray Thee, as they fly their appointed rounds. May they, as well as we, know Thy strength and power, and armed with Thy might may they bring this war to a rapid end. We pray Thee that the end of the war may come soon, and that once more we may know peace on earth. May the men who fly this night be kept safe in Thy care, and may they be returned safely to us. We shall go forward trusting in Thee, knowing that we are in Thy care now and forever. In the Name of Jesus Christ. Amen.

At 1:12 A.M., trucks picked up the crews of the two B-29s assigned to fly alongside the *Enola Gay*: the *Great Artiste*, piloted by Sweeney; and *No. 91*, commanded by Marquardt.

At 1:15 A.M., a truck picked up the crew of the *Enola Gay*. Tibbets and Parsons sat up front with the driver. Squeezed in the back were van Kirk, Ferebee, Lewis, Beser, Jeppson, Caron, Shumard, Stiborik, and Nelson. They all wore pale green combat overalls; the only identification they carried were dog tags around their necks. Beser's was stamped with an *H* for *Hebrew*.

At 1:37 A.M., the three weather-scout planes took off simultaneously from separate runways on North Field. At 1:51 A.M., *Top Secret* took off for its standby role at Iwo Jima.

Duzenbury had spent every available minute since the final briefing with the *Enola Gay*. He always took at least two hours for his "preflight," for whatever Tibbets and Lewis might have thought, the flight engineer *"knew* she was *my* ship."

First, Duzenbury walked slowly around the bomber, checking it visually, "watching out for the slightest thing that didn't look normal," making sure even that every rivet was in place on all the control surfaces. Then, around one, Duzenbury went aboard *Enola Gay* alone, checklist in hand.

Duzenbury went first to his own station, behind Lewis's seat. It took him little time to inspect his instrument panel; he prided himself that it was always in perfect working order. Then he stepped into the cockpit and examined the controls, switches, and dials. After he had verified that all was in order there, Duzenbury made his way back into the spacious area he shared with navigator van Kirk and radioman Nelson. Now it also contained Jeppson's console for monitoring the bomb.

Duzenbury opened a small, circular, airtight door situated just below the entrance to the long tunnel that led to the after end of the plane, swung himself feet first through the hatch, and found himself in back of the bomb.

Using a flashlight, he crawled to the right side of the weapon and onto the catwalk that ran along the length of the bay; from there, he had his first overall view of the world's most expensive bomb. To Duzenbury, who had worked as a tree surgeon before enlisting, it resembled a long, heavy tree trunk. The cables leading into it from Jeppson's monitoring panel, and its antennae, made it look like no bomb he'd ever seen before.

He continued along the catwalk, checking everything as he went, past the nose of the bomb and back along the other side. When he once again reached the fins, he noticed two unusual containers that, he thought, shouldn't be there. Almost unconsciously, he kicked them.

The flight engineer had not been told they contained the explosive powder and tools that Parsons would use later to arm the bomb.

He was about to remove the containers when a bright shaft of light shone through the hatch into the bomb bay. Puzzled, Duzenbury climbed back through the hatch into van Kirk's compartment. The light filled the area. Duzenbury walked forward into the cockpit and stopped, openmouthed.

The *Enola Gay* was ringed by floodlights.

Interspersed between the klieg stands and mobile generators were close to a hundred people—photographers, film crews, officers, scientists, project security agents, and MPs. Dumbfounded and a little annoyed, Duzenbury turned back to his checklist.

The lights and camera crews had been ordered by General Groves, who wanted a pictorial record of the *Enola Gay*'s departure. Only space had prevented a movie crew from flying on the mission.

Now Tibbets stepped from the truck and found himself surrounded by a film crew. He had been warned in a message from Groves that there would be "a little publicity," but in his view, "this was full-scale Hollywood premiere treatment. I expected to see MGM's lion walk onto the field or Warner's logo to light up the sky. It was crazy."

With a touch worthy of an epic production, the "extras" on the asphalt formed an avenue for the "stars" in the crew.

The 509th's commander complied with shouted requests to turn first *this* way, then *that* way, to smile, look serious, "look busy."

Caron peered around owlishly in the bright lights, smiling enigmatically when somebody said he had never before known a tail gunner who wore glasses. He doggedly refused to take off his baseball cap. In common with many on the apron, Caron found the scene "a trifle bizarre. I had to put my guns in their mount, and all the time I was getting stopped to have my picture taken."

Caron had planned to take his camera on the mission, but in all the excitement he had left it on his bunk. Yet in the end he would take the most historic pictures of all. An Army captain thrust a plate camera at Caron and told him, "Shoot whatever you can over the target."

At 2:20 A.M., the final group photo was taken. Tibbets turned to the crew and said, "Okay, let's go to work."

A photographer grabbed Beser and asked for "one last good-bye look."

Beser bridled. "Good-bye, hell! We're coming back!" He climbed up the ladder and through the hatch behind the *Enola Gay*'s nosewheel, suddenly tired of the publicity.

Beser was followed by Ferebee and van Kirk, who, like Caron, were wearing baseball caps; Shumard and Nelson wore GI work caps; Stiborik, a ski cap.

Finally, only Parsons and Tibbets remained below, talking to Farrell. Suddenly the general pointed to Parsons's coveralls. "Where's your gun?"

Parsons had forgotten to draw a weapon from supply. He motioned to a nearby MP, who unstrapped his gun belt and handed it over.

As he said farewell to Farrell, Tibbets had a more immediate concern—the possibility of crashing on takeoff, as he had seen so many planes do during the past weeks on Tinian. The *Enola Gay* was probably the most thoroughly checked aircraft in the world. But no check devised could ensure there would be no last-minute failure of some crucial component.

Smiling and looking relaxed for the clamoring photographers, Tibbets boarded the *Enola Gay*. When he reached his seat, he automatically felt his breast pocket to make sure his battered aluminum cigarette case was still there. He regarded the case as a lucky charm, and he never made a flight without it.

Caron strapped himself in by his twin rear guns; in the event of a crash on takeoff, he believed "there was a marginally better chance of survival in the tail." For luck, Caron carried a photograph of his wife and baby daughter stuck in his oxygen flow-chart. Shumard, squatting in one of the waist blister turrets, had with him a tiny doll; across from him, at the other turret, were Beser and Stiborik. They did not believe in talismans, though Stiborik thought his ski cap was as good as any.

At his station by the entrance hatch to the bomb bay, Nelson fished out a half-finished paperback and placed it on the table beside him. A few feet away, van Kirk laid out his pencils and chart.

Forward of the navigator, Parsons and Jeppson sat on cushions on the floor, listening patiently to the final preparations for takeoff going on around them. Finally, Tibbets called up Duzenbury. "All set, Dooz?"

"All set, Colonel."

Tibbets slid open a side window in the cockpit and leaned out.

A battery of cameramen converged to photograph his head over the gleaming new sign, *Enola Gay*.

"Okay, fellows, cut those lights. We've gotta be going."

Tibbets ordered Duzenbury to start No. 3 engine; when it was running smoothly, he ordered No. 4, then No. 1, and finally No. 2 engine to be fired.

The copilot looked across at Tibbets, who nodded. Lewis depressed the switch on his intercom. "This is Dimples Eight-two to North Tinian Tower. Ready for taxi out and takeoff instructions."

"Tower to Dimples Eight-two. Clear to taxi. Take off on runway A for Able."

At 2:35 A.M., the *Enola Gay* reached her takeoff position.

The jeep that had led the bomber there now drove down the runway, its headlights briefly illuminating the fire trucks and ambulances parked every fifty feet down each side of the airstrip.

At 2:42 A.M., the jeep flashed its lights from the far end of the runway, then drove to the side.

Tibbets told Lewis to call the tower.

Its response was immediate. "Tower to Dimples Eight-two. Clear for takeoff."

Tibbets made a final careful check of the instrument panel. The takeoff weight was 150,000 pounds; the 65-ton *Enola Gay*, with 7,000 gallons of fuel, a 5-ton bomb, and twelve men on board, would have to build up enough engine thrust to lift an overload of 15,000 pounds into the air. Tibbets made a decision:

he would hold the bomber on the ground until the last moment to build up every possible knot of speed before lifting it into the air.

He did not tell Lewis of his intention.

The copilot was feeling apprehensive; he, too, knew that the *Enola Gay* was well overweight, and he sensed that the next few seconds "could be traumatic."

At 2:45 A.M., Tibbets said to Lewis, "Let's go," and thrust all throttles forward. The *Enola Gay* began to roll down the runway.

Tibbets kept his eye on the rpm counter and the manifold-pressure gauge. With two-thirds of the runway behind them, the counter was still below the 2,550 rpm Tibbets calculated he needed for takeoff; the manifold-pressure gauge registered only forty inches—not enough.

In the waist blister turrets, Shumard and Stiborik exchanged nervous glances. Beser smiled back at them, oblivious of any danger. Far forward, at his panel, Duzenbury stirred uneasily. He knew what Tibbets was trying to do, but found himself wondering whether Tibbets "was *ever* going to take her up!"

Lewis stared anxiously at the instruments before him, a duplicate set of those in front of Tibbets. Outside, the ambulances and fire trucks flashed by.

"She's too heavy!" Lewis shouted. "Pull her off—now!"

Tibbets ignored Lewis, holding the bomber on the runway. Instinctively, Lewis's hands reached for his control column.

"No! Leave it!" Tibbets commanded.

Lewis's hand froze on the wheel.

Beser suddenly sensed the fear Stiborik and Shumard felt. He shouted, "Hey, aren't we going to run out of runway soon?"

Lewis glanced at Tibbets, who was staring ahead at the break in the darkness where the runway ended at the cliff's edge.

Lewis could wait no longer. But even as his hands tightened around the control column, Tibbets eased his wheel back. The *Enola Gay*'s nose lifted, and the bomber was airborne at what seemed to Lewis the very moment that the ground disappeared beneath them and was replaced by the blackness of the sea.

Watching the takeoff from his hiding place near the peak of Mount Lasso was WO Kizo Imai. For the past ninety minutes he had observed the lights, the flashbulbs, the cameras, and the people. He could not imagine what it all meant.

When the bomber that was the center of all the attention had taken off, it left from the very runway that Imai had originally helped to build.

Two minutes after the *Enola Gay*, the *Great Artiste* took off, followed at 2:49 A.M. by *No. 91*. Now the three weather-scout planes and three combat planes of Special Bombing Mission No. 13 were airborne and heading, on course and on time, for Japan.

The *Enola Gay* was on the north-by-northwest course it would maintain for the three-hour leg to Iwo Jima. As the plane burrowed through the Pacific night, ten of the twelve men on board busied themselves.

Ferebee had nothing to do and sat relaxed in his seat. There would be another six hours before his specialist skills as bombardier would be called into use. To tire himself now in pointless activity could have a detrimental effect on the role he would play later.

Beser, exhausted from over forty hours without sleep, was slumped on the floor at the back end of the tunnel, quietly snoring. He would be needed to man his electronic surveillance equipment only after the *Enola Gay* passed over Iwo Jima.

Apart from routine orders, Tibbets had not yet exchanged a word with Lewis. Both men were aware that Lewis had tried to take over at the crucial moment of takeoff. Lewis had acted instinctively; he had in no way intended to criticize Tibbets's flying ability. But he could not bring himself to say so. In turn, Tibbets recognized that his copilot's reaction had been perfectly understandable. "It was the response of a man used to sitting in the driver's seat.'' But Tibbets, too, could find no way of expressing himself. And so they sat in uncomfortable silence, Tibbets flying the plane, Lewis watching the instruments and adding a few lines to the log he was keeping. "Everything went well on take-off, nothing unusual was encountered.''

Caron called Tibbets on the intercom and received permission to test his guns. He had a thousand rounds to defend the *Enola Gay* against attack and now expended fifty of them. The sound rattled through the fuselage. In Caron's tail turret there was a smell of cordite and burned oil. Behind him, in the darkness, he watched tracers falling toward the sea.

Satisfied, and for the moment free of responsibility, Caron crawled into the rear compartment of the bomber. There, Stiborik was studying photographs of Hiroshima as the city would later appear on his radar screen. The unreal-looking pictures meant almost nothing to the tail gunner.

Close to 3 A.M., Parsons tapped Tibbets on the shoulder. "We're starting.''

Tibbets nodded, switched on the low-frequency radio in the cockpit, and called Tinian Tower. "Judge going to work.''

As arranged, there was no acknowledgment. But in the control tower on North Field, a small group of scientists studied a copy of a checklist that, on board the *Enola Gay*, Parsons had taken from a coverall pocket. It read:

Check List for loading charge in plane with special breech plug. (after all 0-3 tests are complete)
   1: Check that green plugs are installed.
   2: Remove rear plate.
   3: Remove armor plate.
   4: Insert breech wrench in breech plug.
   5: Unscrew breech plug, place on rubber pad.
   6: Insert charge, 4 sections, red ends to breech.
   7: Insert breech plug and tighten home.
   8: Connect firing line.

9: Install armor plate.
10: Install rear plate.
11: Remove and secure catwalk and tools.

This bald recital gave no clue as to the delicate nature of the task Parsons was to perform.

The naval officer lowered himself down through the hatch into the bomb bay. Jeppson followed him, carrying a flashlight.

The two men squatted, just inside the bay, their backs almost touching the open hatch, and faced the tail end of the bomb. Parsons took his tools out of the box that Duzenbury had kicked during his preflight check.

Ferebee left his bombardier's seat and came back to watch this critical stage of the mission.

To Ferebee, the two men crouching in the bomb bay resembled car mechanics, with Jeppson handing tools to Parsons whenever he was asked.

At 3:10 A.M., Parsons began inserting the gunpowder and detonator. He worked slowly and in total silence, his eyes and hands concentrating on the task. Gently, he placed the powder, in four sections, into position. Then he connected the detonator. Afterward, with sixteen measured turns, he tightened the breech blast, then the armor and rear plates.

The weapon was now "final" except for the last, crucial operation, which Jeppson would perform when he returned to the bomb bay and exchanged three green "safety" plugs for red ones. Until then, the weapon could not be detonated electrically—"unless, of course, the plane ran into an electrical storm."

At 3:20 A.M., the two men climbed out of the bomb bay.

Parsons went forward and informed Tibbets they had finished. Then he sat on the floor beside Jeppson, who was checking the bomb's circuits on his monitoring console.

Five minutes after Parsons and Jeppson completed arming the bomb, in Hiroshima, where the time was 2:25 A.M., the all clear sounded. People emerged from the air-raid shelters.

On Mount Futaba, 2d Lt. Tatsuo Yokoyama staggered sleepily back to his quarters. This was turning out to be a bad night: three alerts and not a sign of a bomber. He dismissed the gun crews and asked his orderly to bring him a pot of tea.

Tibbets stared into the night. The stars were out, pricking the inky blackness of the sky; below them, looking very white, were the clouds. Inside the *Enola Gay*, it was comfortably warm.

Tibbets finally broke the silence in the cockpit by asking his copilot what he was writing. Lewis replied he was "keeping a record." Tibbets did not pursue the matter, and the two men continued to sit, not speaking, peering into the darkness.

At 4:01, Tibbets spoke first to Sweeney and then to Marquardt, both of whom were following some three miles behind. The *Great Artiste* and *No. 91* reported "conditions normal."

At 4:20, van Kirk called Lewis on the intercom to give the estimated time of arrival over Iwo Jima as 5:52 A.M.

Lewis noted this in his log, and then added "we'll just check" to see whether the navigator's estimate turned out to be correct.

By now, Lewis was expanding his log from its original stark timetable to contain such observations as: "The Colonel, better known as the 'old bull,' shows signs of a tough day; with all he had to do to help get this mission off, he is deserving a few winks."

Tibbets, in fact, had never felt more relaxed or less tired. The trip, so far, was "a joyride."

At 4:25 A.M., he handed over the controls to Lewis, unstrapped himself, and climbed out of his seat to spend a little time with each man on the plane.

Parsons and Jeppson confirmed that the final adjustments to the bomb would be made in the last hour before the target was reached.

As he reached Duzenbury's position, Tibbets felt Lewis trim the controls so that the *Enola Gay* was flying on "George," the automatic pilot; the elevators gave a distinct kick as "George" engaged.

Tibbets chatted with Duzenbury for a few minutes and then moved on to Nelson. The young radioman hurriedly put down the paperback he was reading and reported, "Everything okay, Colonel." Tibbets smiled and said, "I know you'll do a good job, Dick." Nelson had never felt so proud.

Tibbets next watched van Kirk make a navigational check. Ferebee joined them, and the three men speculated as to whether conditions would allow them to bomb the "primary." Tibbets said that whatever Eatherly reported the weather over Hiroshima was, he would still go there first "to judge for myself."

Tibbets then crawled down the thirty-foot padded tunnel that ran over the two bomb bays to connect the forward and aft compartments of the *Enola Gay*.

In the rear compartment were Caron, Stiborik, Shumard, and a still-sleeping Beser.

Tibbets turned to the tail gunner. "Bob, have you figured out what we are doing this morning?"

"Colonel, I don't want to get put up against a wall and shot."

Tibbets smiled, recalling that day last September in Wendover when Caron had fervently promised to keep his mouth shut. Since then, the tail gunner had been an example to everybody when it came to security.

"Bob, we're on our way now. You can talk."

Caron had already guessed the *Enola Gay* was carrying a new superexplosive. "Are we carrying a chemist's nightmare?" he asked.

"No, not exactly."

"How about a physicist's nightmare?"

"Yes."

Tibbets turned to crawl back up the tunnel. Caron reached in and tugged at his leg.

Tibbets looked back. "What's the problem?"

"No problem, Colonel. Just a question. Are we splitting atoms?"

Tibbets stared at the tail gunner, then continued crawling up the tunnel.

Caron had recalled the phrase about splitting atoms from a popular science journal he had once read. He had no idea what it meant.

Back in the cockpit, Tibbets disengaged "George" and began the climb to 9,000 feet for the rendezvous at Iwo Jima.

Jeppson went into the navigator's dome; to the east he could see a waning moon, flashing in and out of the cloud banks. Ahead, apart from a high, thin cirrus, the sky was cerulean. All his life Jeppson would remember the grandeur of this night as it began to fade into dawn. By the time the *Enola Gay* arrived over Iwo Jima, the whole sky was a pale, incandescent pink.

Exactly on time, the *Enola Gay* reached the rendezvous point. Circling above Iwo Jima, Tibbets waited for the other two bombers.

At 4:55 A.M., Japanese time, Sweeney's *Great Artiste* and Marquardt's *No. 91* joined the orbit, swimming up to 9,000 feet.

At 5:05:30 (6:05:30 on van Kirk's chart, as the navigator would keep his entries on Tinian time), with daybreak in full flood, the three bombers formed a loose V. Tibbets in the lead, they headed toward Shikoku, the large island off the southeast coast of Japan.

Crossing the pork-chop-shaped Iwo Jima for the last time, Tibbets used his cockpit radio to call Maj. Bud Uanna in the communications center set up on the island especially for the mission. "Bud, we are proceeding as planned."

Through the early-morning static came Uanna's brief response. "Good luck."

At a comfortable 205 miles an hour, the *Enola Gay*, the *Great Artiste*, and *No. 91* headed northward. Aboard all three bombers there was a constant routine of checking wind velocity and calculating drift.

Lewis, with little to do except fill in his log, found his entries becoming cryptic. Finally, when the bomber reached 9,200 feet, he simply wrote: "We'll stay here until we are about one hour away from the Empire."

Beser's sleep was disturbed when an orange rolled down the tunnel from the forward compartment and dropped on his head. He opened his eyes to see Shumard and Stiborik grinning at him. Caron thrust a cup of coffee into his hands. Gulping it down, Beser checked his equipment. He had arranged all the dials he needed to see at eye level when he sat on the floor; instruments he would only listen to were up in the racks that reached to the bomber's roof. Several shelves of receivers, direction finders, spectrum analyzers, and decoders allowed Beser to monitor enemy fighter-control frequencies and ground defenses, as well as radar signals that could prematurely detonate the bomb. His special headset allowed him to listen to a different frequency in each ear.

Beser fiddled with the sets, tuning dials and throwing switches. Into one of his ears came the sounds of a ground controller on Okinawa talking down a fleet of bombers returning from a mission; in his other ear were brief air-to-air exchanges between Superdumbos circling off the coast of Japan. Beser was relieved to hear the rescue craft were on station for the atomic strike.

Suddenly Beser saw the Japanese early-warning signal sweep by. "It made a second sweep, and then locked onto us. I could hear the constant pulse as they continued to track us," he said later.

The element of surprise, which had been counted the *Enola Gay*'s greatest protection, was gone.

The radarman decided to keep the knowledge to himself. "It wasn't Tibbets's worry at this stage. And it would be upsetting for the rest of the crew to have somebody say, 'Hey, they're watching us.' So I just used my discretion."

Sometime after 6:30 A.M., Japanese time, Jeppson climbed into the bomb bay carrying the three red plugs and edged along the catwalk toward the middle of the bomb. The bay was unheated, and its temperature was about the same as that outside the plane, 18° C. Carefully he unscrewed the green plugs and inserted the red ones in their place, making the bomb a viable weapon. As he gave the last plug a final turn, even the ice-cool Jeppson had to reflect that "this was a *moment.*"

Jeppson climbed out of the bay and reported to Parsons what he had done. Parsons went forward and informed Tibbets, who switched on the intercom and addressed the crew. "We are carrying the world's first atomic bomb."

An audible gasp came from several of his listeners. Lewis gave a long, low whistle; *now* it all made sense.

Tibbets continued. "When the bomb is dropped, Lieutenant Beser will record our reactions to what we see. This recording is being made for history. Watch your language and don't clutter up the intercom."

He had a final word for Caron. "Bob, you were right. We *are* splitting atoms. Now get back in your turret. We're going to start climbing."

At 7:09 A.M., Radio Hiroshima interrupted its program with another air-raid alert. Simultaneously, the siren wailed its warning across the city. Everybody tensed for the series of intermittent blasts that would indicate an imminent attack.

Although the Japanese could not know it, Claude Eatherly's *Straight Flush* did not itself warrant an alert.

As the Hiroshima siren sounded, the *Straight Flush* reached the designated initial point, just sixteen miles from the Aioi Bridge. At 235 miles an hour, at a height of 30,200 feet, the *Straight Flush* made a straight run toward the aiming point, following exactly the course Tibbets and Ferebee had selected for the *Enola Gay.*

Eatherly looked for a break in the clouds. At first, he could find none. Then, immediately ahead, he saw a large opening. Six miles directly below, the city was so clear that the crew of the *Straight Flush* could see patches of greenery.

Whooping with delight, Eatherly flew across Hiroshima. Above the city's outskirts, he turned and made another pass.

The break in the cloud was still there, a huge hole ten miles across. Shafts of light shone through the gap, as if to spotlight the target for the fliers.

At about the same time, the planes checking the weather over Nagasaki and Kokura found conditions there nearly as good. All three cities were available for the *Enola Gay*, now at 26,000 feet and still climbing at a steady 194 miles an hour.

At 7:24 A.M., Nelson switched off the IFF. A minute later, on 7310 kilocycles, he received a coded message from the *Straight Flush*.

Cloud cover less than 3/10ths at all altitudes.
Advice: bomb primary.

After Tibbets read the message, he switched on the intercom and announced, "It's Hiroshima."

Minutes later, the *Full House* and *Jabbit III* reported in. Nelson took the transcribed messages to Tibbets, who shoved them into his coverall pocket. He told Nelson to send a one-word message to Uanna on Iwo Jima.

"Primary."

At 7:31 A.M., the all clear sounded in Hiroshima. People relaxed, lit kitchen stoves, prepared breakfast, read the *Chugoku Shimbun*.

WO Hiroshi Yanagita, the Kempei Tai leader who had rounded up some of the American POWs now in their cells at Hiroshima Castle, did not hear any of the night's air-raid alerts. He was in bed, sleeping off a heavy hangover. The sake he had drunk at Field Marshal Hata's party the previous night was taking its toll.

On Mount Futaba, 2d Lt. Tatsuo Yokoyama kept his men at their antiaircraft-gun post. He thought it strange that the lone plane had circled and made a second run high over the city.

He ordered breakfast of rice, soup, pickles, and stewed vegetables to be served to the gunners at their posts, and a similar meal brought to his quarters. As a sign of respect, his aide carried the breakfast tray high above his head—to ensure that his breath did not fall on the food.

Inside Hiroshima Castle, bowls of mush were left on the cell floors of the American prisoners.

At the Shima clinic, the staff changed shifts while the patients had breakfast. As was the custom in Japanese hospitals, the food was prepared and served by relatives. By 7:35 A.M., most of them were hurrying from the clinic to put in another long day for the war effort.

In the center of Hiroshima, at eight, hundreds of youths began work on the fire lane leading to the Aioi Bridge.

Close by, on the grounds of Hiroshima Castle, many of the city's forty thousand soldiers were doing their morning calisthenics. Not far from them, a solitary blindfolded American was also being exercised.

Fifty miles from the Aioi Bridge, the *Enola Gay* flew at 30,800 feet, followed by the two observer planes at a few miles' distance. Van Kirk called out tiny course corrections to Tibbets.

At 8:05 A.M., van Kirk announced, "Ten minutes to AP."

In his cramped tail turret, Bob Caron tried to put on his armored vest. Hemmed in by his guns, and holding the unwieldy camera he had been given just before takeoff, he gave up and put his only protection from flak on the floor.

Beser was monitoring the Japanese fighter-control frequency. There was no indication of activity. Stiborik was glued to his radar screen. Shumard was peering out of a waist blister turret, also on the lookout for fighter planes.

Ferebee settled himself comfortably on his seat and leaned forward against the special bombardier's headrest he and Tibbets had designed months ago at Wendover.

Parsons and Jeppson knelt at the bomb console. All the lights remained green. Parsons rose to his feet and walked stiffly toward the cockpit.

Left alone, Jeppson also stood up and buckled on his parachute. He saw Nelson and van Kirk look at him curiously. Their parachutes remained stacked in a corner.

Van Kirk called out another course change, bringing the *Enola Gay* on a heading of 264 degrees, slightly south of due west. At 31,060 feet and an indicated airspeed of 200 miles an hour, the bomber roared on.

Van Kirk called Tibbets on the intercom. "IP."

Exactly on time, at the right height and predetermined speed, van Kirk had navigated the *Enola Gay* to the initial point.

It was 8:12 A.M.

At that moment at Saijo, nineteen miles east of Hiroshima, an observer spotted the *Enola Gay*, the *Great Artiste*, and *No. 91*. He immediately cranked the field telephone that linked him with the communications center in Hiroshima Castle and reported what he had seen. The center was manned by schoolgirls drafted to work as telephone operators. Having written down the details, one of the girls telephoned the Hiroshima radio station. At dictation speed, the announcer wrote down the message. "Eight-thirteen, Chugoku Regional Army reports three large enemy planes spotted, heading west from Saijo. Top alert."

The announcer rushed to a nearby studio.

It was now 8:14 A.M.

Tibbets spoke into the intercom. "On glasses."

Nine of the twelve men slipped the Polaroid goggles over their eyes and found themselves in total darkness. Only Tibbets, Ferebee, and Beser kept their glasses up on their foreheads; otherwise, it would have been impossible for them to do their work.

Before covering his eyes, Lewis made a notation in his log. "There will be a short intermission while we bomb our target."

With thirty seconds to go, Ferebee shouted that Hiroshima was coming into his viewfinder. Beser informed Parsons that no Japanese radar was threatening the bomb's proximity fuse.

Tibbets spoke quickly into the intercom. "Stand by for the tone break—and the turn."

Ferebee watched the blacks and whites of the reconnaissance

photographs transform themselves into greens, soft pastels, and the duller shades of buildings cramming the fingers of land that reached into the dark blue of Hiroshima Bay. The six tributaries of the Ota River were brown; the city's principal roads a flat, metallic gray. A gossamer haze shimmered over the city, but it did not obscure Ferebee's view of the aiming point, the T-shaped Aioi Bridge, about to coincide with the crosshairs of his bombsight.

"I've got it."

Ferebee made his final adjustments and turned on the tone signal, a continuous, low-pitched hum, which indicated he had started the automatic synchronization for the final fifteen seconds of the bomb run.

A mile behind, in the *Great Artiste*, bombardier Kermit Beahan prepared to switch open the bomb doors and drop the parachute-slung blast gauges earthward.

Two miles behind, Marquardt's *No. 91* made a ninety-degree turn to be in position to take photographs.

The tone signal was picked up by the crews of the three weather planes, including Eatherly's, now about 225 miles from Hiroshima and heading back to base.

It was heard on Iwo Jima by McKnight, still sitting in the pilot's seat of *Top Secret*. McKnight told Uanna, "It's about to drop."

Precisely at 8:15:17, *Enola Gay*'s bomb-bay doors snapped open, and the world's first atomic bomb dropped clear of its restraining hook.

The monitoring cables were pulled from the bomb, and the tone signal stopped.

The *Enola Gay*, suddenly over nine thousand pounds lighter, lurched upward ten feet.

Caron, in the tail, gripped the plate camera and, blinded by the welder's goggles, wondered which way to point it.

Tibbets swung the *Enola Gay* into a diving right-hand turn.

Ferebee shouted, "Bomb away," and turned from his sight to look down through the Plexiglas of the *Enola Gay*'s nose.

He saw the bomb drop cleanly out of the bay and the doors slam shut. For a fleeting eyeblink of time, the weapon appeared to be suspended by some invisible force beneath the bomber. Then Ferebee saw it fall away. "It wobbled a little until it picked up speed, and then it went right on down just like it was supposed to."

On the ground, Lieutenant Colonel Oya stood at a window of Second General Army Headquarters and peered up at the *Enola Gay* and the *Great Artiste*. The two bombers seemed to be diving toward the city.

Field Marshal Hata, having tended his garden and prayed at his shrine, was dressing for the communications meeting.

Kempei Tai officer Hiroshi Yanagita snored insensibly in his bed.

Tatsuo Yokoyama, stripped to the waist in the midsummer heat, was raising a bowl of rice to his mouth, chopsticks poised.

The announcer at Radio Hiroshima reached the studio to broadcast the air-raid warning.

On the fire lanes, supervisors blew their whistles, signaling thousands of workers, many of them schoolboys and -girls, to run to their designated "safe" areas.

Aboard the *Enola Gay*, Tibbets pulled down his glasses. He could see nothing. He yanked them off. In the nose, Ferebee had not bothered to put his on.

The *Enola Gay* was coming to the end of its breathtaking turn and was now some five miles from Ferebee's AP, heading away from the city. Tibbets called Caron. Again, the tail gunner reported there was nothing to see.

Beser at last managed to switch on the wire recorder. Stiborik turned up the brightness on his radar screen so he could see it through his glasses. Duzenbury, his hand on the throttles, worried about what the blast would do to the *Enola Gay*'s engines.

Jeppson counted. Five seconds to go.

In the bomb, the barometric switch tripped at five thousand feet above the ground. The shriek of the casing through the air had now increased to a shattering sonic roar, not yet detectable below.

On the ground, Kazumasa Maruyama was on his way to pick up Mayor Awaya, as he did every morning before work.

At Radio Hiroshima, the announcer pushed the button that sounded the air-raid siren and, out of breath, spoke into a microphone. "Eight-thirteen, Chugoku Regional Army reports three large enemy planes spotted, heading—"

The bomb's detonator activated 1,890 feet above the ground.

At exactly 8:16 A.M., forty-three seconds after falling from the *Enola Gay*, having traveled nearly six miles, the atomic bomb missed the Aioi Bridge by eight hundred feet and exploded directly over Dr. Shima's clinic.

Spad Pilot

from *Skyraider*

BY ROSARIO RAUSA

A legend in U.S. Navy carrier aviation, Paul Gray was the leader of the strike during the Korean War that inspired James Michener's The Bridges at Toko-Ri. A veteran of thirty combat missions in the Pacific during World War II, he was the commanding officer of VF-54 flying from the USS Essex during the Korean War and served a tour as commanding officer of the Riverine Patrol Forces during the Vietnam War. Paul Gray had a dozen commands and earned more combat decorations than any other officer in the U.S. Navy before he retired as a captain in 1969.

The airplane Gray flew in Korea, the AD-4 Skyraider, was almost as tough as he was. Known to Navy pilots as the Spad, this propeller-driven attack plane also served in Vietnam, where it was a faithful mount for both U.S. Air Force and Navy pilots. Still, as the following excerpt describes, Gray used up Spads at a fearful rate.

PAUL GRAY AND THE SKYRAIDER WENT TOGETHER LIKE PATTON and tanks. Like the attack bomber, this pilot was durable and could take punishment. He took the reins of VF-54, based aboard the carrier USS *Essex*, in 1951. Before long he was leading attacks on targets of opportunity with great effect. His method: go in low and press for accuracy. The targets were bridges, railroad tracks, railroad cars, trucks, troop emplacements, and supply depots. Forward air controllers (FACs) on the ground or in U.S. Air Force spotter planes aloft often coordinated attacks, vectoring the bombers toward the targets. Most missions took place during the day. Sorties were often an arduous, butt-busting four and a half hours in length. Casualty rates were high. Gray's squadron, for instance, suffered 25 percent losses on the cruise, which lasted twelve months in 1951–52. Seven pilots were killed.

A native of St. John, Kansas, Gray was a thirty-five-year-old in Korea, who kept in shape with workouts in the ship's gym. This helped to sustain him on the long combat flights and certainly didn't work against him when he had to crash-land his ADs.

"We seldom got over a thousand feet above the ground," said Gray, "and frequently returned to the ship with holes in the Skyraider's skin from small-arms fire. But the AD was a marvelous machine and could carry the same tonnage in bombs as the four-engine B-17 bomber of just a few years earlier. [A couple of years later at Naval Air Station Dallas, Texas, an AD took off with load of fuel and ordnance totaling 26,739 pounds, an amount equal to a DC-3 transport carrying twenty-four passengers.] It was a perfect aircraft for close air support and the other bombing and strafing duty which characterized the interdiction mission."

For the ADs, a typical close air-support mission load included four hundred rounds of 20-mm ammunition, three 500-pounders, and a dozen five-inch rockets.

Demonstrating a mild disdain for the "call-sign" system with which pilots identified themselves by an officially designated name followed by a three-digit side number, Gray's group decided on a Walt Disney theme. Gray became Snow White and his wingmen Dopey, Grumpy, Sneezy, and so forth. It was not long after he implemented this system that Gray's Skyraider took a hit while over enemy territory.

"Happily for me," said Gray, "shortly after I went into the sea a South Korean picket boat came along and pulled me to safety."

There was more to it than that. Gray's Skyraider sank quickly beneath him after he splashed into the water. Somehow he unlatched himself from the cockpit, but, as he put it, "I was weighted down by my survival equipment, which included pistol, ammunition belt, Mae West, and various other items. I couldn't quickly locate the CO_2 cartridge toggles of the Mae West, even though they were floating somewhere directly in front of me. I started to sink but got to the toggles in time, and the South Koreans then hauled me out of the water."

On board the carrier the crew received the good news from Grumpy, Gray's wingman orbiting overhead. "Snow White is safe!" he reported with a sharp ring of exuberance in his voice.

Wonsan Harbor, where Gray ditched, incidentally, is a major seaport on Korea's east coast. Shielded from storms by a natural barrier of mountains, it is ice-free in winter. It was, therefore, a reasonably accommodating place to ditch an airplane as long as survivors weren't left in the frigid waters too long in the nonsummer seasons.

Gray's philosophy of go-in-low-for-accuracy had its drawbacks. When a bomb released from a fast-moving aircraft explodes, it inevitably sends a pattern of fragments skyward. The pilot has only fractions of a second to pull up and away if he releases at low altitude, where he stands a chance of sustaining hits from his own weapon.

Several days after his first dip in Korean waters, Gray angled his Skyraider toward the mouth of a tunnel in which the enemy had stowed a locomotive. He pickled off (released) a 1,000-pounder and banked swiftly away. The bomb apparently struck just at the mouth of the tunnel, a good hit. Fragments from it slammed into his AD, however, producing ominous thudding sounds. The plane was barely flyable, and since taking it to the ship was in doubt, Gray advised his wingmen that he would try to reach an emergency landing strip called K-55. Somehow he managed to coax the wounded plane southward across the thirty-eighth parallel to the field, where he landed.

On the ground at K-55, mechanics examined the bird, shook their heads, and declared it "dead." It was scrapped, and Gray was flown out to the *Essex*. Within twenty-four hours he was aloft in another Skyraider over North Korea on a combat mission.

A few days later Gray swept in low over a target, collected

no less than fifty-nine holes in the skin of his attack bomber from ground fire, told the carrier that he thought he could recover on board, and proceeded to do so with minimum dramatics. It was almost like another day at the office for Paul Gray.

Fortunately, this plane could be repaired, although the sight of those holes angered one Andrew Syzmanski, a lieutenant (junior grade) and VF-54 maintenance officer tasked with patching up the aircraft on board the *Essex*. A native of Brooklyn known as much for his salty language as his great repair skills, "Ski" could only ask the rhetorical question, "What is he trying to do? Bust 'em up faster than I can fix 'em?"

Sometime later as Gray was attacking a column of North Korean trucks, an enemy artilleryman caught Gray's Skyraider in his gunsight reticle. He fired a stream of 37-mm shells toward the speeding naval plane, and one of the charges tore into the AD's engine. Flames erupted over Gray's cowling. Instinctively, one of his wingmen transmitted the dreaded message back to the ship: "Snow White has been hit!"

Gray zoomed to altitude and turned his bomber toward the sea and the *Essex*, fifty miles away. He quickly discovered that when he pulled back his fuel-mixture control lever (located with the throttle and propeller controls on the port console), thus shutting off the flow of gasoline to the engine, the blaze went out. Of course that also caused the engine to stop. But by manipulating the mixture, intermittently he was able to fly a little, glide a little, fly a little, glide a little.

In this manner he guided his aircraft over the mountains and plains and reached the water, where the temperature was thirty-five frigid degrees.

"At that temperature you could freeze to death, even with an exposure suit on, in less than half an hour," said Gray. "Indeed, gloveless hands would be useless in five minutes." (Anti-exposure garments, called "poopy" suits by the fliers, covered the body from neck to feet and were worn over thermal underwear. They were made of waterproof, rubber-type materials and were tightly sealed at the wrists. Large boots were actually integrated with the suit and were part of it.)

Gray spotted an American destroyer moving slowly through the churning sea and descended toward it. He ditched in the vicinity of the ship, extricated himself from the disintegrating airplane, and slipped into the sea. The inferno that was the R-3350 was quenched by the briny ocean.

That was shoot-down number three.

Some weeks later Gray was hit again but managed to limp into K-15, another emergency landing strip south of the thirty-eighth parallel, for shoot-down number four. Some people were beginning to believe that VF-54's skipper led a charmed life.

North Korea didn't look at it that way. Newspaper accounts began to mention the exploits of Snow White and his entourage of naval pilots, who were scoring heavily against bridges, trains, trucks, and supply emplacements.

Take the attack on Kap Son, for instance. An enemy base constructed at the foot of a mountain slope near the Yalu River in North Korea, it became the focal point for one of the most daring raids of 1951, if not the whole war.

Intelligence sources had learned that a high-level meeting between North Korean and Chinese Communist officials was to take place there. Gray was selected to lead an attack against the base, a perilous three hundred miles from the *Essex*. He and his wingmen would have to go without cover from friendly jet fighters.

After examining charts and analyzing the placement of triple A (antiaircraft artillery) and radar detection sites, he decided to take his flight in low. The plan was to rendezvous after the launch, go feet dry (cross the coastline), and descend to treetop height, skimming over the rugged terrain, which, hopefully, would conceal the aircraft from the probing radar eyes of the enemy. Eight Skyraiders and eight Corsairs, heavily loaded with 1,000-pound bombs and napalm, were catapulted from the *Essex* in snowy weather. Formed into a loose cruise formation, the sixteen heavily laden planes began their journey.

Navigation at low altitude (in later years such flights would be called sandblowers) is difficult enough even over familiar ground because the pilot's perspective is radically different from that which he experiences at altitude. Careful preflight planning combined with precise timing and relentless tracking along the prescribed route are critical.

About an hour and a half after leaping from their mobile runway, Snow White and his troops spotted the target—principally a collection of closely spaced, simple, barracks-type buildings. Gray signaled his wingmen to add power for the run-in.

A stunned and bewildered gathering of Chinese and Koreans heard the thunder of sixteen piston-driven power plants, then saw the wave of planes homing directly toward them.

"Stand by for the pull up," transmitted Gray over the radio as he approached a preselected initial point.

His wingmen followed Gray in fanlike progression as he pulled his Skyraider steeply skyward, trading airspeed for altitude. Peaking out over the encampment at about 5,000 feet, he banked sharply, pushed the nose over, and dove down. One after the other the Skyraiders and Corsairs followed, releasing their weapons in sequence and racing away to clear the target area.

The first assault lasted only a minute or two but produced a holocaust of orange-red balls of fire followed by a towering display of brown-black, debris-filled clouds. Repeated runs using 500-pounders and then napalm completely burned and leveled the site.

"The beauty of it," remembered Gray, "was that not one bomb hit outside of a city-block square. Every one was on target." Days later intelligence sources reported that the attack was extremely successful and that 510 of the enemy were killed. There were no American losses.

Shortly thereafter the word was passed that the North Koreans were offering $10,000 for heads of a naval pilot named Paul Gray and his wingmen.

"That's a lot of money today and was a helluva lot more back then," said Gray. "I was flattered in a way, despite how disquieting it is to know someone has put a price on your person. This action also influenced my thinking in that if I were hit, I would try, if at all possible, to avoid bailing out over land risking capture. I would take my chances with the sea."

It was no surprise when superiors began to notice signs of fatigue in Snow White. He developed what someone called a nervous twitch. The *Essex*'s flight surgeon told him he ought to step down for a while and rest. In fact, it was decided to officially ground him, which meant his complete removal from the flight schedule.

"It was a terribly cold winter morning," recalled Gray. "The wind was strong and laced with ice as it whipped across the flight deck. But I was airborne and on the way to the target before the word was passed to me that I wasn't supposed to fly."

North of a place called Munchon, Gray was executing a strafing attack when .50-caliber ground fire ripped into his plane. Parts of the propeller blades were shot away. Despite this he managed to get the plane over water. The Skyraider vibrated horribly en route, and Gray was destined for another arcticlike dip in Wonsan Harbor. He crashed into roiling whitecaps.

Snow White was down again. The message was received in grim silence throughout the carrier. Squadron mates in the ready room paused in their card games. Five times Commander Gray had ridden a Skyraider down to earth or ocean. People were thinking, "The odds can't be with him this time."

And yet they were. The destroyer USS *Twinning* hurried alongside the stricken flier forty minutes after he crashed. The ship dispatched a crew in a rescue boat and retrieved Snow White from the freezing deep. The card games resumed. A wit in the group drafted a sign that was posted in the ready room: "Use Caution When Ditching Damaged Airplanes in Wonsan Harbor. Don't Hit Commander Gray."

That was the last time Gray crashed an airplane, but it was not his last mission. He did take a rest as ordered but went on to fly ten more combat hops before the *Essex* was finally relieved on station and sent home.

Ia Drang Valley

from *Chickenhawk*

BY ROBERT MASON

The helicopter was first widely used in actual combat during the Vietnam War. Mobility is one of the critical ingredients to victory on the modern battlefield, and the helicopter seemed just the instrument to provide it. The air-assault concept was born—little choppers moving troops quickly and efficiently to the point where they were most urgently needed. Yet the lightly armed helicopters were easy to shoot down. The short-term solution was to arm other choppers with machine guns and use them to defend the lift machines. Gunships were born. Specialized machines would follow, the Cobra about 1967, then the Apache of the Gulf War. Fifty years before, the fighter plane was born of military necessity in a similar manner.

Prior to the arrival of the Cobra, the helicopters of the mid-1960s could fairly be compared to World War I fighters. They had about the same speed, climb rate, ceiling, and were similarly armed with a couple of machine guns. They were equally vulnerable to ground fire, yet in the 1960s enemy infantry were armed with vastly more firepower than World War I soldiers possessed. Flying air-assault troop-lift choppers into and out of hot landing zones was a bloody, thankless business that required tremendous skill, nerves of steel, and brass balls. Just why sane men volunteered to fly and fight in these aerial death traps is one of the unsolved mysteries of the aviation age.

What follows is a selection from Chickenhawk by Robert Mason, easily one of the two or three best books on the Vietnam helicopter war yet written. Flying as a copilot on a "slick," a UH-1 Huey troop-lift chopper with two door guns, Mason is experiencing his first major battle. The year is 1965.

"THE LONGEST WEEK BEGAN ON A SUN-DRENCHED SUNDAY MORN-ing in a small clearing, designated Landing Zone X-Ray, in the Chu Pong foothills. Intelligence had long suspected the Chu Pong massif of harboring a large Communist force fed from the Cambodian side of the border. X-Ray seemed like a likely spot to find the enemy, and so it was." I read this in *Time*, the week after the Tea Plantation incident.

The results of nearly two weeks of searching and probing by the Cav were hundreds of dead NVA soldiers and a very good idea of where to find the main force of three NVA regiments. On November 14 our battalion lifted the First Battalion, Seventh Cavalry (Custer's old unit) into LZ X-Ray, where they were expected to make contact. Our sister company, the Snakes, made the first assault in the morning and received very little opposition. By early afternoon, though, the two companies of the Seventh Cav they had lifted in had been surrounded and suffered heavy casualties. Our company was assigned to support the Snakes, to lift in reinforcements.

We picked up the troopers at the Tea Plantation, eight to each Huey. It was easy to tell where we were going. Although we were still fifteen miles away, the smoke was clearly visible from all the artillery, B-52 bombers, and gunship support concentrated around the LZ to keep the grunts from being overrun. As we cruised over the jungles and fields of elephant grass, I had the feeling this was a movie scene: the gentle rise and fall of the Hueys as we cruised, the perspective created by looking along the formation of ships to the smoke on the horizon, the quiet. None of the crews talked on the radios. We all listened to the urgent voices in the static as they called in air strikes and artillery on their own perimeters, then yelled that the rounds were hitting *in* their positions.

LZ X-Ray could accommodate eight Hueys at once, so that was how the ships were grouped in the air. Yellow and White in the first group; Orange and Red in the second. Leese and

I were Red Two. As we got closer to X-Ray, the gap between us and the first group got bigger to allow time for them to land, drop off the troopers, and take off.

Five miles away, we dropped to low level. We were flying under the artillery fire going into the LZ.

A mile ahead of us, the first group was going over the approach end of the LZ and disappearing into the smoke. Now the radios came alive with the pilots' calling in where the fire was coming from. The gunners on all the ships could hear this. Normally it was helpful, but this time, with the friendlies on the ground, they could not fire back. Yellow and White were on the ground too long. The artillery still pounded. The massif behind the LZ was completely obscured by the pall of smoke. We continued our approach. Leese was on the controls. I double- or triple-checked my sliding armor panel on my door side and cursed the Army once again for not giving us chest protectors. I put my hands and feet near the controls and stared at the scene.

"Orange One, abort your landing. Fire in the LZ is too heavy," a pathfinder called from X-Ray. Orange flight turned, and we followed. There was a whole bunch of yelling on the radios. I heard two ships in the LZ call out that they were hit badly. What a mess. Orange flight led us in a wide orbit two miles away, still low level. Now A-1Es from the Air Force were laying heavy fire at the front of the LZ along with the artillery and our own gunships. What kept everybody from flying into each other I'll never know. Finally we heard Yellow One call to take off, and we saw them emerge from the smoke on the left side of the LZ, shy two ships. They had waited in the heavy fire while the crews of the two downed ships got on the other Hueys. One crew chief stayed, dead. One pilot was wounded.

We continued the orbit for fifteen minutes. I looked back at the grunts, who were staring at the scene. They had no idea what was going on, because they had no headsets.

"Orange One, make your approach," the pathfinder called.

Apparently a human-wave attack by the NVA on the LZ was stopped. "Orange One, all eight of the ships in your two flights are keyed to pick up wounded." "Keyed" meant that they had groups of wounded positioned to be loaded first.

"Roger. Red One, copy?"

"Red One, roger."

Orange One rolled out of the orbit and we followed. The A-1Es were gone, but our gunships came back to flank us on the approach. Even with the concentration of friendlies on the ground, the gunships could fire accurately enough with their flex guns and rockets, so the grunts allowed them to. Our own door gunners were not allowed to fire unless they saw an absolutely clear target.

We crossed the forward tree line into the smoke. The two slicks that had been shot down were sitting at the front of the LZ, rotors stopped. That made it a little tight for eight of us to get in, but it was okay. The grunts jumped off even before the skids hit the ground. Almost before our Hueys had settled into the grass, other grunts had dumped wounded men, some on stretchers, into our ships. No fire. At least nothing coming our way. Machine guns and hundreds of rifles crackled into a roar all around us as the grunts threw out withering cover fire. The pathfinder, hidden in the tree line somewhere, told us everybody was loaded and to take off to the left. Orange One rogered and led us out. Fifty yards past the perimeter, some of the ships took hits, and we cleared all our guns to fire. Our ship was untouched.

After we dropped off the wounded, Leese and I were delayed by taking some men to an artillery position, separating us from the rest of the company for a half hour.

We were on our way to rejoin them when we saw a fighter get hit near X-Ray. It was a prop-driven A-1E. This scene, too, was right out of the movies. Orange flames burst from the root of his right wing and billowed back toward the tail, turning into coal-black smoke. The flames flared thicker than the fuselage and in moments hid the multipaned canopy. The pilot was either dead or unconscious. The plane screamed toward the ground from about 3,000 feet, not more than half a mile from Leese and me. Black smoke marked its path as it streaked into the jungle at a steep angle, exploding instantly, spreading wreckage, and bursting bombs, unspent ammo, and fire forward, knocking down trees.

I made the mistake of calling our headquarters to tell them of the crash.

"Roger, Red Two, wait one," was the answer in my phones.

"Ah, Red Two, Grunt Six has relayed instructions that you are to proceed to the site of the crash and inspect same."

I wanted to go flying around where an Air Force plane just got shot down like I wanted to extend my tour. Leese advised flying by very fast and taking a quick look-see. I dumped the Huey from 3,000 feet, using the speed of my dive to swoop over the burning swatch in the jungle.

I told headquarters to tell Grunt Six that nobody had jumped out before the plane had hit and that there now remained only some smoldering pieces of airplane and some exploding ammo in the middle of the burnt clearing.

"Ah, roger, Red Two, wait one."

Whenever they asked you to wait, you knew they were up to no good.

"Ah, Red Two, Grunt Six says roger. But the Air Force wants you to land and do an on-site inspection."

Leese shook his head. "Negative, HQ," I radioed, "this area is hot. We will return to do a slow flyby and check it again, but we know there's nobody left." Leese nodded.

Now, you would think that that would be good enough. I had just volunteered the four of us in our lone Huey to fly back over a very hot area to double-check the obvious.

It was not good enough. The Air Force commander, via a relay through our HQ radio, wanted more.

"Red Two, the Air Force wants you to land and inspect the crash site for survivors," announced the voice in my flight helmet.

I told them to wait one, that I was doing another flyby to check it out.

While our guy at HQ got back to the Air Force commander, Leese and I and Reacher and the nervous ex-grunt who was our gunner approached the crash site. I wanted to be sure this time. I slowed to about thirty miles an hour just above the trees surrounding the new clearing. I started to circle the smoke and flames below us when we heard explosions. Leese, who always stayed off the controls, said, "I got it." He took the controls and dumped the nose of the Huey to accelerate. "Probably just some leftover ammunition from the fighter exploding," he said, "but I want to come back around in a fast turn just in case." He glanced out his window. "Somebody shot down this guy, and they're still around here somewhere." Leese began a turn to the left to circle back to the smoke. He picked up speed fast, and when we got to the clearing again, he banked hard to the left. We all sank into our seats feeling the pressure of at least two g's as Leese put the Huey into an almost ninety-degree bank. I looked across at him in the left seat, through his side window, and directly down to the wreckage. I had never experienced such a maneuver in flight school. My first thought was that the Huey would disconnect from the rotors, that the Jesus nut would break.

The view was, however, unique and totally revealing. And we were moving so fast we would be harder to hit.

From this dizzy vantage point we could see a few metal parts that hadn't melted and the flashes of exploding ammo. We hoped that all his bombs had gone off in the crash. We radioed that the pilot was definitely dead.

"Ah, roger, Red Two, wait one." We circled at 2,000 feet about a mile away.

"Red Two, this is Preacher Six." Major Williams was now on the horn. "I have just talked to the Air Force, and I agreed that you would land to do an on-site inspection."

Leese, in his capacity as aircraft commander, answered. "Preacher Six, Red Two. We have already confirmed that no one is at the crash site, alive or dead. We have already risked more than we should have to determine this."

Leese should have known better than to try to be logical.

"Whether you have risked enough is my decision, Red Two. You are ordered to proceed to the crash site and land. You will then have your crew get out and inspect the wreckage firsthand. Over and out."

There was silence. I'm sure Leese considered telling him to stuff it, but he had to play his role.

He played it correctly. "Affirmative."

We were now back at the wreckage, circling once again in a scrotum-stretching Leese special. The left side of the Huey was really straight down. After two of these furious turns, he pulled away to set up his approach. He had decided not to try to land in the wreckage-strewn clearing itself because we wouldn't be able to land far enough away from the fire and the exploding ammo. Just behind the point of impact, there was a natural thin spot in the jungle where a few bare, seventy-five-foot trees stood. It certainly wasn't big enough to put a Huey there, but that's where he was headed. Leese was going to show me another trick.

He settled into a hundred-foot hover directly over the tall trees and moved around searching for the right spot to play lawn mower. He had Reacher and the gunner lean out to watch the delicate tail rotor. He found what he liked and began to let the helicopter settle down into the trees.

He had picked the spot perfectly. The tail boom with the spinning rotor on the end had a clear slot to follow down to the ground. The main rotor only had to chop a few two-inch-thick branches off some trees, a maneuver not even hinted at in flight school. When they hit the first branches, it sounded like gunfire.

Splintered wood flew everywhere. Treetops towered above us as we chopped our way down. We settled to the ground amid swirling debris, ass end low on a gentle slope covered with dense undergrowth. There was a moment of silence as the twigs and leaves settled around us. Nothing had been broken.

Reacher and the gunner grabbed their rifles and leapt into the thick tangle of weeds, galloping toward the still-exploding wreckage. The cords from their flight helmets trailed behind them.

Leese and I sat at the bottom of the vertical tunnel he had cut, our heads swiveling on nervous lookout. So far, only the sound of exploding ammo occasionally popped over the sound of the Huey. Reacher and the gunner disappeared through the thicket of trees between us and the wreckage.

We waited.

Whump! Whump, whump! Mortars! From wherever they were hiding, the NVA launched their worst.

We were alone. HQ had not sent a gunship for escort or even another slick to watch over us. Leese and I looked at each other as the mortars got closer. His mouth was thin and his jaw was tight. I wondered if this was as bad as landing gliders. In the dense foliage around us I heard the mortars crashing heavily, shaking the air, searching for us. They sounded like the footfalls of a drunken giant. A big crunch nearby, then one to the side, then another behind us as the invisible giant staggered around trying to stomp us. The NVA were good with their mortars, but it took time to zero in on a new target like us. Since they couldn't see us from where they were, they had to walk the rounds back and forth until they got us.

Just when my fear was at an all-time high, Reacher and the gunner finally broke through the thicket to release us from the trap. They were both pale with fear as they dove on board. Leese had never let the Huey relax, so to speak. He had been ready to go at any second. As the two men hit the deck, Leese went.

He climbed back up through his tunnel in the trees like an express elevator and nosed the Huey over hard just as the rotor cleared the treetops. A mortar went off below just as our tail cleared the last tree.

Reacher told us that there was not even a little piece of the pilot left, and the Air Force commander was finally satisfied. "Not only that," I fantasized he would write to the widow, "but I sent four suckers from the Army right back in there to make sure your husband was dead."

Leese and I joined our company for the next lift after a trip to the Turkey Farm for refueling.

X-Ray was quiet this time. We dropped off the troopers and picked up wounded. At the hospital tent next to the runway at Holloway, I couldn't believe how many bodies were piling up outside the tent. Williams radioed that Leese and I and another ship could fly over to our camp and shut down because he wouldn't need us for the last lift in. I looked at the pile of dead and shivered.

Back at our camp, Sergeant Bailey leaned out of the operations tent and yelled that the company was on its way back to Holloway. Two pilots had been hit.

Leese and I had been lying back for ten minutes at the Big Top, drinking coffee and enjoying every minute away from the gaggle. As Bailey yelled, I noticed the whole battalion on the horizon coming up from the south. Getting closer, the swarm was so noisy it sounded like a war all by itself. It wasn't too hard to imagine how the VC kept track of where we were.

The battalion broke into trail formation a few miles south, and the string of Hueys looped around, landing from the west. Leese and I were downwind from the flight line, and a warm, sweet breeze of burning kerosene from the turbines drifted by us.

The Hueys lined up side by side. Engines were shut down, and the pilots jumped out, carrying their gear. The crew chiefs waited patiently to tie the blades down and postflight their machines. As the pilots got closer, we could hear some whooping and yelling in their midst. It wasn't what we expected to hear after the news of the wounded.

At the Big Top, it was obvious why they were happy. The two wounded pilots, both from the other platoon, were walking with them, grinning and laughing with the rest. The blood from their wounds had dried in their hair and on their faces.

Both men had been hit in the head on the last lift. One had been shot from the front and the other from the side. Both were clutching their helmets, pointing at the holes. One guy had had a bullet hit the visor knob on the forehead portion of his flight helmet. The bullet had crushed his helmet and glanced off. His scalp was bleeding.

The other lucky soul walked around holding his helmet with a finger stuck into the holes on each side of it. Dried blood matted his hair on each side of his head. It was a magician's illusion. The bullet had to have gone through his head, from what we could see. We wanted to know the trick.

"I figured it out on the way back," he said. "I mean, after I stopped feeling for the holes on each side of my head and asking Ernie if I was still alive!" He was still pale, but he laughed. "The bullet hit while we were on short final to X-Ray. Luckily, Ernie was flying. It felt like somebody had hit me on the head with a bat. It blurred my vision. First I thought that a bullet had hit me on the helmet and somehow bounced off. Ernie first noticed the blood. He'd turned to tell me about a round going through the canopy in front of him when he saw it." I could imagine the guy seeing the jagged hole in the side of his friend's flying helmet, blood dripping down his neck. "I reached up to feel my helmet and felt the hole on the right side, but Ernie said the blood was coming from the other side. I put my left hand up and felt *that* hole! I pulled both hands down quickly, and they were both bloody! I felt the helmet again. Two holes all right. Two wounds all right. One on each side of my head. I couldn't believe I was still alive!" He passed the helmet around while he continued his story. "See, it hit here." He pointed in front of his right ear. "The bullet hit this ridge of bone and deflected up between my scalp and the inside of my helmet. Then"—he shook his head in disbelief—"then it circled around inside the top of the helmet and hit this ridge of bone on my left side." He pointed. "It was deflected out here, through the helmet and on through the canopy in front of Ernie!" He beamed. I saw the path the bullet made as it tore its way around through the padding on the inside of the helmet and the two wounds on each side of his head. I shook my head. God again?

As soon as he finished his story, a jeep drove him and the other pilot across the airstrip to the hospital tent. As I watched them go, I saw the eastern sky fill with a huge formation of helicopters coming from the direction of An Khe. The Cav was sending the 227th to join us. That's about as near to full strength as the Cav got.

I joined Resler and the rest of the pilots going over to the compound for chow. About a hundred of us walked across the runway, spread out, talking to our buddies under the twilight sky. We passed the hospital tent, where the smell of blood was strong and body bags concealing grotesquely contorted corpses waited in the shadows.

The next morning, Leese and I stayed behind when the company left. We left a half hour later, to go on a single-ship mission before joining them later.

We had an easy mission to an artillery unit. We were supposed to drop off some radios, the mail, and the unit's commander, who was dropping by to talk shop with his boys. When he was finished, we were to take him back to Pleiku and then join our company.

The grunts were in the middle of a fire mission. Twenty steel barrels grouped on the north side of the clearing pointed eagerly toward the sky in the south. Concussion rings sprang away from the muzzles in the high humidity. The guns rocked back. They were shooting at targets five miles away.

They cleared us to come in, but kept on firing. The landing spot was in front of the guns.

Landing at artillery positions was a thrill. They were always in the middle of a fire mission, and they would keep firing until the ship was just about in front of the first tube. Naturally the final decision about what was too close for comfort was entirely up to the man pulling the lanyard on the cannon. The timing varied a lot. It depended on the mood of the gunner, which in turn depended on whether or not a helicopter had ever blown his tent away.

This was only my second landing into an artillery position. I set up my approach to the clearing in front of the guns and cautiously crept in, constantly reminding them on the radio that I was coming. As I crossed the trees, they were still firing. I glanced at the blasting muzzles on my left and realized that we were beginning to line up on the barrels. They stopped firing. I looked into the black muzzles and watched smoke drift lazily out as I flew through the still-turbulent air in front of them.

Someone decided to resume firing.

I was so close to the guns, looking right down their barrels when they went off, that I thought they had made a mistake and blown us apart. The sound went through me. My chest vibrated. The shock of the explosion rocked the helicopter. I landed and checked the seat. Clean.

The artillery commander told us he'd be about an hour, so I got out and walked around the place.

Twenty 105-mm howitzers were grouped together on one side of the circular clearing. They took up about one fourth of the available space, the rest being kept clear for helicopters.

Spent brass casings glittered in the grass. They took these, eventually, to a large cargo net laid out near the middle of the clearing to be carried away by a Chinook when it was full.

I walked around behind the guns to watch the crews work. They were in the middle of a big salvo, going toward X-Ray, and the pace was hectic. The explosions were more than loud; they shook my body and my brains. I stuffed toilet paper in my ears and kept my mouth open. This was supposed to keep your eardrums from bursting.

One man near each gun took a chain of four or five powder bags out of the shell casings and tore off one of them. He threw it into a nearby fire, where it flashed brilliantly. The strength of the charge was controlled by discarding packets not needed for the distance they were shooting. After adjusting the charge, the man put the round—the business end of the package containing high explosives or white phosphorus—onto the open end of the brass casing. Ready to fire, the shell was stacked on a pile near the gun crew.

A hundred shirtless men worked, sweating, in practiced synchronization in the hot, stagnant air of the clearing. I watched them fire round after round in a fifteen-minute barrage that finally ended when the command "Cease fire" was shouted down the line.

When the thunder stopped, the quiet was startling. The men in the crews began clearing away spent casings and rearranging some of the litter around them, but they were clearly interested in the outcome of their efforts. I heard calls of "How'd we do?"

The aerial observer several miles away, at their target, radioed the news. "A hit. Body count over one fifty." A few isolated cheers sprang from among the twenty crews. Their sweat-covered backs glistened in the sun as they sat down for a smoke break.

Theirs was an odd war. As they worked feverishly in tree-walled clearings dotted here and there, away from everyone else, their enemy remained unseen, and the measure of their success or failure was a radio call from an aerial observer counting bodies. The work was hard and the noise was oppressive. During the month-long battle of Ia Drang valley, it went on twenty-four hours a day. Could a man ever really sleep in such cacophony? I tried it once and couldn't.

I talked to some guys in the crews, and they liked their job, especially as an alternative to being a trooper or a door gunner on a Huey. Their only real danger, aside from their guns blowing up, was being overrun. So far this hadn't happened in the Cav.

They asked me a lot of questions about what was happening. They could see the big flights of choppers heading south. They were having more fire missions with big body counts. The pace was quickening. They were excited about the idea of trapping the NVA. Maybe, just maybe, the enemy could be surrounded and killed. Maybe after suffering such a defeat, they would give up. We could all go home. It seemed possible. We were winning, weren't we?

*　　*　　*

The number of wounded we were carrying was growing fast. That week Leese and I flew more than a hundred wounded to the hospital tent. Other slicks carried a similar number.

When there was room and time, we carried the dead. They had low priority because they were no longer in a hurry. Sometimes they were thrown on board in body bags, but usually not. Without the bags, blood drained on the deck and filled the Huey with a sweet smell, a horribly recognizable smell. It was nothing compared to the smell of men not found for several days. We had never carried so many dead before. We were supposed to be winning now. The NVA were trapped and being pulverized, but the pile of dead beside the hospital tent was growing. Fresh recruits for graves registration arrived faster than they could be processed.

Back at our camp, I was feeling jittery after seeing too much death. I heard that two pilots had got caught on the ground.

Nate and Kaiser had gone to rescue them. Nate was almost in tears as he talked to us in the Big Top. "The stupid assholes. They had been relieved to return for fuel. But you know Paster and Richards: typical gunship pilots. Somehow they think their flex guns make them invulnerable. Anyway, on the flight back they were alone and spotted some VC or NVA or somebody on the ground and decided to attack. Nobody knows how long they were flying around there, because they called after they got hit. When Kaiser and I got there about ten minutes later, the Huey was just sitting there in a clearing looking fine. There were two gunships with us, and they circled around first and took no fire. Kaiser and I went behind the grounded ship. When we landed, I saw a red mass of meat hanging off a tree branch. It turned out to be Paster, hanging by his feet with his skin ripped off. There was nobody else around. The guns kept circling around and a Dust Off landed behind us. I got out, Kaiser stayed with the ship. The medic jumped out and ran with me." Nate kept patting his breast pockets, looking for his pipe. He never found it. "Paster's skin hung down in sheets and covered his head. The bastards had even cut off his cock. They must have just started on Richards, because we found him lying half-naked about a hundred feet away in the elephant grass. His head was almost off." Nate stopped for a second, looking pale. "I almost threw up. Richards and I went to flight school together. The medics cut Paster down and stuffed him into a body bag." He shook his head, holding back tears. "Remember how Richards always bragged about how he knew he'd survive in the jungle if he got shot down? Shit, he even went to jungle school in Panama. If anybody'd be able to get away, it'd be Richards."

Nate's story hit hard. I remembered Richards and his jungle-school patch. Big deal, jungle expert. You got a hundred feet on your one big chance to evade the enemy. All that training down the drain. The thought of his wasting all that training brought tears to my eyes.

The pace remained hectic. The next day several assaults were made to smaller LZs near X-Ray to broaden our front against the NVA. Farris was assigned the command ship in a company-size flight, a mix of ships from the Snakes and the Preachers. We were going to a small, three-ship LZ. He picked me to be his pilot.

Everyone was tense. Radio conversations were terse. The grunts in the back looked grim. Even Farris looked worried. The NVA were being surrounded, and we knew they had to fight.

Farris and I would be in the first group of three to land. The company, each ship carrying eight grunts, trailed out behind us.

As the flight leader, Farris had the option to fly from any position in his flight. He chose the second ship. A theory from the developmental days of the air-assault concept said that the flight commander supposedly got a better idea about what was happening from the middle or even the end of the formation. Really big commanders flew high above us, for the best view of all.

I think this was my first time as a command-ship pilot, and I was all for survival. I would've been very happy flying the brigade commander up there at 5,000 feet, or Westmoreland to his apartment in Saigon. It's amazing how many places I considered being besides there.

In assaults, we usually started drawing fire at 1,000 feet, sometimes at 500. This time we didn't.

At 500 feet, on a glide path to the clearing, smoke from the just-completed prestrike by our artillery and gunships drifted straight up in the still air. There had to be one time when the prep actually worked and everybody was killed in the LZ. I hoped this might be it.

Fighting my feeling of dread, I went through the automatic routine of checking the smoke drift for wind direction. None. We approached from the east, three ships lined up in a trail, to land in the skinny LZ. But it was too quiet!

At 100 feet above the trees, closing on the near end of the LZ, the door gunners in Yellow One started firing. They shot into the trees at the edge of the clearing, into bushes, anywhere they suspected the enemy was hiding. There was no return fire. The two gunships on each side of our flight opened up with their flex guns. Smoke poured out of them as they crackled. My ears rang with the loud but muffled popping as my door gunners joined in with the rest. I ached to have my own trigger. With so many bullets tearing into the LZ, it was hard to believe anyone on the ground could survive.

The gunships had to stop firing as we flared close to the ground because we could be hit by ricocheting bullets. Still no return fire. Maybe they *were* all dead! Could this be the wrong spot?

My adrenaline was high, and I was keenly aware of every movement of the ship. I waited for the lurch of dismounting troopers as the skids neared the ground. They were growling and yelling behind me, psyched for battle. I could hear them yelling above all the noise. I still can.

My landing was synchronized with the lead ship's, and as our skids hit the ground, so did the boots of the growling troops.

At the same instant, the uniformed regulars from the North decided to spring their trap. From at least three different directions, they opened up on our three ships and the off-loading grunts with machine-gun crossfire. The LZ was suddenly alive with their screaming bullets. I tensed on the controls, involuntarily leaning forward, ready to take off. I had to fight the logical reaction to leave immediately. I was light on the skids, the troops were out. Let's go! Farris yelled on the radio for Yellow One to go. They didn't move.

The grunts weren't even making it to the trees. They had leapt out, screaming murderously, but now they dropped all around us, dying and dead. The lead ship's rotors still turned, but the men inside did not answer. I saw the sand spurt up in front of me as bullets tore into the ground. My stomach tightened to stop them. Our door gunners were firing over the prone grunts at phantoms in the trees.

A strange quietness happened in my head. The scene around me seemed far away. With the noise of the guns, the cries of the gunners about everybody being dead, and Farris calling for Yellow One to go, I thought about bullets coming through the Plexiglas, through my bones and guts, and through the ship and never stopping. A voice echoed in the silence. It was Farris yelling, "Go! Go! Go!"

I reacted so fast that our Huey snapped off the ground. My adrenaline seemed to power the ship as I nosed over hard to get moving fast. I veered to the right of the deadly quiet lead ship, still sitting there. The door gunners fired continuously out both sides. The tracers coming at me now seemed as thick as raindrops. How could they miss? As a boy I made a game of dodging raindrops in the summer showers. I always got hit eventually. But not this time. I slipped over the treetops and stayed low for cover, accelerating. I veered left and right fast, dodging, confounding, as Leese had taught me, and when I was far enough away, I swooped up and away from the nightmare. My mind came back, and so did the sound.

"What happened to Yellow Three?" a voice said. It was still on the ground.

The radios had gone wild. I finally noticed Farris's voice saying,

"Negative, White One. Veer left. Circle back." Farris had White One lead the rest of the company into an orbit a couple of miles away. Yellow One and Yellow Three were still in the LZ.

I looked down at the two ships sitting quietly on the ground. Their rotors were turning lazily as their turbines idled. The machines didn't care, only the delicate protoplasm inside them cared. Bodies littered the clearing, but some of the thirty grunts we had brought in were still alive. They had made it to cover at the edge of the clearing.

Farris had his hands full. He had twelve more ships to get in and unloaded. Then the pilot of Yellow Three called. He was still alive, but he thought his partner was dead. His crew chief and gunner looked dead, too. He could still fly.

Two gunships immediately dove down to escort him out, machine guns blazing. It was a wonderful sight to see from a distance.

Only Yellow One remained on the ground. She sat, radios quiet, still running. There was room behind her to bring in the rest of the assault.

A grunt who found himself still alive got to a radio. He said that he and a few others could keep some cover fire going for the second wave.

Minutes later, the second group of three ships was on its way in, and Farris told me to return to the staging area. I flew back a couple of miles to a big field, where I landed and picked up another load of wild-eyed boys.

They also growled and yelled. This was more than just the result of training. They were motivated. We all thought that this was the big push that might end it all. By the time I made a second landing to the LZ, the enemy machine guns were silent. This load would at least live past the landing.

Somebody finally shut down Yellow One's turbine when we left. Nobody in the crew could. They were all patiently waiting to be put into body bags for the trip home.

Why I didn't get hit I'll never know. I must have read the signs right. Right? They started calling me Lucky after that mission.

*   *   *

That afternoon, while the sunset glowed orange behind Pleiku in the distance, Leese and I and some others walked over to the hospital tent.

We came to see the bodies. A small crowd of living stood watching the growing crowd of dead. Organization prevailed. Bodies on this pile. Loose parts here. Presumably the spare arms and legs and heads would be reunited with their owners when they were pushed into the bags. But graves registration had run out of body bags, and the corpses were stacked without them.

New arrivals, wounded as well as dead, were brought over from the helicopters. A medic stood in the doorway of the operating tent diverting some of the stretchers away. Some cases were too far gone. Bellies blown open. Medics injected morphine into them. But morphine couldn't change the facts. I stared at one of the doomed men, fifty feet away. He saw me, and I knew that he knew. His frightened eyes widened, straining to live. He died. After a few minutes somebody came by and closed his eyes.

A new gunner, a black kid who had until recently been a grunt, had come over with me and Leese. We stayed back, but he had gone closer to the pile of bodies just to look. He started wailing and crying and pulling at the corpses and had to be dragged away. He had seen his brother at the bottom of the heap.

Two days later there was a lull in the fighting, at least as far as our company was concerned. We were given the day off. You could hear a collective sigh of relief. Compared to Happy Valley, this was *action*, and living through a year of it seemed unlikely.

What do you do on your first day off after weeks of action when you're feeling tired, depressed, and doomed on a hot, wet day at Camp Holloway, Vietnam? You get in a deuce-and-a-half and go into Pleiku and drink your brains out. That's what you do.

*   *   *

Normally, the Cav carried only its own troopers, but we hauled ARVNs one day. I had heard stories about their unwillingness to fight.

"When you land at the LZ, make sure your door gunners cover the departing ARVNs," Williams said at the briefing. "There have been several incidents of so-called ARVNs turning around and firing into the helicopter that just dropped them off. Also, you may have a few on your ship that don't want to get out. If this happens, have *one* gunner force them out. The other gunner should be covering him. If your gunner has to shoot, make sure he knows to stop shooting when he gets the one who made the wrong move. A wrong move is turning around with a rifle pointed at you. We're flying this one lift today as a favor. We won't be doing it again." Williams gave his flock a paternal look. "Keep your eyes open."

I was amazed. This was the first time I had heard the rumors verified. In the months to come, I would hear as much about being wary with the ARVNs as I did about the Cong. If neither was to be trusted, who were our allies? Whose war was this, anyway? The people who had the most at stake wouldn't get out of the choppers to fight?

But we lifted the South Vietnamese without incident this time. We flew them to a big LZ from which they were supposed to patrol the newly liberated Ia Drang valley and maintain the status quo of allied dominance. Within twenty-four hours they were pinned down by the VC. In two months we would return to retake the valley.

While we waited for a couple of hours to load the ARVNs, I saw a body lying in the field when we landed at the pickup zone next to Holloway. A piece of rope still cinched his neck.

I walked back and asked Resler, "What's the story on that guy?"

"He's a Chinese adviser," Gary said. "The same one we gave to the ARVNs yesterday for questioning." He looked toward the body. "You see him up close yet?"

"No."

"Well, he must have answered one of their questions wrong, because they took a chunk out of the side of his head as big as your fist." He grimaced. "His brains are leaking out. Want to go see him?"

"No. I've seen enough brains to last me."

"Hey, look at those guys." Gary pointed toward the body, about two hundred feet away. Two soldiers from the adviser compound were setting up a pose for a photograph. One man knelt on one knee behind the body while his friend moved around looking for the best angle for a snapshot. He took a few shots, but apparently the pose wasn't lively enough for him. He had his friend grab the dead man by the hair and raise the gory head off the ground, brains dripping. He posed like a man holding a dead gazelle.

With the ARVN in place, the Cav's mission was done. We only killed people; we did not take land. Such was the war of attrition.

By November 26, America had won its first large-scale encounter with the North Vietnamese Army. The Cav and the B-52s killed 1,800 Communists. The NVA killed more than 300 GIs. The Ia Drang valley campaign was one of the few battles in which I saw clearings filled with NVA bodies. In all, I might have seen a thousand of their corpses sprawled in the sun, rotting. We left them there.

The Cav waited a few days before looking for its missing. That gave the bodies time to get ripe enough for the patrols we lifted out to find them. It was the only way a dead man could be found in the tall elephant grass.

They did not growl now. Stacked on the cargo deck, they still fought, frozen inside their rubber bags, arms and legs stiffly askew. The smell of death seeped out of the zippered pouches and made the living retch. No matter how fast I flew, the smell would not blow away.

"We cut the enemy's throat instead of just jabbing away at his stomach. This is just the beginning," said one of our generals in *Life* magazine.

A Filthy Little War

from *Thud Ridge*

BY JACK BROUGHTON

First published in 1969 at the height of the Vietnam War, Thud
Ridge *became an instant classic. The author, Jack Broughton,
was an F-105 Thunderchief ("Thud") pilot who had survived
the experiences he wrote about. What he had to say was
startling to an American public unaccustomed to acrimonious
debate about the proper use of fighting forces from the military
leaders who led us during wartime.*

*Broughton's indictment of the criminal stupidities of the
upper echelons of the U.S. Air Force and the Department of
Defense has since been expanded into almost countless volumes by other writers, but it was raw, powerful, and fresh
when* Thud Ridge *first exploded on an American public
stunned at the sacrifices being demanded to prosecute the
war. Broughton also posed a moral question for which our
nation still has not found an answer—should American lives
and treasure be sacrificed by political leaders in limited wars
that they have no intention of trying to win? Alas, this is the
burden of empire, a burden that most Americans still instinctively reject.*

In the selection from Thud Ridge *that follows, Colonel
Broughton and his wingman, whom he refers to as Ken but
who was at the time Major, later Brigadier General, Kenneth
Bell, fight the system to rescue a Thud pilot who ejected over
Laos. They almost die in the attempt and ultimately fail. Here
is the entire Vietnam experience in fifteen pages.*

JOE CAME TO US AS AN ADMINISTRATIVE OFFICER, EVEN THOUGH HE
was a rated pilot. He was not a Thud driver by trade, but he
scrounged an hour here and an hour there until he could leap
all the hurdles and qualify himself for combat. He had a hell of

a time mastering the art of hanging behind a tanker and refueling in flight, but he did it. Joe—another one of my boys who had not managed to graduate from the toughest postgraduate school in the world, the school that demanded a hundred missions over the North in a Thud for a diploma. He was now simply Tomahawk four, down over the North.

I split my flight into elements of two to search more effectively and headed for the coordinates that were supposed to represent the spot where Joe was down. As I entered the new area, I knew even more than before that time would be a big factor. It was a fantastic-looking spot. The hills rolled up into small mountains and farther south leaped into the sheer sawtoothed karst that dropped violently to the winding riverbed far below. The sawtooths were already shading the huge trees rolling from ridge to ridge underneath them, and my first thought was of two big hopes. I hoped he hadn't landed on top of one of those sharp knobs, and I hoped we had a good, gutty chopper driver sitting in the wings. I hoped half-right.

I swung my element a bit north of due west and started a gradual turn that would allow me to get a good look at the land below and would bring me out of the orbit about over the sharp peaks to the south. I did not have long to wait, and halfway through my first turn a new, strong, and definite rescue beeper came up on the inside of my turn. I grabbed a quick directional steer on him and called my number two man, who verified both the beeper and the steer. We wrapped those Thuds around to the left like we were driving midget racers, and although the force of the turn nearly knocked them out of the sky, we were able to roll straight and level before we got to the spot on the ground where the beacon was telling us our fourth downed comrade of the afternoon was waiting for us and for the help we could bring.

The steering needle swung to the left and then to the tail and I knew I had him pinpointed. "Tomahawk four, Tomahawk four—this is Waco on emergency. If you read me, turn your beeper off."

Like the cut of a knife the screecher shut off and the small, clear voice said, "This is Tomahawk four. I read you loud and clear, Waco. I am okay and awaiting pickup."

I almost pulled my beast into a stall as I told the world on the radio that I had found Joe. "Waco two, I've got his position spotted. Get up to altitude and get us some Spads and some choppers in here on the double. Tell them no sweat on MiGs and tell them we have to hurry. We're far enough south so they ought to be able to get the job done without making it a big production." I swung around for the spot and yanked my sweaty map out from under my left buttock, which is still the best map holder ever devised for a fighter plane, and prepared to get some good coordinates for the rescue guys. "Joe, turn your beeper on now." I fixed right over the beacon and said, "Okay, Joe, turn it off, and if I just flew right over your position, turn it back on for two seconds, then back off." The reply was just like the survival movies and I knew that I was right and that Joe was both in good shape and as sharp as he could be.

I relayed the coordinates, and since the rescue system had been alerted by Tomahawk lead on his way out for fuel, it was not too long before two different Spads, but still using the call sign Nomad, arrived on the scene and went to work like a couple of old pros. They took over and my job reverted to that of top cover. These Nomads were doing it properly.

"Okay, Tomahawk four—Nomad here. Turn your beeper on for ten seconds." He lined up and said encouragingly, "Okay, good steer, I'm lined up on you. Turn your beeper on and leave it on till I tell you to turn it off." Completing his pass, he got a good low-level swing and was able to bend his little bird around in a tight turn that allowed him to keep the area in view. "Okay, Tomahawk, beeper off. Are you on top of that ridge I just flew over?"

"Nomad—Tomahawk. I am on the east side of the ridge you just flew over, about halfway down to where it levels off into a little plateau. I have plenty of flares."

This Nomad showed a completely different picture of the rescue pilots than the one we had just attempted to work with. He was sure enough of the position and condition of his man and knew how critical the time was, so he called the controllers on his second radio and directed that the choppers start inbound on the now relatively short trip that they had to make. All the terrain there was relatively high in elevation, which would make the choppers' job more difficult, but all in all, things smacked of possible success. Pulling up abruptly over the suspected spot, Nomad announced, "Rog, Tomahawk, think I've got you. The choppers will be here in a few minutes. Get ready for pickup and give me a red smoke flare now so I can be sure I get them to the right spot from the right approach direction." Joe, like many of us, figured that those flares and the radio were two of the most valuable pieces of cargo you could carry, and he had several extras strapped to the outside of his anti-g suit. He took one out, carefully selected the end that would emit a thick red smoke that would float up through the trees to stain the twilight sky and momentarily show both his position and the direction of the wind before it drifted away into nothing, held it skyward, and pulled the lanyard. "Rog, Tomahawk four, I've got your smoke. Sit tight for a couple of minutes."

But the minutes dragged, the sun sank lower, and the haze thickened. I had been stooging around on the deck for quite some time and could not delay too long before departing for the night rendezvous with the tanker that I now had to have, or else I would have to park this bird of mine in the jungle. But I knew the tankers would be there. Where in hell were those choppers?

"Tomahawk four—this is Nomad. I hate to tell you this, old buddy, but one of the choppers thinks he has a rough engine and has turned back, and the other one has decided he will go with him in case he has any trouble. We can't get another one up here tonight, so I guess you better pull up a log and try and get some rest. We will try and get back in the morning—and by the way, there is a stream about fifty yards downhill from you if you get low on water. C H I Dooey [Thai for 'sorry about

279

that'], old buddy." At least the Spad driver got right to the point. He knew we were screwed and so did Joe.

"Roger, this is Tomahawk four, understand. Thank you. I'll be waiting for you in the morning."

I couldn't believe it. So what if one of the choppers did have a rough engine—we'd had rough engines all afternoon. If the first one decided he was going to crap out, so what—why did the second one want to go back in case of trouble? We had trouble we hadn't used yet right here, and we had the rescue in our hip pocket. I still can't believe it. I try to think nice things about the situation and about the actions and decisions I saw that day, but I can't.

I stumbled off to find the tanker that would give us what we needed for the trip back to base. But we weren't through yet. Nomad's wingman split the evening ether with, "Mayday, Mayday, Mayday—Nomad lead is hit and on fire." In his frustration he had wandered too close to someone on the ground, and once again unseen small arms had scored a hit.

Oh, boy, what next! I knew that Nomad was far slower than we were and the only place that he could be was behind us, so I forgot the fuel and wheeled 180 degrees and back we went.

"Nomad—this is Nomad four. You're on fire. Bail out, bail out, *bail out!*" The wingman repeated his call. "Bail out, you're on fire."

With lots of calm, Nomad came back and said, "Negative."

Not negative because he was not on fire, but negative because he was not about to park his Spad over the dark noplace where he knew four fellows had withered in the sunlight. He was not about to leap into what would have been either death or prison, knowing there would be no rescue for him that night. He knew what the odds were, and he was going to take his chances with the machine. He was not about to become number five if he could help it. There is little doubt that he knew he was on fire. In a bird like the 105, you cannot see the wing, and besides the wing seldom burns. In the Spad you can see the wing, and he was burning severely from the wing root. His judgment was

swift, and I am sure that his head was filled with many thoughts
of things other than himself as he made his move.

He rolled his flaming Spad over onto her back and dove for
the deck. His wingman got the natural impression that he had
lost control of the machine, and that resulted in a few more
panic-stricken calls in the black, unfriendly night. Down he
went, pointed at the hills, the hills he could not see but those
he knew were there. If he got the ancient warrior going fast
enough, he could blow the flame out. He could starve the fire,
he could divert the airflow, and the fire would go out and he
could limp home. And if not—why not try. He did, and it
worked, and while it was working, his wingman and the Thud
drivers still left in the area marveled and wondered what the
next step would be. The next step was a big batch of silence
and lots of hard breathing. After what seemed like four hours
and could not possibly have been more than a minute, the not-
so-calm-but-ever-so-pleased voice of Mr. Nomad announced that
the fire had gone out, that he was pulling the nose up, and
that he had plenty of fuel to get back to his homedrome. The
night was black, but not nearly as black as my thoughts. I
wheeled once again, and more than seven hours after I left Ta-
khli I touched down on that remote piece of concrete and unstrapped from the belts that bound me to the machine. I was
beat but I was not through fighting.

I got on the hot line to the big bosses as soon as I got into the
operations building and found them ready to talk. They were, of
course, anxious to hear what had happened from my view, and
I told them. I was anxious to know what had happened from
the rescue guy's point of view, but nobody was ever able to
explain that to my satisfaction.

While I cleaned up the details and grabbed a bite to eat, we
got the word "go" on my proposal for a combination rescue
effort and MiG sweep for the next morning. It was already close
to midnight, and morning meant something like 4 A.M. for this
one, so the press was on again.

Morning came quickly, but the challenge pushed aside the

need for rest. The weather in the area where Joe had parked was as advertised—rotten. The clouds had stacked up against the hills, and the electronic guys who had been watching the spot all night reported no signals, but cloud right down to the deck.

Despite the fact that Joe was in a rather lightly populated region, there are very few areas up there that don't have enough people to give a downed airman a rough time. There was little doubt that they knew exactly where he was, and his chances of getting out were diminishing by the hour while the weather that hampered us made it that much easier for the bad guys.

When nothing good had been reported by Tuesday morning, we realized that if we were to do any good on the now slim hope that Joe was still on the loose and still waiting for us, we were going to have to get the ball rolling ourselves. The afternoon mission seemed to provide a good vehicle, and I loaded it with our best people. It was an interesting one as it was headed for one of the better targets right in downtown Hanoi, and although everyone knows that your chances of coming back from one of those are not the greatest, there were always people crawling over each other trying to get on them. That is something about a fighter pilot that is both unique and hard to describe. Tell him you are going to send him to hell, and that things will be rougher than he's ever seen, and he will fight for the chance to go. He may be petrified half the time, but he will die rather than admit it, and if he gets back, most of the time he will tell you that it might have been a bit rough but not so rough that he doesn't want to go back and try to do it just a little bit better next time.

This mission was especially attractive as we were to be allowed to provide our own MiG cover flight for a change. On an approach somewhat similar to the sweep of the day before, we were to take one flight without bombs whose only job was to fly like the normal strike aircraft but go get the MiGs if they showed. I was forced to take that flight in the face of the wails of my three squadron commanders. My flight call sign for this one was Wabash, and I picked myself three sharp flight leaders from the squadron and put them on my wing. That's how I wound up with Ken on my wing as Wabash two. We charged around the course despite the fact that the weather forecast was quite dismal. (The weather is seldom what you would call really good, but there was quite a bit of doubt that we would get in that day.) We got down into the MiGs' backyard, but they did not rise to the bait. They knew better than we did what the weather was downtown and figured we were just spinning our wheels and would not be able to get in to our primary target; there was little sense in exposing themselves. They were right. We had to divert about three-quarters of the way down the Ridge and eat another frustration pill.

The rest of the flights went to their alternative targets. As soon as I canceled the primary strike, I headed for the last spot we had seen Joe. Once in the area, it was no problem to identify the exact position, and I split my Wabash flight again, to cover more area, and set about the job of trying to raise some sign of Tomahawk four. I switched to the emergency channel I knew he would be monitoring—if he still had his radio, if the battery was still working, and if he still had the freedom to operate the radio as he wished. All three were pretty big ifs by this time, but the events of Sunday had left such a bitter taste in all of our mouths that we wanted to exhaust every possibility. As I moved, I alternated radio calls with "Tomahawk four, Tomahawk four—this is Wabash lead. If you read, come up on your beeper," and the next circuit I would give him, "Joe—this is Wabash lead. If you read me, Joe, come up on emergency channel. Give me a call on emergency, Joe."

And up came the beeper. Weak to be sure and with nowhere near the piercing tone that it had belted out a couple of days ago, but it was there. It was so weak that I could not home in on it the way I wanted to and thus could not get a really accurate fix, but it was very close to the same area. "Tomahawk four—Wabash. I read your beeper. If you read me, shut your beeper off now." There was always the possibility that Joe, or whoever had his beeper, had not actually read my earlier transmissions but had simply turned it on when he realized that the Thuds overhead were looking, not simply passing by. Of course, if the wrong people have the beeper and you sucker in a little too close, you are liable to be met with a blast of ground fire. Even though we all knew this and even though we have lost some machines and people to this ruse, when you pick up the scent that could be one of the guys, you acknowledge this possibility and press on regardless.

The beeper operator responded perfectly and the pitifully weak beep left the air as directed. I called my element lead and told him to get back to the tankers as fast as he could, pick up a load of juice, and come back to relieve me. While he was gone, I continued to work the beeper but could not pin it down to a specific ridge or group of bushes. I would start in on it, get my directional indication, and then it would fade, just like a weak radio when you are trying to catch the prime line or note of music on your favorite radio program. Try as we might, neither my wingman, Ken, nor I could get what we wanted out of the beeper, nor could we get any voice contact.

While we were working our hearts out in a vain attempt to get the specifics I knew so well I would need if I was to persuade my bosses to launch the rescue fleet again, my element was encountering delays on the tanker rendezvous, and this was the first indication that a more exciting afternoon was ahead. I did not want to leave the scene until I had at least the other part of my flight in the area where they could give one more try for something that would be a firmer hat hanger when I tried to sell the case. We played our fuel right down to the minimum and they were not back yet. The time of day indicated that we would not be able to get the show in gear and get back that night, but there was time for the element to work a bit longer. They did not show, as they were hung up on the tanker, and I played the fuel to the point that everything would have to work just right on the way back, or Wabash one and two were in trouble.

I had in effect bet heavily on the fact that the ground controllers and the tankers would appreciate the seriousness of the situation, and that they would do their job of getting me where I was supposed to be, and get a tanker up to us in time to avert fuel starvation and the resultant loss of machines and maybe people—like me and my wingman.

When I could wait no longer, I called the element and brought them up to speed on my results so far. I told them to get back in as soon as they could and repeat my efforts. If they got nothing better than I did, they were to hit the tankers again and head for home where we would recap the situation and make our pitch for another rescue attempt. This accomplished, Ken and I reached for all the altitude we could get and I started screaming for ground control to get me with a tanker, quickly.

As we leveled at maximum altitude, we should have been within voice range of the control people. We called and called but received no answer. I knew we were transmitting okay, as I could hear and talk to other fighters and tankers in the area, but none of us could get the control guys to answer or assist. I turned my internal radio gear to the emergency position, which is supposed to knock every ground controller right out of his chair as he sits in his darkened room and surveys the air picture, but to no avail. We desperately needed help and nobody would help. As Ken and I tried not to believe the story our gauges were telling us, we both knew that it was most doubtful that we would be able to get ground-control direction to a tanker in time. We didn't know why they wouldn't answer, but we knew time was eating fuel, and things looked grim as Ken punched the mike button and passed that simple phrase that means more to a fighter pilot than all the fancy emergency calls: "Boss, I'm hurting."

One of our tanker friends was listening and was trying as hard as we were to rock someone off his seat and get some steers going. He advised us that he was blasting away with both of his big radios on all channels and, like us, could get nothing. We started to try a freelance rendezvous and hookup with him using his internal gear and ours, but it became immediately apparent that we were just too far apart and that there was not enough fuel left to get us together.

Then someone awoke to that lonely cry of emergency to the north and the radio spoke to us, "Aircraft on emergency, what's your problem?" I spit out my answer as tersely as I could, but I obviously did not have the regular crew chief, as I got the most frustrating of answers, "Stand by."

I couldn't stand by and barked back, "Listen, I can't stand by, I have two Thuds at minimum emergency fuel and I have got to get to a tanker right now. Give me a steer to the nearest tanker, quickly, or we are both going to flame out."

As I looked over the side at the rough green carpet below, I subconsciously remembered that this was the area where the little people skin captives alive. Some of the more vivid horror stories I had heard made a fast lap around my head, only to be jarred out of position by my friendly controller's reply to my desperate plea: "Emergency aircraft—this is control. I am having trouble hearing you and don't quite understand your problem. Proceed further south and give me a call later and I will set up a tanker for you."

Balls, better that clod should have been looking down at these headhunters than me. I hoped he fell out of his swivel chair and bumped his little head on his scope. The tankers screamed at him and Ken and I both screamed at him and he wouldn't come back up on the air. But someone in that center must have heard and understood, because within about thirty seconds a new voice came booming through loud and clear from the center, but unfortunately as he shoved Clodley out of the way and took over the scope, he must have alerted all other control agencies within a zillion miles that he had two birds about to flame out, because all at once we had more help than we could use. They all wanted to help now, and they all wanted to do it at once. Within sixty seconds we had calls from every ground operator who could get a hand on a mike and who could make his mouth work. They each wanted us to cycle the emergency equipment, they each wanted an identifying turn or a dogleg, and they each wanted a detailed explanation of the problem. It was tough to get a word in edgewise, but Ken finally managed to get through with, "Boss, I'm down to five hundred pounds." I had seven hundred, and either quantity is about enough to take a Thud around the block, and that's all.

The next two minutes were critical and it was clear that the controllers were out of control. I held the mike button down for a few seconds hoping to cut a few people out and announced, "Okay, all control agencies shut up and listen. This is Wabash lead. I've only got a couple of minutes of fuel left and I must have a tanker. Now, whichever one of you has good contact with me and has me identified for sure, take control of me. Sit back and take a deep breath and go to work. You've got to do it right, and if you don't, I'm going to park these two birds in the jungle, and so help me if I do, I'll walk back and kill you. The rest of you get off the air."

One kind soul accepted the challenge and tried to get with the program, but he was unsure of himself and his resources and he was stumbling. When Ken came through with, "Two hundred pounds, boss," I figured we had about had the stroke.

Then out of nowhere came the clear voice of White tanker. "Wabash—this is White. I think I have a beacon on you. I've passed all the gas I am authorized to for the day, and I just have enough to get back to home base, but if you are hurting as badly as I think you are, I'm willing to give it a try. Have to land at an intermediate base and get my wrist slapped. Deviation from plans, you know."

At last. Someone who sounded like he knew what was going on. "Rog, White—Wabash here. You call the shots, but make it quick."

"Okay, Wabash, turn to zero nine zero and drop down to twenty-four thousand. I should be about forty miles back on the inside of your turn. Okay, Wabash, roll out, roll out. Steady on. Now look at eight o'clock. Eight a little low."

"Okay, Ken, we're going past him. There he is about seven to you. A little low."

"I got him and I'm showing zero on the fuel."

"I've still got two hundred pounds. Go get him. Pull your nose up and roll back to your left. You'll fall right down on top of him."

As Ken rolled up over his left shoulder and let the big nose fall through, there that big fat beauty was, and Ken's engine started chugging as the pumps reached for the last drops of fuel.

"White—Wabash two. Got you in sight and I'm flaming out now. Toboggan. Go down. Go down. I'm flamed out. Hold two fifty and go down. Come on, fellows—give me a chance—toboggan."

"White, he's flamed out, *stuff that nose down*. He's got to coast up to you. Don't miss, boomer."

As the big load with the lifesaving fuel pushed over into a dive, the now silent Thud coasted into position behind him, and Ken almost sighed as he said, "Come get me, boomer." And the sarge in the back end of the tanker lay on his belly, took hold of the controls of his flying refueling boom, aimed one time, and rammed the boom into the Thud's nose. As the hydraulic locks bit into the receptacle, Ken was hooked up and being towed along for the ride. As the fuel poured into his tanks and the engine restarted, I was delicately charging into position on his wing as my fuel needle bounced on and off the empty mark. As his tanks registered a thousand pounds, he disengaged and slid to the side while I moved into the slot, and before I chugged to silence, the same expert gentleman stuck me and the fuel flowed. After I filled up, Ken came back on the boom and filled up and we left for home.

"Nice save, White. Where are you going to land?"

"I'll have to go into your place."

"Good, we'll see you on the ground. Beautiful crew, and that boomer is absolutely gorgeous."

"Glad we could help. See you later."

All the way home I didn't even talk to all the various control guys whose areas we passed through. They were all very efficient now that we didn't need them, and it was not because I was pouting that I didn't talk. I just didn't trust myself to speak to them at the moment, as I am sure that I would have hurt someone's feelings. My next task was to get on the phone to my big bosses, which I did as soon as I got on the ground and again thanked White Tanker for his save.

One of Ken's additional duties, for he was a wing staff weenie, was running our Standardization and Evaluation program. The program directed that masses of records be kept on each pilot certifying that each was up-to-date on all the recurring courses of instruction and examinations as the various headquarters saw fit. Even in war we got inspected by inspection teams of as many as forty-five men from each of our headquarters, as often as four times a year. They stayed in Bangkok and commuted to the jungle daily in our C-47 gooney bird. It was an almost unbelievable farce, but they got combat pay for it.

A few days after we landed from this particular flight, Ken stopped by the office and advised, "Boss, you were due for a headquarters proficiency flight check," and handed me my report card. It said, "Colonel Broughton was given a proficiency evaluation while flying as Force Commander on a combat strike mission. His demonstrated ability to command and control an entire strike force is outstanding. He was able to cope with several critical and unforeseen problems with cool and decisive action. Flight was debriefed." We almost laughed ourselves sick.

It takes a lot of maneuvering of forces and some significant changes in plans to mount a sizable rescue effort such as we would need to try what I wanted to try. I thus had to convince those further up the line that we could be relatively sure of gaining something from the effort. If you launch for this purpose, you have to give up some more routine mission that you are scheduled for, and this often causes raised eyebrows in some quarters. I guess they knew I felt quite strongly about this one, and since we had verified that signals were coming from the area, and since we knew that Joe appeared to be in good shape, I got the okay for the next day. We provided the fighter cover and configured for that specific mission. The rescue people came up with the Spads and the HH-3C Sikorsky choppers, better known as the Jolly Green Giants, and we prebriefed to rendezvous crossing the border. We staggered our fighters so we could have good cover through both the search and the rescue, should that come to pass. It didn't come to pass. The Spads looked and got nothing. No noise and nothing visual. We escorted them back out through the quiet countryside where nothing moved, and nobody even fired a round that we saw. That was officially the end of the attempt. We had done all we could.

The next day, leading a flight, Ken was able to swing back over the area again. He repeated our previous pattern, and bigger than hell the beeper came up on command. He called for voice contact expecting the same void that we had received two days before, but this time the beeper talked to him on the emergency channel. Only problem was that it was talking in an oriental voice. It was not until then, on that Thursday afternoon, that the mission we had started on Sunday was finally all through.

The Professionals

from *On Yankee Station*

BY JOHN B. NICHOLS AND BARRETT TILLMAN

The American public was not in the mood for heroes during the Vietnam War, but there were plenty of them in the military's ranks. In this excerpt from their book On Yankee Station, *John Nichols and Barrett Tillman tell of one such man, Lt. Comdr. Mike Estocin, an A-4 Skyhawk pilot. The supreme tragedy of Vietnam was that the lives of so many men like Mike Estocin were squandered without purpose.*

FLYING ESCORT ON IRON HAND SORTIES GAVE FIGHTER PILOTS greater appreciation of the attack community. Perhaps the bravest man I ever knew, and one of the finest aviators, was Lt. Comdr. Mike Estocin of VA-192. We flew together in Air Wing 19 off the *Ticonderoga* in 1967, and Mike was on a roll. He seemed to wage a personal war against SAM batteries, and he wasn't content merely to suppress them. He wanted to destroy them.

On 20 April 1967, Mike led a three-plane flight against Haiphong, in the face of heavy SAM opposition. Mike called out the missiles, led his flight against three sites, and took out all three. But his A-4E sustained blast damage, and he pulled off to check his airplane. Satisfied he could stay in the air, he returned to the target to launch his last Shrike.

By the time Mike egressed, he was losing fuel at a horrible rate. He estimated that he had five minutes of flight time remaining. Providentially, a KA-3 tanker was close enough for him to plug in, and they flew formation back toward the task force. The Skyhawk was pumping fuel overboard through holes in the wings, as the KA-3 passed far more fuel than Mike was using.

None of us who saw that picture can ever forget it: the little A-4 hooked up to the "Whale," flying a long straight-in to *Tico* with Mike radioing instructions to the tanker pilot: "You're half a ball low, take it up." Mike Estocin was a precision aviator.

Finally, between two and three miles from the ramp, the tanker unhooked and pulled up. Mike was committed; he had fuel for one pass at the deck. Then his airplane caught fire.

But it didn't matter. He made an excellent landing, the fire crews doused the flames, and Mike opened the canopy. He tossed down his helmet to a crewman, alighted from the cockpit, and walked across the deck, not even looking back. Another day, another dollar.

Six days later I flew Mike's wing during a strike on petroleum facilities in Haiphong. It was the second Alpha of the day, with clear skies and unlimited visibility.

We coasted in ahead of the strike group at 21,000 feet, headed for Site 109 north of the city. As the strike pulled off target and headed for the beach, Mike called, "The site is up!" We turned directly toward the SAM site.

Our radar controller, noting the strike was outbound, queried, "Are you feet wet yet?" Mike answered, "Negative," as we continued northward, my F-8 stepped up in a right-hand SAM box.

Moments later Red Crown came back: "The strike is all feet wet. What is your position? Are you feet wet?" There was apprehension in his voice.

I glanced over and saw Mike leaning forward, obviously looking for the SAM he knew would come. Then we both saw the liftoff, straight ahead about eight miles. Mike called it, and I acknowledged. The SA-2 arced up, the booster separated, and the missile continued head-on. I waited for Mike's turn to offset the SAM's heading, but we maintained course.

In retrospect, it's apparent what happened. Mike, the dedicated Iron Hand, was closing the range for a high-percentage shot at the site. He ignored the SAM, concentrating on firing a Shrike.

He waited too long. The SAM exploded off the A-4's left

nose, rolling the Skyhawk almost inverted to starboard. In a steep-diving, right-hand turn, Mike's airplane shed debris while trailing heavy flames from the belly.

Following, I was relieved to see the Skyhawk begin a pullout, coming level at about 2,000 feet. I was closing rapidly, and to prevent an overshoot I extended my speed brakes and finally had to lower my wheels and raise the variable-incidence wing. We were making about 160 knots, still decelerating.

Fire was visible from Mike's wingroot as I flew close aboard to starboard. I heard the high warble of another SAM closing in. My F-8 was rocked by the missile's passing and I felt the explosion behind me. It was that close. But I was more concerned with Mike.

Now very close to his right wing, I could see Mike leaning well forward in his seat, but he didn't turn to look at me. There was no response to my calls, so I went to guard frequency and summoned the ResCAP. We were directly over Haiphong, headed for the water, so there seemed a chance Mike could make it.

I crossed to port, and it was then I knew my hopes were baseless. The left nose and cockpit area were heavily damaged. The 350-pound SAM warhead had done its job. Mike's airplane had many large holes and the port intake was smashed. For lack of anything else to do, I crossed back to starboard. We were about three miles from the water, descending to 1,000 feet.

Then, ever so slowly, the Skyhawk began a left-hand roll. I followed to about ninety degrees, then realized Mike wasn't going to recover. I returned to level flight as the A-4 went inverted and seemed to hang in midair for a few seconds. Suddenly the centerline tank blew off and both Shrikes fired. The circuits were apparently burned through, punching off the drop tank and launching the missiles.

Then the nose came through and the Skyhawk impacted from inverted. I flew around the crash site at 500 feet, looking for a parachute. There was none. Flak increased, and that was no place to be low and slow. The ResCAP, still inbound, asked if there was a chance. I said negative, and the CAP remained off-shore as I came out.

Mike Estocin received a posthumous Medal of Honor, and more recently, a ship was named for him. His aggressiveness and airmanship were unquestioned. He got the job done, but he wanted more. We had kept the SAMs down while the strike went in and made a safe getaway. As soon as the bombers cleared the beach, our job was over.

Whether Mike chose to ignore the SAM launched at us or whether he misjudged its closure is open to conjecture. We did not turn even slightly so that the closure rate and proximity could be discerned better. Perhaps the SAM fooled him because it came from straight ahead.

In any case, Mike wasn't satisfied with merely suppressing the missiles. He wanted to shoot those people, just as he'd done six days before. But that was an inherent risk in playing the electronic game of tag over North Vietnam. The desire to win could overshadow one's sense of preservation, and it cost us some of our best men.

It's a lesson we will profit by studying.

Carrier Pilot

from *The Heart of a Man*
BY FRANK ELKINS

Frank Elkins was a U.S. Navy A-4 Skyhawk pilot during the early years of the Vietnam War. He kept a diary that his wife inherited after Frank was killed on October 13, 1966. She edited the diary and it was first published in 1973. The charm of the diary is that it was not written to be read by the public—it contains the intimate thoughts of a brave young man very much in love and facing combat, an honorable man keenly aware of the duty he owes to his country and his shipmates. One wishes that Lyndon Johnson and Robert McNamara had the courage to read this diary after it was published, but probably they didn't. Life isn't like that.

August 24, 1966

ONCE I GOT TO SLEEP YESTERDAY, I DREAMT AND TOSSED AND rolled. I had a dream about some girl I didn't know. I don't seem to dream about Marilyn that much. I guess, regardless of what else may be said, Barry is right in that man, in the primitive state at least, is not a monogamous creature. But if I found it necessary to look for other women here, loving Marilyn the way I do, and knowing that she is mine only, I couldn't get up in the morning. . . . It's not a moral thing with me; I just don't want to disappoint Marilyn in any way, don't want any secrets to come between what we share.

One thing that's really difficult about being married to her is that my attitude is now not as good as it was when I felt that I had nothing really to lose. I enjoy living more than some, and if I'm killed, surely there are plenty who will say, "Too bad," and mean it. But I've never felt that the world would be greatly altered. I've lost that attitude, though it's the best possible frame of mind to be in when you know there's a good chance you won't make it back. It's those who have too much to live for; they're always the ones who get it. And me, I've got too much to live for now. I have to keep my longings and daydreams in check, or I'm afraid I'll lose something that's really necessary to get me through all this.

After 2300 I was half-awake. I had already checked the schedule and knew where my 0300 strike would be. Checking the schedule is always a mistake. If you don't know where you're going on a hop, you can't really worry because you can't form pictures of the terrain and the flak and the hills where you might be forced to parachute down in the pitch, milky black. But I had seen the schedule, and I knew that I was to go into the area of heavy fire at checkpoint 32 in the middle of Brandon Bay, to follow the roads west for twenty miles, then turn north and reconnaissance that part of the road up to checkpoint 38, then turn back southeast to the coast.

Lying there in bed, I mentally dodged bullets and shells, called Bob a hundred times giving him instructions, and struggled the way one will do in a dream when he doesn't know what he's fighting; I just tense up against whatever it is I'm to go up against, although tensing up doesn't do anything either. I lay there for half an hour doing this, the way in the afternoons in high school before a night football game, I would lie upstairs and mentally make touchdowns and fantastic razzle-dazzle football plays. Except in this case there was the tough load of having to shepherd Bob in and out of there as well as just live through the whole thing. And, unlike the football game, there's no great thrill about looking forward to a night armed-reconnaissance hop; there's only the dread of the dark, of not seeing anything worth bombing and yet risking your very ass every minute of the night, keeping track of yourself and another man over hostile territory, making bombing runs when a mistake in navigation might drive you into a mountain or hillside, or, even easier, cause you to drop a bomb where the elevation puts you down in your own bomb fragmentation pattern and blow yourself out of the air. Hell, even night hops in the States were dangerous, and people flew into the ground and killed themselves, just because there's so damned much that you have to take care of, keep track of, and get done.

But, add all this to a murky, milky, black night, with no horizon and rolling variable terrain, and lights out in both aircraft, bullets, flak, the possibility of SAMs and MiGs, a wingman who, even though I think he's the damned best in the squadron except for Barry, is nevertheless the section leader's responsibility, and then, take all that to bed with you when you know you've got to get up in a couple of hours, right in the middle of the night, and face all that garbage. Try to get a little rest under those circumstances.

I gave up and wrote Marilyn a letter instead.

After the hop is over and you are back on the ship, it's virtually impossible to remember how much you dreaded going out there at night. It's true; even now I can't really put myself in the helpless, inadequate mood I was in before manning aircraft this morning.

During the brief in Air Intelligence, you know you're going and you listen carefully. Then back in the ready room, you begin to dread it and you go on briefing though, even though you're beginning to look for a way out, to hope that you're really not going out, that the spare will be launched in your place, that you'll be late starting, that you'll have no radio, or a bad ALQ, or something—anything—that'll give you a decent, honorable out of that particular night hop. After the brief, waiting to suit up and man aircraft, you really dread it most then. A cup of coffee and another nervous call to the head, and you're told to man your aircraft for the 0300 launch.

Up on the flight deck, you start looking for something wrong; you go all the way around the aircraft, looking for that little gem that'll be reason enough to your conscience and your comrades to refuse to go out. And it doesn't come. You never give up though, first the damned radio works, and the damned ALQ works, and the damned TACAN works . . .

August 25, 1966

It's 0800; at 0230 I briefed Bob Smith and the spare, Darell, for a night armed-reconnaissance hop. At 0400 we manned aircraft. At 0400 Bob was launched, and as I was taxiing up on the cat, I noticed his aircraft, at about one-half a mile forward from the ship, start a hard left turn. Then I noticed he was descending rapidly, and I grabbed for the mike key. I couldn't say a word before aircraft, bombs, and everything hit the water and went up in a 1,500-foot fireball. No ejection. No chance for survival.

There was no horizon, clouds everywhere, perfect vertigo weather. I suspect that this is what happened. Disorientation or a bad gyro.

Since then I've been in sort of a daze. I guess, flying with Bob every day, I got to be much closer to him than I had meant to be. Also, he was really my first wingman, and there's a lot to that too. Sort of like he was mine. And he was really coming along too. He was as good as anybody I ever met at that experience level. Gone. What a waste.

He has a kid brother aboard who is an enlisted man. I went down with the chaplain and told his brother about Bob's death this morning. He looked so sad. I finished and went out on the catwalk and cried for five minutes or so.

And the war goes on. I flew my second hop. I guess if the spare hadn't been down, I'd have been expected to fly the one on which Bob was killed. On the second hop Bob and I were scheduled to go out again. Richard was in his place. When I went back to the ready room, I expected to see Bob there ready to brief. Damn it all, it's just too bad. Engaged and to be married the first couple of weeks back from this damned place. Zap. Over. Gone. Written off.

It's a tough blow. I liked Bob, and he was so doggoned good in the air. We really didn't pal around much on the ground, but oh what a pleasure to fly with him on my wing. He held the tight formation just like I do with three years' less experience than I have. And he used his head and could be trusted. We were just getting so we could feel what the other was thinking and doing in the air. Lately, almost nothing had to be said, for we each already knew what to expect from the other. And now it's gone, and I don't think it'll ever be exactly the same. At least not this cruise. Oh, God, what a loss to the squadron, to his girl, to his brother and family.

August 27, 1966

I don't like to admit this, and if I get killed and Barry reads this as I have given him permission to do, I think it may make him cringe as it would me if I were reading the same thing in his journal. However, the truth is, I downed an aircraft on deck for a bad gyro, and it just wasn't the truth.

It was a 2300 brief with Ralph and Bost as spare. I briefed for a flight in the area of north Brandon Bay, following the route over to checkpoints 38 and up to 41. We were to look for traffic on the road. I intended to go, for I knew after having seen Bob go in the night before, I needed to have a terrifically hard hop turn out successfully before I could have my confidence restored. I intended to go, but the dread of it was in my mind all the time. When we manned aircraft at 0100, I began meticulously looking for something wrong with the aircraft, but there was nothing really wrong.

I started, checked and rechecked everything, and everything was still working. Going through my mind right then was all the camaraderie that Barry, Tom, T.R., and I have had about not giving a damn when the going got rough and when things were most hairy, and how that what I really wanted from God right then was not the strength to endure, but just a good, safe way out. I did wrong; I can't feel any other way about that. But my conscience hasn't bothered me like I thought it might. I called, "416, in and up," and I thought that I had my head problem solved and that I was going out and solve my lack of confidence right then.

But as I taxied up on the cat, I looked to 10:30/11:00 and thought I could see Bob's lights zooming by and the fireball blazing and blinding. I couldn't see the horizon and I tried to concentrate on checking my instruments and takeoff checklist. But right then, without thinking or anything else, I called, "This is 416, on cat number two. I'm down. Bad gyro." I chickened out and didn't fly.

I flew the second hop of the day and put a big hole in a bridge near Caobang.

All this happened yesterday.

Today, I briefed at 0100 with the XO as his wingman on the same route I was to fly last night when I showed yellow. When we got to the aircraft, it was last night's scene all over again. Scared. Dread was engulfing me. No horizon. But, knowing that things weren't going to get any better until I had gone out on just such a night as this—thunderstorms everywhere, fog, soup, rain, no horizon—I wouldn't be up to myself again. So, taxiing up on the cat, there was Bob's fireball again, looking at me from 10:30, but I gritted my teeth and went ahead. Tearing down that cat, I was 100 percent adrenaline. I ran my seat down and was all instruments and no visual. I got into the air okay, and suddenly I knew I had it made, faced the devil and grinned him down.

The rendezvous was blacker'n ever and in the goo and hairy again, but I never really sweated it. I got on the XO's wing, and here we went. Terrible weather, but I was suddenly all guts. North Vietnam couldn't get to me since I had beaten the Frank

Elkins devil. I overcame the weakling, the mama's boy, the guy about whom Billy said, "Give the ball to Elkins. He'll dance across the goal." And I didn't give one rat's ass if the whole world was shooting at me, I had already won.

Fritz had an electrical failure and, after one try for the deck, punched out. He was being rescued as we were landing.

Then I heard Maverick Two call, "This is Magic Stone 403. I've lost you in the clouds, Darell."

Darell said, "Roger, make a twenty-degree right turn." He did and the ship had him on radar and was talking to him.

Then Benny called, "I've lost my gyro and external lights."

Darell said, "Roger. Pull your emergency generator."

"Roger, but I don't think it'll do any good; I've still got my standby gyro, and I've got it under control."

"Roger. As long as you've got control."

But Benny lost the rest of his gear, lost his lights, calmly took off his kneeboard, and sold the aircraft to the fish. Bingo. Pop-up and out into the free airstream for a nylon letdown into the saltwater bath. The helo got him out after half an hour or so. He's okay, and I'm taking him on two hops tomorrow.

Since Bob's death, I've decided to retire the "Genghis" flight call—that'll be mine and his. I was Genghis One and Bob was Genghis Two, and there won't ever be another Genghis flight as far as I'm concerned.

This week has been like a bad dream. Since Bob got killed, the whole squadron seems different to me. Never knew I thought so much of Bob. Never realized how comfortable I was flying with him, and probably I did better not to know. Damn, I never meant to let myself get close to anybody out here where a death is something you have to expect and prepare for. But without knowing it, I guess I did.

August 28, 1966

Commander Stone of the Spad squadron just had an engine fire and jumped out at Hon Me. He was fired upon during the rescue operation, but nobody else was hurt. He was banged up a little and burned, but he's being flown back here right now. That makes nineteen airplanes we've lost in actual combat operations, not to mention the other crunches.

My own flights were uneventful: I'm beginning to recover from that bout I was having with my nerves.

August 29, 1966

Bad news today. We'll be extended on the line until September 8, which means I won't be seeing Marilyn until the ninth.

Along with the announcement night before last that we would be extended, they gave us a sort of conciliatory boon; we were given three days as white carrier. That is, we fly days only for three days, until the first. Red, white, and blue carriers; white has the day shift, blue flies noon-to-midnight, and red has the gruesome midnight-to-noon shift.

Late this evening I went out with Bost for a typical no-control, no-plan, confused two hours of pure hair, up in the island area to the north, just south of China. On earlier flights, SAMs had been fired at everyone in that area. That damned Bost had us going around at 10,000 feet, right in the most vulnerable area, at the most vulnerable altitude. We were looking for SAM sites, and boy, I got a full half hour of eye strain, not to mention mental indigestion. We drew a lot of fire from an automatic-gun site. I saw two tracers fly over my right wing and then a couple go under the wing. There's a tracer bullet about every eighth round in the ammo belt; at least that's the way we did it in the North Carolina National Guard. So, for every tracer bullet you see, there are seven or so more invisible bullets zigging around. The tracer helps the gunner see where he's shooting and, incidentally, gives the aviator a sporting chance, not to mention a little fear.

Dammit, I don't feel right saying, "Come on, September ninth." It should be September 5.

September 4, 1966

Yesterday was an eventful day for me.

Tim asked me the night before if I minded being sent into the dreaded island area around Cac Ba, Hon Gay, and the Haiphong harbor channel area on Bost's wing. That's like asking a turkey on Christmas Eve if he minds laying his head on the block of wood while you're filing your ax.

I said something like, "Hell, yes; it might save some lesser wingman's life, so I'll go." But when it came time to go, I began to wish I had uttered sentiments similar to those of other junior officers who have flown that particular tactical position.

We accompanied the strike group up to a point just east of the island area. At that point, the strike group, led by the CO, proceeded farther north to a coast-in-point. Don and I broke off to the east and flew in to begin monitoring the fan-song radars on our Shrike missiles. Only hitch here was that the ship had run out of Shrikes, and there I was with only a load of bombs, in the worst SAM/flak area outside of Hanoi/Haiphong, with no passive radar to tell me when I was being tracked or painted by SAM or fire-control radar sites.

As the skipper rolled in, I got myself steeled somehow and flew in there like a madman, looking down gun barrels and directly at SAM sites known to be active, and went tearing into that area, found the SAM site that had fired on most of us, and laid my stick of bombs right across that momma. Bingo! Zap and away!

I was still in a hell of an area though and went dodging out the Haiphong channel at 2,000 feet. Back at the ship, CAG and the skipper met me in the ready room, slapping me on the back and hollering congratulations. Tim cursed me properly because he and I have been plotting for a week on various ways to get up there and hit that particular site. After secure last night, we got a message from the admiral personally congratulating the two of us. Since Bost was leading the flight, he gets credit for my hit as well. Both of us are being recommended for Distinguished Flying Crosses for the flight.

Hotdoggin' It

from *Low Level Hell*

BY HUGH L. MILLS, JR., WITH ROBERT ANDERSON

During the Vietnam War the college-educated sons of the middle class who lusted for high adventure joined the Navy and Air Force and learned to fly jets. The high-school-educated sons of the working class joined the Army and learned to fly helicopters. Fate placed a few of the Army pilots into hunter-killer squadrons, platoons of OH-6 or OH-13 scout helicopters and Huey gunships, then after 1967, the heavily armed Cobras. The job of the scout pilots was to find and kill enemy soldiers. Flying low and slow with their observer and gunner, these men dueled head-to-head with enemy assault rifles, machine guns, artillery, and mortars. They fought without the computers, infrared optics, laser designators, and guided weapons that would soon revolutionize war in the air. They fought without parachutes. The majority of them were killed or wounded.

The aviators of World War I would have perfectly understood this deadly game and the men who fought it. History will probably regard the scout and Cobra pilots as the last of the true fighter pilots.

This selection is by Hugh Mills, who was a twenty-one-year-old OH-6 scout pilot in the Big Red One (the First Infantry Division) in Vietnam. His helicopter, called a Loach, was flown from the right seat. The left seat was empty. A gunner armed with an M-60 machine gun sat behind the pilot, also on the right side of the machine. A fixed 7.62-mm minigun was mounted on the left skid. A heavily armed Cobra gunship flew top cover.

In this selection Mills was on his way to a conference at brigade headquarters. His Cobra teammate was a pilot named Paul Fishman, call sign Three Four. Whimsically Mills chose to fly at low level. He had been in-country eight months and, as this selection reveals, had not yet succumbed to the emotional carnage caused by too much flying, too much dying. After you read this, you might wish to reread the excerpt by James McCudden.

AS SOON AS WE CLEARED THE BASE BOUNDARY, I FLIPPED MY WEAPONS system to ARM and the fire selector switch to FIRE NORM, then settled in for the flight at an altitude of about twenty feet off the ground. After a couple of minutes I heard Three Four check in with Lai Khe artillery. They reported that they were firing 105s into the northern area of the Iron Triangle, meaning that we would have to either detour up north around Lai Khe or head south to the Saigon River and follow it on up to Dau Tieng. Rather than go north, which was farther out of our way, Paul gave me a heading for the river. We turned west, picked up the Saigon River, and started following its general course around the southwestern edge of the Iron Triangle. I was cruising along right on top of the trees and holding airspeed at a consistent ninety knots.

I was relaxed. So was Parker. He was sitting on his little jump seat just watching the scenery go by. The collective control was resting on my left knee; I had hold of the cyclic and was flying the airplane with my left hand. With my right hand I was leisurely puffing on a cigarette. My right foot was dangling outside the cockpit door. It was another beautiful morning in sunny Vietnam.

We came up on the vicinity of our FSB Kien. It was just a few more minutes from there to Dau Tieng, and I was having so much fun that I thought I would play a little "pop-up" for the rest of the way. I dropped the bird down to an altitude of about two feet and moved the airspeed up to a hundred knots, then up to one hundred and ten. As we ripped along, I would yank back on the cyclic, which tilted the rotor disk to the rear, and pop the bird up and over the rice dikes and treelines. Then I'd shove the cyclic stick forward again, which tilted the blades sharply forward and pushed the nose down, and drop to two feet. I was just plain hotdoggin' it, and I loved it!

My antics didn't escape my gun pilot, however. As always, Paul was carefully watching me. "Hey, One Six, what the hell are you doing down there?"

"I'm having a ball," I answered. Then I warned Parker to hang on for the next pop-up as yet another treeline loomed ahead through my bubble.

It was still early in the morning, and the semidarkness made it difficult for me to see really well. But the approaching treeline looked clear of obstacles on the other side, making it a piece of cake to pop up over the trees and then right back down again without missing a beat. I could just barely make out a rice paddy on the other side with a dike going through the middle of it. No sweat.

I closed in fast on the treeline, waited until the very last split second, then jerked back a chestful of cyclic stick. The little OH-6 jumped straight up about forty feet as though she had suddenly been kicked in the tail boom by a Missouri mule.

As we leapt up to the crest of the trees and the OH-6's nose depressed for the letdown on the other side, I looked forward through the bubble. Spread out across my front from left to right was a string of thirty NVA soldiers in column, walking on the paddy dike, taking their own sweet time.

I was moving very fast and very low, so the sound of my engine and blades was muffled by the vegetation, and my Cobra was high and too far behind me to be seen or heard. The enemy was taken completely by surprise.

When I popped up over that treeline, doing more than a hundred knots and less than thirty to forty yards off their left flank, those poor bastards were thunderstruck.

I could tell as soon as I saw the column that these guys were NVA regulars. Unlike guerrillas, they were loaded down with equipment, such as mortars, SGMs, radios, and web gear. It looked like an NVA heavy weapons platoon. They had probably scouted the open ground ahead, satisfied themselves that there was no potential danger, then started to move the whole platoon across. And at that very instant, up I bounced over the treeline, catching them bare-assed in the open with no cover and no place to run.

Snapping back from my initial shock at seeing a whole column of enemy soldiers strung out across my front, I started to look at them more carefully. My eyes focused on their point man. He was no more than thirty yards in front of me, frozen in place, staring right at me. Then he started to jerk up his weapon.

I hit my radio transmit switch and yelled, "Dinks! Dinks! They're right under me!" Then I squeezed the minigun trigger to two thousand rounds a minute. My initial blast caught the wide-eyed point man square across his belt line and literally cut him in half.

I kicked hard right pedal, held the bird's nose down, and spun around in order to bring the minigun to bear on the rest of the column. Squeezing the minigun trigger again—this time all the way back to four thousand rounds per minute—my second burst raked through the next four men. The bullets slammed them to the ground in a cloud of dust, debris, and body parts.

The paddy dike now seemed to explode as the NVA soldiers shot back at me, running every which way trying to find cover. I again broke hard right in order to bring Parker's M-60 to bear on the maze of trapped enemy in the clearing below.

He ripped off a three-to-four-second burst, then keyed his intercom button. "Level out, sir. Level it out!" he yelled at me.

The right turn I was executing was so sharp that Parker couldn't fire without the risk of hitting the bird's tilted rotor blades. I slammed the cyclic stick to center, leveling out the aircraft, and instantly heard Parker's M-60 go to full bore. He had caught a group of three NVA soldiers trying to make it out of the clearing and back to the jungle. He dropped them all in their tracks.

I was pulling the ship around for another circle over the mass of enemy confusion when Three Four's voice suddenly erupted in my earphones. He was shouting, "One Six, One Six, what the hell's going on down there? What have you got? What have you got down there, One Six?"

"Dinks . . . I got dinks, lots of dinks," I blurted. "We've got 'em trapped. They're running all over the place!"

I didn't hear his reply because Parker was going crazy with his 60. Besides, I had just spotted an NVA with an AK-47 rifle running toward the jungle. Another soldier was running in front of him and they were both hell-bent for election.

Determined not to lose them, I pulled the bird hard around to come up on their rear. It was then that I noticed all the shooting that was coming up at us from the ground. There was a constant stream of AK-47 fire, and I could hear rounds beginning to impact the aircraft. But I was still not going to let those two soldiers make it back into the jungle. I pulled up to about forty yards behind them. They knew I was on their tail and they were running for their lives.

As I raced up the trail behind them, I noticed that one of the soldiers had a large black rice-cooking pot strapped to the back of his pack. It was the size of a large wash bucket and was bouncing furiously up and down as he ran. I pulled the nose down a little, watching the bottom of the cooking pot come into view through the crosshairs grease-penciled in front of me on the bubble's Plexiglas. I touched a shade of right pedal, then I pulled off a short minigun burst.

My rounds walked right up the trail behind the last man, then tore into the bottom of the rice pot. The man pitched forward to the ground. So did the soldier running in front of him. My bullets had apparently gone through the last man and hit the soldier in front, killing them both. There were nine enemy down in less than a minute of battle.

I jerked the bird around in a hard right turn to get back over the main group of trapped enemy soldiers. Again, intense ground fire poured up. We offered a pretty choice target at only five to seven feet off the ground, and I could hear bullets ripping and snapping all through the aircraft. I was trying to bring my minigun to bear on Charlie again, and Jimbo's 60 was firing in long, sustained bursts.

Things were so frantic that it took me a while to realize that Three Four was yelling at me through the headset. "Get out of there, One Six . . . get the hell out of there and let me in!"

I snapped back to reality. "Roger, Three Four. One Six is out to the west."

As soon as Paul saw my tail kick up, he was rolling in and firing rockets. I could see his 2.75s impacting the rice paddy and the nearby jungle. The last pair of rockets that he fired into the swarming enemy soldiers in the clearing contained nail flechettes. From my circling position nearby, I saw the puffs of red dye explode as the nail-flechette canisters blew open and saturated the whole area with thousands of nail-like metal spears.

As Three Four broke from his last firing pass and headed back to altitude, I punched my transmit button: "One Six is back in from the east on BDA." I pulled back into the clearing from the east, made a couple of fast turns over the area, and discovered that there were still plenty of people moving around. They were still shooting at me, and Parker opened up again with his M-60 on everything he saw moving. I could hear more of Charlie's rounds impacting the aircraft, and I wondered how much more punishment the OH-6 could take.

Coming around again, I engaged two more enemy soldiers with the minigun and knocked them down. Continuing the turn, I saw Parker's rounds splatter up the dust around two more, then slam them both to the ground.

Out of the right corner of my eye, I saw another NVA jump up from the ground and start to run toward the center of the clearing. Just as I was coming around, I saw him dive into some bushes. It was a small vegetated spot, out there all by itself— the only piece of cover in the clearing.

I hit the intercom and told Parker, "Shoot into the bushes. An NVA just jumped in there. Spray the bushes . . . he's got no place to go. Get 'im!"

Parker yelled back, "I can't, sir, I'm out of ammo!"

I could hardly believe it. In several minutes, Jim had gone through thirty-two hundred rounds of M-60 ammo. "Okay," I said, "I'll pull around and take him with the mini. Hang on!"

I whipped around, zeroed out airspeed, eased the nose down, and squeezed the minigun trigger back all the way to the stick. Nothing happened. It didn't shoot. All I heard was the gun motor running. I was out of ammo for the minigun.

I punched the intercom again. "I'm dry on the minigun, too, Jimbo. Do me a Willie Pete."

Parker yanked a dark lime green canister off the bulkhead wire, pulled the pin, and held the grenade outside the aircraft ready to drop on my command.

As I came up on the man's hiding place, I keyed the intercom again. "Ready . . . drop!" The grenade sailed down right into the center of the bushes. I accelerated away just as the explosion erupted in the vegetation, sending up arms of hot-burning white phosphorus.

I called the gun immediately. "Okay, Three Four, target my Willie Pete. Hit my mark, hit my mark! One Six is out."

As I headed out, I glanced back at the little vegetated area. The man was running frantically out the other side of the scrub. Patches of his clothing were burning fiercely where fragments of the white phosphorus had landed on him.

He had taken about five steps when Three Four's first rockets came in. They were the last he ever took. One of Fishman's rockets impacted directly between the man's legs.

As Three Four rolled out and away from his firing pass, I got on UHF. "Good rocks, Three Four. One Six is back in. You better scramble the ARPs because I've still got beaucoup people moving on the ground and lots of equipment lying out in the open all over the place."

Of course, the guys back at the troop had been monitoring our transmissions, so Three Four's request was almost after the fact. The next thing I heard over the radio was, "Okay, Three Four, this is Darkhorse Three. Stand by over the target area.

ARPs are saddled up and about to be under way, and I've scrambled another hunter-killer team to relieve you. Stand by.''

As I arced back down over the clearing, more enemy rounds came up at the airplane. I jigged and jogged, trying to keep the remaining bad guys corralled and to convince them that I still had ammunition. Parker had resorted to a backup M16, which he promptly emptied on anything that moved. Then he hauled out a twelve-gauge Ithaca pump shotgun that he had stashed under his jump seat and shot it point-blank until it was dry.

I followed his lead and pulled my Colt .357 Python out of the shoulder holster. I was able to shoot the big revolver out the cockpit door by hooking the collective stick on top of my left leg, holding the cyclic with my right hand, while resting my left elbow on my right forearm and firing with my left hand. I'm sure I didn't hit a damned thing with the Colt, but I may have scared a few NVA to death. Every time I fired that .357, which had Super Vel magnum cartridges in it, flames shot about a foot and a half out the muzzle and it barked like a howitzer.

As I emptied the last .357 round, I got a call from Bob Davis (One Three) telling me that he and his gun were now on station. While I was taking him on a high-speed pass of the battle area, I heard him say, ''Damn!''

''What's the matter, One Three?'' I jumped back at him. ''What have you got . . . what the hell have you got?''

''Damn, One Six, I've got nothin', and that's the trouble. I count about twenty-two bodies down there and you guys didn't leave a thing for us!''

On the way back to Phu Loi (I never did make the meeting in Dau Tieng) I keyed the intercom and told Parker, ''Let's get a red smoke rigged on your M-60 so we can let the boys back home know that we stung Charlie today.''

I heard him chuckle. ''Sir, the red smoke is already there.'' I glanced back and saw it already wired to the muzzle of his machine gun.

We made our traditional pass of the base trailing a stream of billowing red smoke. The field personnel waved and cheered us on. Hundreds of people worked on the base, and when the hunter-killer teams came back home trailing red smoke, you could hear them slapping each other on the back and yelling, "Hey, our guys did good today!"

It was a morale booster for us, too. We knew we were doing the job that we had been sent to Vietnam to do. Maybe, just maybe, we had shortened the war a few minutes or hours.

As quiet and reserved as Jim Parker was, his emotions showed as we came back into base and settled the bird down near the revetment. My emotions probably showed, too.

I cut the battery switch, then twisted around in my seat to look back at my crew chief through the open panel in the bulkhead. Jimbo broke into a broad grin and shot me a big thumbs-up. That said to me, You did good, sir. We stuck it to Charlie pretty hard today.

I nodded and smiled back, then gave him a thumbs-up. That was my way of saying, Good job yourself, Georgia farm boy. I wouldn't have survived that engagement today with any lesser man in the crew chief's cabin.

By that time, Paul Fishman had walked over to the ship. He clapped his arm around my shoulder as we walked together toward the ops bunker. "Goddamnit, Mills," he said, "you scare the shit out of me! If you don't quit mixing it up down there for as long as you have a tendency to do, you're going to get your ass shot full of holes. And I'll just be sitting up there at fifteen hundred feet watching it happen!"

I told him the truth when I answered, "I scare the shit out of myself sometimes, Pauly, and this was one of those days that I nearly scared myself to death!"

The base maintenance guys went over my OH-6 after we got back, and their report scared me even more. Altogether, about twenty to twenty-five enemy rounds had impacted the airplane. My airspeed indicator had been shot out. The altimeter had a round through it, smashing it to pieces. The armor plate under Parker's seat had been hit twice. The armor around my pilot's seat had been hit several times from the rear, indicating that enemy bullets had gone through the crew chief's compartment, missing Parker but smashing into the back of my seat armor before ricocheting somewhere else in the ship.

Also, Parker's M-60 door gun itself had caught an AK-47 round near the front sight, right between the barrel and the gas operating tube. The almost impossible hit put a neat half-moon gouge in the bottom of the barrel and blew the gas cylinder right off the gun.

Then there were four or five NVA bullet holes in the Plexiglas of the bubble, a couple more in the tail boom of the aircraft, and at least three through the rotor blades. For good measure, one AK slug had gone into one side of the engine compartment and exited on the other—completely missing any engine vital, without which we would have gone down into the middle of those thirty or so bad guys.

The way I figured it, between the NVA and our Loach, in just the 120 seconds of that battle, somewhere between eight thousand and ten thousand rounds of ammunition had been fired in a jungle clearing no bigger than half a football field. And through it all, that miraculous little OH-6 kept flying. Even more miraculous was the fact that neither Parker nor I was hit. Man . . . we both must have been living right!

That same day when the ARPs got back from their ground sweep, we found out just how much havoc we had actually caused those enemy soldiers we had caught on the paddy dike. We learned that there were two POWs and twenty-six KIA— four more dead than the twenty-two bodies Bob Davis had quickly counted from the air when he relieved me. Also, ARP leader Bob Harris brought back a load of enemy weapons and equipment that his platoon had found strewn around on the ground after the fight was over. Among the recovered items were numerous late-issue AK-47 assault rifles, a 60-mm mortar, a skid-mounted SGM machine gun, and two Russian handguns.

But, to me, the most interesting piece in the lot was the rice cooking pot that was strapped to the back of the soldier I caught running off into the jungle. The ARPs had found it on the jungle trail, took it off the body, and brought it back to show me the twenty-four minigun slug holes right up through the bottom of the pot!

The enemy unit that we jumped in the clearing had definitely been identified as a heavy-weapons platoon belonging to the Dong Nai. We had been hunting those bastards for a long time. Now we had found them and stirred them up pretty good by destroying one of their crucial subunits in that jungle clearing.

After rehashing the morning's activities, I finally dropped off to sleep, knowing that I was going to be back out at first light the next morning looking to find the Dong Nai again. I wanted to help deliver the coup de grâce.

The next morning, 29 August, we went back out and searched and searched. Nothing. It looked as though, after a day of scouring, we were going to go home empty-handed. It was getting late and we had found absolutely no evidence of recent enemy activity, let alone any traces of the Dong Nai Regiment itself.

It got to be last light and I finally keyed the intercom. "It looks like a dry run, Jimbo. We've lost 'em again."

I decided to make one more run before heading home, so I pulled in low over a strip of trees that ran from southeast to northwest right near FSB Kien. Watching intently in the fading light along the edge of the treeline, I suddenly spotted people.

Coming into view low, out my right door, was a group of what could only be enemy soldiers, lying on the ground at the base of a couple of trees. They were being perfectly still, weapons resting across their chests, and they were looking straight up at me. They apparently thought that if they didn't move, I'd pass them by unseen. But they looked ready to shoot if they had to.

I punched the intercom to Parker. "Don't move a muscle . . . don't do anything. We've got beaucoup bad guys right below us . . . right below us in the treeline."

"I see them, Lieutenant," he came back calmly. "Looking up at us like they're waiting for us to make a move."

I jumped on Uniform to Sinor in the Cobra. "Three One, I got dinks, out my right door in the treeline now. Mark, mark. When I break, you roll."

Sinor answered, "Roger, One Six, on your right break."

"Breaking . . . *now!*" I jerked the ship hard over on her right side to get out of Sinor's way. In the split second that I put the ship into the turn, the enemy opened up on me with everything they had.

Sinor was back on Victor to me instantly. "You're taking fire, One Six . . . heavy fire, heavy fire! Break left . . . break left now."

Just as he finished his transmission, I heard a loud impact on the aircraft and felt a sharp burning, stinging sensation in my right hip. I bent forward to look down at the cockpit floor. I didn't see anything that looked like a bullet hole. But leaning forward was painful as hell.

I continued my turn out for about five to seven seconds before I noticed that my seat was beginning to fill up with blood. "Ah, son of a bitch!" I groaned. "If I had only flown right on by them instead of making a break and settin' them off."

Then it became obvious that my body just didn't feel right from the waist down. I keyed the intercom. "Hey, Jimbo, I'm bleedin' like a stuck hog. I've been hit."

"Do you want me up front to help?" he asked.

"No," I answered, "just hang on tight. I can still fly this thing, but I don't know for how much longer. I'm going to try to put her down at Contigny."

Thank God I was close to that fire support base, because I was beginning to feel woozy. Contigny had a small helicopter landing area within the wire near the center of the complex, and I managed to put the bird down in that spot. Parker jumped out of the back, stuck his head in the cockpit, and calmly asked, "Whatcha got, Lieutenant?"

"What I got, Jimbo," I said, looking for bullet holes and rubbing my hip, "is an AK round in my ass!"

"I see what happened, sir," Parker said as he pointed to the instrument panel. There was the bullet hole I had been looking for. An AK round had come up through the instrument panel, hit the inner side plate of my seat armor, and ricocheted into my hip. After going through both cheeks of my backside, the bullet then hit the other side of my seat armor, ricocheted again, and flew back out of the airplane through the floor of the ship!

Just then a young soldier came running up to the helicopter. "What can we do for you, Lieutenant?"

"Have you got a surgeon here?" I asked.

"Yes, we do, sir. What do you need?"

I very tenderly lifted myself out of the cockpit and stood—a little wobbly—outside the aircraft. "Well, buddy, I've been shot in the butt."

A smile broke across the young infantryman's face. "But, sir, that's not a very dignified place for an officer to get shot."

"Be that as it may, Private," I fired back, "I'm still shot in the ass, and would appreciate it all to hell if you would please get the surgeon!"

The battalion surgeon just happened to be at the firebase, and it wasn't long before he came out to the helicopter carrying his little aid bag.

Parker wanted to stay with the airplane, and I noticed that quite a little crowd of soldiers was beginning to gather around him and the ship. They were interested in looking over the OH-6 and asking Parker questions about it, but in typical Loach crew-chief manner, Parker shrugged off their queries. I overheard him tell one man, "Keep your hands off . . . don't touch the fuckin' helicopter!"

But when the doctor got me over to the aid bunker and dropped my flight suit, the crowd wandered over, seeking some new entertainment. As my posterior came into open view and the doc began his examination, I began to hear a lot of one-liners followed by muffled yuks and snickers. By that time my fanny hurt so bad I didn't care.

Finally, after probing and sending spears of pain through my punctured buttocks, the doctor said, "You're awfully lucky, Lieutenant. No bones were hit. It's a through-and-through flesh wound, but you'll have a beautiful scar to show off."

Finally the doctor told me I could lift my flight suit back up, and a Dustoff was ordered to take me into Doctor Delta.

"But I don't want a Dustoff," I said. "I've got an aircraft out there on the pad and I've got to get it home. I'm sure as hell not going to leave it out here all night."

The battalion doctor stiffened at my response. "No, you're not flying! We'll take care of your gunner here tonight while Dustoff gets you to the hospital, so just go on out there and secure your helicopter."

When I told Parker what the doctor had said, his eyes got as big as dishes, then his boyish face screwed down into a hard frown. "Oh, no, you don't, sir," he said to me. "If you think I'm staying out here at a firebase in these boonies, you're crazy."

It was about a twenty-minute flight back to Phu Loi. The only way I made it was to roll over in the pilot's seat so I was resting on my left hip. Also, Parker sat up front with me and I let him fly to take the strain off.

But God, my ass did burn and hurt. I didn't know why it was throbbing so badly, but I *did* know what the burning was. The doc had told me that the AK-47 round that passed through my buttock was a tracer!

A few minutes out of Phu Loi I radioed ahead and made the mistake of telling operations, "I'm coming in. One Six is hit. I have been treated at FSB Contigny, but I'm going to need help getting in off the flight line. Get me some help off the line when I get down."

Unfortunately my help was Davis and Willis. I could hear Willis laughing even before I got the aircraft shut down.

"Tell me it's not true," he kept saying. "Tell me it's not true that you've been shot in the ass!"

"Okay, okay, you miserable bastard," I answered. "I'm shot in the ass. Now help me get the hell out of this aircraft!"

"My God," Willis went on, "get an ambulance, call in a specialist. This is severe, this is crass. Our fearless leader has been shot in the ass!"

The next day, our troop first sergeant, Martin L. Laurent, came over to the hootch and announced, "Well, Lieutenant, you got your first Purple Heart, and the flight surgeon has grounded you for the next several days."

I realized my wound was minor, just a scrape compared to the wounds that so many other guys suffered. I was lucky. Even so, every nerve ending in my tail screamed for the next several days, reminding me that a .30-caliber tracer round through the fanny was not as much fun as Willis tried to make it.

The Last Ace

BY STEPHEN COONTS

A fighter pilot who scores five victories has been regarded as an ace since World War I. As this is written—in the summer of 1995, eighty years after the first ace, Roland Garros, scored his fifth victory—one can legitimately ask if the era of the aces is over. Will the ace fighter pilot prove to be a phenomenon of the twentieth century, as unique to his time and place as the Japanese samurai or the English longbowman?

The collapse of communism ended the threat of an all-out conventional or nuclear conflict between the two largest superpowers—the Soviet Union and the United States—and their allies. Simultaneously, extraordinary advances in computers, lasers, composite construction, metallurgy, miniaturization, and a host of other fields obsolesced entire weapons systems at an ever-accelerating pace and drove the cost of new, state-of-the-art systems into the realm of pure fantasy.

In his 1983 book, Augustine's Laws, *Norman Augustine pointed out that in every decade since the Wright brothers, the cost of warplanes has quadrupled. He noted that if that trend continues, by the year 2050 the purchase price of one fighter will consume the entire American defense budget. The trend appears to be continuing: ten years after Augustine's observation the U.S. government's first buy of B-2 bombers was a mere twenty airplanes . . . for $2.2 billion each!*

Manned strategic bombers are today artifacts of a bygone age. It is beyond dispute that airplanes costing $2.2 billion each are purchased for political reasons, not military ones.

They are too expensive to be flown for training purposes, too expensive to bear the political risks of a training accident, too expensive to be exposed to hostile fire, and too few to be a military factor in future conflicts.

As this is written, governments throughout the world are drastically reducing the sizes of their air forces. This course of events is perhaps inevitable, but it has profound implications for future armed conflicts. The 1991 Gulf War proved that a second- or third-rate power cannot hope to contest air superiority today or in the foreseeable future with a superpower, which by definition is a nation that can field well-trained, modern armed forces equipped with state-of-the-art weapons.

One suspects that in future conventional wars the inferior air force will be destroyed on the ground or flee to a neutral country. If a nation cannot contest air superiority, one wonders exactly how it could sustain a conventional army on a future battlefield. The answer may well be that it cannot, and if so, conventional wars as we knew them in the twentieth century will not occur again.

In any event, one can confidently predict that fighter pilots in the twenty-first century will come in two varieties—they will either be highly trained specialists flying state-of-the-art superplanes with sophisticated, computerized weapons systems, or they will be undertrained cannon fodder flying obsolete equipment cast off by a superpower or some cheap volksplane with limited capabilities. Whichever, we can predict that since air forces will continue to shrink, there won't be many fighters or fighter pilots. Future conventional wars will be almighty short, with durations measured in hours, not years, and there will be drastically fewer targets aloft for winged warriors to shoot at. The chances of any individual pilot achieving five kills under such circumstances are poor indeed.

The Israeli Air Force, which has fought more conflicts in the jet age than any other power, is notoriously closemouthed about the records of its active-duty pilots. Still, Israel is known to have at least two high-scoring aces on active service as this is written; one with seventeen kills, one fifteen.

The Vietnam War may prove to be the last war on this planet in which the aerial conflict lasted long enough for pilots to become aces. The American side of the seven-year Vietnam conflict produced only two, Navy Lieutenant Randy Cunningham and Air Force Captain Steve Ritchie. Both scored five victories in F-4 Phantoms, then were removed from combat by their respective services.

Legend has it that there was at least one Vietnamese ace, Colonel Tomb, with thirteen victories scored in MiG-19s. Tomb was supposedly the fifth and final victim of Randy Cunningham and his radar intercept officer, Willie Driscoll.

Cunningham scored his last three kills on just one mission on May 10, 1972, one of the most eventful days of that long war. Laser-guided bombs—LGBs—were first used by the Americans that day against two of the most heavily defended, brutally tragic targets in North Vietnam, the Paul Doumer Bridge in Hanoi and the railroad bridge at Thanh Hoa. Both bridges fell, finally.

Perhaps it was coincidence, but that day the North Vietnamese elected to launch their largest aerial effort of the war against inbound American strikes. That they still had intact airplanes at usable airfields with which to oppose the Americans illustrates not the military genius of the North Viet communists, but the grotesque stupidity of the American politicians who committed their nation to an Asian war and then foully mismanaged it. As usual in that war, the execrable decisions of these criminal incompetents would this day cost American lives.

And it was on this day, May 10, 1972, that Steve Ritchie scored his first kill. Let's fly now with the pilot destined to become the last American ace as the battle for air supremacy in the skies over North Vietnam reaches a grand crescendo.

THE BRIEFING FOR FLIGHT CREWS IN THE 555TH FIGHTER SQUAD-
ron at Udorn Air Force Base, Thailand, began before dawn, at
5 A.M. The briefing always began at this ridiculously early hour,
according to sour GI humor, so that the crews would have more
time for weather delays, which occurred almost every morning
at this time of year.

Capt. Steve Ritchie, a 1964 graduate of the U.S. Air Force
Academy, was on his second combat tour in Southeast Asia. On
his first tour he flew 195 combat missions and helped inaugurate
F-4 Fast-FAC missions, in which the Phantoms' crews called in
aerial strikes in areas too hot for the slower prop or turboprop
machines flown by conventional forward air controllers. This
morning Steve and his guy in back, or weapons system operator—WSO—in Air Force terminology, Chuck DeBellvue, were
scheduled for another such mission.

Ritchie was in a grim mood. Two days before, on the eighth
of May, he had finally engaged an airborne MiG. He was flying
as a wingman, yet when his flight lead's weapons system
malfunctioned, Ritchie got the communist fighter in his sights.
He was just a trigger squeeze away from launching a missile
when he broke off. He was below bingo fuel, the fuel state
necessary to return to base safely, so he terminated the encounter. For two days the memory of that moment, and that decision,
has haunted him.

The North Vietnamese rarely committed their meager air
forces to aerial combat. More than half the American fighter
pilots who flew north of the DMZ never even saw an enemy
plane airborne, and only a few got a shot.

Although Ritchie's decision to break off was dictated by
squadron doctrine and his years of training, still . . . He now felt
that he had had a rare opportunity, and he had blown it. Worse,
the enemy pilot was still alive, still had an airplane that was a
lethal threat to every airborne American. The thought that that
pilot might someday kill one of Ritchie's friends gnawed at
him mercilessly.

He is still stewing when he learns that the number three pilot of a flight of four Phantoms scheduled to precede the bombers to Hanoi this morning has failed to appear for the brief. Ritchie quickly volunteers to fly in his place.

The call sign of the flight will be Oyster. The flight leader is Maj. Bob Lodge, a close friend of Ritchie's and a '64 classmate from the Air Force Academy. Lodge is on his third combat tour and has a reputation as the best highly experienced combat flight leader in Asia. Ritchie considers him to be a superbly competent fighter pilot, a man destined for a great Air Force career. It is an honor, Ritchie feels, just to fly with him. Lodge's wingman will be 1st Lt. John Markle. Ritchie's wingman will be 1st Lt. Tommy Feezel.

Lodge has concocted a special plan. On several previous missions North Vietnamese MiGs have orbited northwest of Hanoi, near the Yen Bai airfield, while waiting for American strikes on their way to Hanoi. When the Vietnamese GCI controllers felt the time was right, they vectored the MiGs southwest toward the inbound Americans.

Predictability is vulnerability in combat, so today Lodge hopes to ambush the Vietnamese. His plan is to lead his flight into North Vietnam at a few hundred feet above the treetops, below the radar horizon of the communists. He hopes to establish an orbit at a location that will allow him to remain undetected by enemy radar. Then, when the MiGs leave their orbit to attack the inbound American strikes, Lodge's flight will pop up and execute a surprise head-on attack.

Timing will be crucial to the success of this plan. Fuel will be critical, time on station too short. And yet, if Lodge can get his flight into position at just the right time, perhaps they will be able to break up the MiGs' attack on the Americans. Maybe the Americans will even get a shot or two.

The key to being in the right place at the right time will be knowing where the MiGs are. The Americans have a top-secret gadget to help solve this problem, the APX-81, a black box that tells the U.S. pilot the distance and bearing to the enemy aircraft, and what kind of aircraft the enemy is flying. Three of the four aircraft on this morning's mission will be equipped with this device.

When Lodge finishes briefing the specifics of this mission, he has a few words to say about emergencies. Although F-4 crews are trained to eject if their aircraft is visibly on fire, Lodge recommends staying with the aircraft and flying it to a safe area, if possible, before ejecting. Then he makes a comment that Ritchie has heard before: Lodge says that since he has a Special Intelligence clearance, he will not eject over enemy territory. He does not want to take the chance that he will spill critical intelligence information if captured and tortured by the North Vietnamese.

Ritchie ponders that comment for a few seconds and wonders what it would be like to knowingly choose to die when one has only to pull a handle to live. He doesn't doubt Lodge's sincerity—no one who knows Bob Lodge has ever doubted that he means exactly what he says, all the time—but Ritchie tells himself that if he gets into that situation, he will eject if humanly possible.

And then the brief is over. Time for breakfast. Time for the stomach to get queasy as a weather delay is announced. Time to think of home and family, to fret, to ponder, to reflect, and for some, to pray.

The mission timing slides and everyone updates their notes, fusses over this chore. Fortunately, today, the weather delay is not long, so it is soon time to suit up, then preflight the planes and weapons.

Each F-4D is armed with four Sparrow missiles and four heat-seeking Sidewinder missiles. They are loaded for bear.

Almost as if it were preordained, the mission goes exactly as planned, which is rare enough in ordinary human affairs and rarer still in war. Today there are no mechanical problems, take-off goes exactly as briefed, Oyster flight rendezvouses with the refueling tankers and is soon on its way to North Vietnam on schedule. Even the weather is cooperating: scattered clouds at the lower levels, clear above, visibility excellent for Southeast Asia at this time of year—apparently a little beyond seven miles.

Lodge leads his flight to the preplanned orbit position west of Hanoi at a height of two or three hundred feet, which the Americans hope is below the coverage of North Vietnamese radar. The four F-4 crews observe strict radio silence. The North Vietnamese must know this flight is airborne, Ritchie muses, because their intelligence system is excellent, but perhaps they can be kept in the dark about its mission and location until the trap springs. Perhaps.

Lodge is keeping the power up but cannot afford to use afterburner. The Phantoms are racing above the trees at about five hundred knots. If they are jumped by MiGs, they must have a high energy level—speed—or they will not survive. Yet speed costs fuel, so the heavy fighters cannot stay long.

Lodge, Markle, and Ritchie carefully monitor their APX-81s for indications of MiG activity. Feezel, on Ritchie's wing, lacks the magic box, so he is flying formation and wondering what is going on.

The boxes reveal the presence of MiGs, about thirty miles north. MiG-21s. Circling. Waiting for their Ground Control Intercept (GCI) controller to vector them in on the Phantoms on their way to Hanoi to deliver their laser-guided bombs.

The MiGs must turn this way soon, or Lodge will have to head in their direction and begin to climb, which will reveal his presence to the enemy radar operators. What Lodge cannot do is placidly wait for more than a few minutes. The F-4s are burning fuel at a prodigious rate.

Ritchie is working hard, monitoring the APX-81, flying a loose, fluid formation, glancing occasionally at his engine and fuel gauges—warily eyeing the jungle rushing past just beneath his plane—and in the back of his mind, still simmering over the missed opportunity of two days before. A professional fighter pilot, he wishes he had handled that once-in-a-lifetime chance differently. The fact is, he doesn't really expect to get a shot today. Life doesn't work that way. Oh, Lodge has two MiG kills to his credit already, but most guys never even see one. The odds are Ritchie has seen his first and last MiG and blown his chance. Augh . . .

The APX-81 chirps nicely.

The MiGs are thirty miles north.

No, they are closing the range. They must have turned southward, be accelerating downhill from 25,000 feet to bounce the incoming American strike, which is still well south of Oyster flight, heading northeast toward Hanoi.

Lodge seems to think so, too. He levels his wings headed north and engages his afterburners. The Phantoms slip past Mach 1.

They are four supersonic bullets now, hurling northward just above the trees.

Lodge and his wingman, Markle, increase their separation. The plan is for both of them to shoot as the formations close.

"I got 'em," Chuck DeBellvue tells Ritchie from the rear cockpit. He has the MiGs on radar. The two formations are not closing precisely head-on. The MiGs are slightly left of the Phantoms' course, and if they maintain their heading, should cross in front of the Phantoms from left to right.

Now Lodge lifts his nose, bringing the flight of four Phantoms into a climb. The afterburners are fully engaged. The Phantoms quickly leave the jungle floor . . . and are immediately illuminated by enemy radar.

Ritchie adds the electronic countermeasures to his cockpit scan: the communists could launch a surface-to-air missile at any time. A SAM will reduce an F-4 to a flaming wreck in a millisecond if the pilot doesn't visually acquire and properly evade the flying telephone pole coming at him at Mach 2.

The MiG-21s are still too far ahead to be visible—over twenty miles away—yet Ritchie glances through the gunsight glass anyway. DeBellvue has the radar locked onto one, so there is a dot on the glass that tells Ritchie where the radar is looking.

Too far. Too far.

In fact, the MiG-21s are so small—about half the size of an F-4—that Lodge and Markle will shoot before they get close enough to acquire them visually. This exception to the Vietnam rules of engagement that require a visual ID before shooting is a narrow one, permissible only because Lodge's flight is "first in," that is, the first friendly flight into enemy territory.

The fighter formations race toward each other. The four MiGs are still coming, so the GCI controllers must not yet have had time to tell the enemy pilots of the oncoming Phantoms.

Ritchie is totally focused—this time and place, this moment, is the only reality as the seconds tick by and the formations streak toward each other.

A Sparrow ignites under Lodge's wing and races forward off the rail, leaving a trail of white smoke. And another.

Two Sparrows shoot forward from Markle's fighter.

The four smoke trails disappear straight ahead into the vast, hazy blue of the sky.

The MiGs are at eight miles, now seven . . . and two fireballs erupt in the sky ahead.

Both Lodge and Markle have scored!

The formations continue to close. The two remaining MiGs streak across in front of the Phantoms from left to right as the Americans turn hard to close in behind, a classic bounce.

Ritchie sees the remaining enemy planes, two tiny silver specks. He is on Lodge's left wing, so he will take the left MiG, Lodge the right.

DeBellvue has a radar lock on the MiG, which is about six thousand feet ahead. Now comes the hard part: Ritchie must follow every turn of the MiG, keep it in the radar's field of view for four seconds while the seeker in the nose of the Sparrow gets in phase with the plane's radar. When properly phased in, the missile will home on the energy being reflected from the enemy plane, if the complex seeker in the missile functions properly. Alas, Sparrow missiles have a mere 11 percent reliability rate.

Ritchie isn't pondering reliability rates just now—he is intent on keeping the tiny silver MiG-21 in sight, on counting the four seconds, on not squeezing the commit trigger on the stick too soon.

Time's up! Ritchie squeezes the trigger.

Nothing happens, of course, because over ninety electromechanical functions must occur in the missile before it can fire—and that mechanical dance takes another second and a half, during which Ritchie must continue to follow every twist and turn of the MiG ahead.

At this stage a second and a half is a lifetime to wait, so Ritchie releases the trigger and squeezes it again. This commits a second Sparrow to fire.

Now the first Sparrow ignites with a flash and shoots forward off the rail. A heartbeat later the second goes.

Ritchie watches the tableau ahead intently—the silver speck of the enemy plane, the smoke trails converging upon it. He must keep the enemy plane within the cone of his radar, keep it illuminated with his radar beam so that the Sparrows can guide upon the reflection.

If these two Sparrows miss, he will squeeze off two more, then begin blasting with Sidewinders.

The MiG is turning hard, has achieved a good angle off . . . and the first Sparrow misses.

The second is leading too much . . . yet at the last instant it turns . . . and detonates as it passes under the nose of the MiG.

Pieces fly off the enemy plane.

Before Ritchie can decide if he must shoot again, the enemy pilot ejects.

A kill! Three MiGs down, one to go.

Ritchie looks right, toward Bob Lodge and his wingman, John Markle. Lodge is behind the fourth MiG-21, Markle slightly to his right . . . and almost in formation with Lodge are two silver MiG-19s.

Ritchie is horrified. All his elation is instantly gone.

"Oyster Lead, break right. Break right, Bob. MiGs at your six, break right!" Ritchie shouts into the radio.

The MiG-19s must have been following the MiG-21s, and the Americans inadvertently turned neatly in front of them to engage the 21s.

Ritchie probably has MiGs on his own tail, but he can't rip his eyes off Lodge's fighter. As he watches, the MiGs pull their noses up and yo-yo high to let Lodge extend out. They overran him, now they are maneuvering to open the distance.

"Oyster Lead, *break right now!*"

Yet Lodge doesn't break. He and his WSO, Roger Locher, are intent on the MiG-21 ahead of them. Lodge must have committed a missile, be waiting for it to fire—target fixation.

The MiG-19s settle in behind Lodge at a range of about six hundred feet and open fire with 30-mm cannons.

The cannon shells immediately register strikes on the F-4. Sparkles appear all over the Phantom where the shells are plastering it.

A spurt of fire erupts from the F-4. It lazily rolls upside down. Now it begins a flat spin, rotating like a Frisbee, on a downward arc.

"*Bail out, bail out, bail out!*" Ritchie shouts into the radio.

Ritchie has his nose stuffed down, the afterburners on full, as a wave of anguish and desperation sweeps over him. In the space of seconds the tables have been turned—the American ambush of the MiGs has become a MiG ambush. The odds are not three against one, but at least five against three. MiG-19s are much more maneuverable than F-4s: to engage them in a turning dogfight would be dangerous, and the Phantoms don't have enough fuel.

He looks again for Lodge. The Phantom is still burning, still spinning when it disappears into a cloud. He sees no parachutes.

Inside the stricken Phantom, a conscious Bob Lodge tells Roger Locher to eject if he wishes. The fighter is inverted, spinning, passing seven thousand feet. Locher pulls his ejection handle. He will land only five miles from the Yen Bai airfield and evade capture for twenty-three days, then be plucked from the jaws of the tiger in one of the most daring rescues of the Vietnam War. Apparently Bob Lodge chooses, as he always said he would, not to eject. He is never heard from again.

Steve Ritchie scans behind one more time, then glances ahead. The ground . . . it is rapidly coming up at him.

Ritchie pulls out of his dive, looks behind for his wingman. Feezel is there, thank God!

Ritchie looks ahead . . . and is staring at a giant tree on a ridge. Coming straight at him. He is going to crash into it.

He jerks the stick back and slams the rudder over. Miraculously, the now-supersonic Phantom misses the tree by inches.

There is no elation at Udorn when Ritchie, Feezel, and Markle land. There is no word from Lodge or Locher. The flight has shot down three MiGs but lost one of their own, a very poor trade. Losing two good friends is damn rough.

Ritchie feels drained. Yet somehow he feels he has made up for breaking away from the MiG two days before, so that nightmare disappears, never to return.

On May 31, 1972, with Capt. Larry Pettit as his WSO, Ritchie shot down another MiG-21. On July 8, with Chuck DeBellvue in the backseat, he scored a double, two MiG-21s.

Ritchie was now the subject of intense interest within the Air Force, which desperately wanted an ace pilot to lionize after all the bloody years of conflict in this no-win war. A cheer for an ace would be a cheer for all the men who never came back, all the mechanics, all the pilots, all the support personnel, all of those men and women who had done their best in an unpopular war simply because their country asked it of them.

Ritchie got his chance on August 28, 1972. As fate would have it, he was flying the same aircraft in which he had scored his first kill. Chuck DeBellvue was again in the backseat.

Like the initial contact on May 10, Ritchie closed the MiG almost head-on, with a combined closure speed of 1,200 miles per hour. This day he was not "first in," so he was unable to fire until he had visually identified the MiG.

The two planes were within two miles of each other when he saw it.

Ritchie turned hard to get behind the MiG, which continued

on course, descending. Now he fired two Sparrows . . . out of range. Two misses.

With afterburners plugged in, Ritchie used the raw power of the Phantom to close the distance as the MiG dove for the clouds ahead. Ritchie squeezed off his last two Sparrows. The first one missed left, frightening the enemy pilot into a right turn, squarely into the oncoming last missile, which converted the tiny silver fighter into a mushrooming fireball.

Chuck DeBellvue stayed in Southeast Asia to complete his tour and helped another pilot, Capt. John Madden, score two kills, giving him a total of six as a weapons system operator. At this writing he is still serving on active duty in the U.S. Air Force as a colonel.

And Steve Ritchie?

Well, he is happily married and living in Colorado. A brigadier general in the Air Force Reserve, he devotes much of his time to helping the Air Force recruit good people. Yet if you saw him in civilian clothes, at dinner or in a mall or on his Harley, you would never suspect that this soft-spoken man with graying blond hair and a charming grin was a fighter ace, the last of the breed.